A song for Alexander Ogorodnikov

The Big Lie slowly draws the mask aside:
the secret guards of power make their threats
and guilty priests all whisper their regrets.
The God of life has nowhere to abide.

Death haunts the Gulag, taking for his prize
the ones whom pain has beaten down and broken.
But he who fights off grief, by Life awoken:
"Where is your victory, O Death?" he cries.

And floating there on power's watery gloom
We see them shining: islands of pure light,
For suffering men, a refuge in their night.
The God of life has come to make his home.

Refrain

He lives for all his brothers,
he speaks for all the others.
Protests of truth and honor,
a whole life long.

PATRICK LATEUR

DISSIDENT FOR LIFE

*Alexander Ogorodnikov and the Struggle
for Religious Freedom in Russia*

Koenraad De Wolf

Translated by
Nancy Forest-Flier

William B. Eerdmans Publishing Company
Grand Rapids, Michigan / Cambridge, U.K.

Original edition © 2010, Uitgeverij Lannoo, nv.
Original title: *Dissident voor het leven. Aleksandr Ogorodnikov
en de strijd voor religieuze vrijheid in Rusland*
Translated from the Dutch language
www.lannoo.com

Published 2013 by
Wm. B. Eerdmans Publishing Co.
2140 Oak Industrial Drive N.E., Grand Rapids, Michigan 49505 /
P.O. Box 163, Cambridge CB3 9PU U.K.
www.eerdmans.com

Printed in the United States of America

18 17 16 15 14 13   7 6 5 4 3 2 1

Library of Congress Cataloging-in-Publication Data

Wolf, Koenraad de.
[Dissident voor het leven. English]
Dissident for life: Alexander Ogorodnikov and the struggle for religious freedom
in Russia / Koenraad De Wolf ; translated by Nancy Forest-Flier.
p.   cm.
Includes bibliographical references (p.   ).
ISBN 978-0-8028-6743-8 (pbk.)
1. Ogorodnikov, Aleksandr Ioil'evich, 1950-
2. Dissenters — Soviet Union — Biography.
3. Dissenters — Russia (Federation) — Biography.
4. Russkaia pravoslavnaia tserkov' — Clergy —Biography.
I. Title.

DK275.O46W6513 2013
281.9092   dc23
[B]

2012032304

The illustrations are taken from the personal collection
of Alexander Ogorodnikov.

Contents

CONTENTS

III. ISLANDS OF HOPE

"This Story Ought to Be Told to *All* Generations"

In the early 1980s, just after I had been elected to Parliament, the NGO Jubilee Campaign asked for my support for the young Soviet dissident Alexander Ogorodnikov, who had just been sent to the Gulag. His case immediately captured my interest. Ogorodnikov was not one of those protesters who carried out noisy human rights campaigns. He worked in silence, building up an underground Christian Seminar.

Three things about him fascinated me. First, in a society that was controlled by the KGB from beginning to end, he had succeeded in creating a network with branches in more than ten cities of the former Soviet Union, thereby reaching a few thousand believers — surely a feat without precedent in the history of the Soviet Union. In addition, Ogorodnikov — a young man in his twenties — called his group the "Christian" Seminar. He himself was an Orthodox convert, as were all his friends who lent their support to this initiative. But they welcomed other Protestants and Catholics to their meetings as well. That ecumenical approach was also a first. Finally, his unimaginable idealism, his courage, and his spirit of self-sacrifice also touched me. When given the option to leave the country, he firmly declined because he wanted to change "his" Russia from the inside out. His willingness to sacrifice himself also meant that when he was imprisoned he was parted from his wife and newborn child.

This book describes in great detail the turbulent history of Ogorodnikov and the Christian Seminar during the period 1974-78. Slowly the net closed in around the group. All those responsible for keeping the Seminar alive were arrested, put through show trials, and deported to Soviet camps. Inevitably, as the leader of that group, Ogorodnikov was the first in a long line of detainees.

At the beginning of the 1980s, news of Ogorodnikov was replaced by a disquieting silence. We could only imagine what atrocities were taking place in the Gulag. We carefully followed the publications issued by the Keston Institute in Oxford, which systematically gathered information on the dissidents via the underground press, or *samizdat,* which often traveled to the West at a snail's pace. And as long as no death announcement was published, there was hope. Several times I myself approached the British prime minister and the minister for foreign affairs, and they made representations — all without results.

I vividly remember, years later, at the end of 1986, that two farewell letters from Ogorodnikov reached the West — six months after they had been smuggled out of the camp in Khabarovsk. They made a huge impression on me, and they still do today, though twenty-five years have elapsed. Jubilee Campaign responded to Alexander's letters by immediately launching a campaign throughout the United Kingdom. Hundreds of thousands of posters and postcards of Alexander were distributed. I often visited Saint James Church in Westminster in the heart of London, where the Reverend Richard Rodgers and the Orthodox monk Athanasius Hart had gone on a hunger strike to obtain Ogorodnikov's release. When Alexander was finally set free in February 1987, we threw a huge party.

Although Ogorodnikov had spent years in hell and had barely survived the horrors of the Gulag — including a few lasting physical injuries — and the KGB had destroyed his marriage, Alexander continued his struggle. What fascinated me was that he did this without any form of bitterness or hard feelings, and with that perpetual smile on his face, but at the same time with a rarely seen determination. When you've survived the Gulag, you're no longer willing to compromise on anything. Alexander's priority was to obtain religious freedom. But he also saw this as an opportunity to realize his life's ambition: to change "his" Russia from the inside out. As a pioneer, his accomplishments were astounding. He founded the first free school in the Soviet Union, as well as the first soup kitchen and the first shelter for orphans. He also went into politics, but that step was not a success because of his unwavering scruples. When he visited the West for the first time, in 1989, he was my guest in Liverpool where, among other things, we visited the Beatles Museum. Alexander had told me that it was his overhearing of the prison guards listening to Beatles music that had helped him defeat the isolation in which he was kept. He told me how he had learnt some English through the music and through conversations with a prisoner in the next cell with whom he was able to have secret conversations via a broken pipe. Alexander also visited Liverpool's cathedrals, the Roman Catholic Church of Our Lady of Good Help in Wavertree, where the organist played the traditional Russian anthem in his honor, and a Baptist church in Accrington, where the congregation had kept him faithfully in their prayers throughout his captivity. One member of the congregation in Liverpool told him that she had his photograph in her kitchen and prayed for him daily. I think it was the first time that Alexander realized how much his courageous stand had touched people way beyond his homeland and from every walk of life.

AFTER THE EXTRAORDINARY changes that came in 1989, I organized support for Alexander's social activities, and I also helped with the delivery of the first printing press that had ever been legally imported into the Soviet Union. Our contacts have lessened over the years, but I am full of admiration when I read here that Ogorodnikov is still carrying on his struggle — often all alone. While we tend to use grand and lofty language to talk about solidarity, Ogorodnikov goes to the Moscow train stations and the metro three times a week to get food in the hands of needy people. And right up to the present day, this "eternal dissident" is a thorn in the side of the powers that be in the Kremlin. The fact that in 2011 his shelter in Buzhorova is wired for electricity but still is not connected to the grid, after ten years of operation, beggars the imagination. And only because he refuses to pay bribes to corrupt bureaucrats. A man who has survived the Gulag doesn't pay bribes.

At the moment, Ogorodnikov is risking a new two-year prison sentence because a contractor who guaranteed the rebuilding of the shelter in Buzhorova in 2009 is believed to have hired illegals.

Alexander Ogorodnikov's life story is far from over, but it testifies to a rare courage and sacrifice. It is our duty to tell it to all generations.

DAVID ALTON

Setting

Just who is this "eternal" Russian dissident, Alexander Ogorodnikov? Search his name on Google, the well-known Internet search engine, and you come up with about 7,800 entries, the first few hundred of which are particularly informative. Ogorodnikov, born in 1950, grew up in the Russian city of Chistopol, and as a boy he was active for some time in *Komsomol,* the Communist youth movement. He broke with Communism, however, and after a long search he finally converted to the Russian Orthodox faith. In 1974 Ogorodnikov secretly founded the Christian Seminar, which soon branched out into ten cities in the Soviet Union. He was also active in samizdat, the underground press. After much provocation by the KGB, the Soviet secret service, he spent a year in hiding, and when he refused to leave the country, he was imprisoned on November 20, 1978, in a concentration camp of the Gulag, the government agency that administered the Soviet Union's penal colonies and labor camps. Ogorodnikov the religious dissident was convicted three times and spent five years in "Perm-36," the notorious "camp of death." On February 14, 1987, he was freed, thanks to the intervention of President Ronald Reagan and Prime Minister Margaret Thatcher.

Ogorodnikov immediately resumed his religious activities and continued to fight for freedom of religion, which in 1990 became a fact. He also became active again as a journalist and founded the Christian Democratic Union of Russia (CDUR): the Soviet Union's first Christian Democratic party. But his attempt to change society by political means did not result in the success he had hoped for. Ogorodnikov set up the first nongovernment school in the Soviet Union, but because of the great social need his activities gravitated to the social sphere. In Moscow he opened the first soup kitchen for the homeless, which served about 1.8 million free meals between 1991 and 1997. But after a violent attack by the police (condemned by the European Parliament), the soup kitchen was forced to make way for a restaurant and nightclub intended for the regime's elite. In April 1995, Ogorodnikov set up the "Island of Hope" in Buzyurova, a village just outside Moscow. This was the first private shelter for street children, orphans and teenage mothers. Ogorodnikov also runs a number of shelters in Saint Petersburg, Moscow, and Chechnya, and he distributes food to the homeless in the railway stations of Moscow three times a week, thereby caring for two to three hundred people a day.

His brother, Boris, entered the Pskov-Pechory monastery under the name Raphael in 1975. He and CDUR secretary Sergei Savchenko were both murdered, in 1988 and 1989 respectively, and Alexander narrowly escaped an attempted murder in 1996. But after thirty-five years, Ogorodnikov is still on the firing line. He is still a dissident, although today it is mainly in the figurative sense of the word. Grounded in the power of his faith, he takes up the daily fight against the indifference and cynicism that characterize the bureaucracy and the mafia in order to fulfill his ultimate dream of a more humane Russian society. He remains a potential threat to the Russian secret service because of his journalistic activities. Until 2008 Ogorodnikov was still the editor-in-chief of a religious publication.

WHAT STRUCK ME as I researched Ogorodnikov and his life was the unprecedented cruelty of the Russian bureaucrats and police, which I, as a Westerner, could barely comprehend. It's a thread that runs not only through Ogorodnikov's life story but also through the entire history of the Soviet Union (1922-91) and present-day Russia (1991-present). Thus, in order to gain a proper understanding of his eventful life, I have found it essential to keep referring back to the broader historical and social context, which also explains why both elements in this book are so closely interwoven. This book begins, then, with a brief historical review of the czarist regime, the Bolshevik Revolution of 1917, and the rule of Communist leaders Lenin, Stalin, and Khrushchev. It also weaves in the life stories of Maxim Ogorodnikov and Yemelian Firsov, Alexander's grandparents, and his parents, Iol Ogorodnikov and Margarita Firsova. From the late sixties on, the biography of Alexander Ogorodnikov keeps pace with the evolution of Russian society.

The book is divided into three parts. The first part is a reconstruction of how Ogorodnikov evolved from a Communist youth to a religious dissident; the second part deals with his imprisonment in the Gulag (1978-87); and the third part describes his life after his release from the Gulag — up until today.

The organization of the text is strictly chronological, with subheadings that mark the transition from the social context to Ogorodnikov's own personal fortunes. One final note: For the sake of readability I have opted for a running narrative without source notes. A list of the sources that I consulted can be found in the back of the book.

KOENRAAD DE WOLF

"We Don't Want Any New Martyrs"

Autumn 1977. After being interrogated by the secret service, Alexander Ogorodnikov was shoved into a car that drove far out of the capital and into a forest, stopping in a clearing a few miles farther on. There Ogorodnikov stood eye to eye with seven men, their rifles at the ready. Out of a nearby dacha emerged a couple of other men dressed in black. One of them gave a sign and said, "You are free." But the seven men formed such a tight circle around him that he could barely move.

"I can't get away," he said. "They won't let me out."

Suddenly he saw a narrow opening and bolted through it. He expected to be shot in the back at any moment, but it didn't happen. The men came up behind him and encircled him again. Roughly pushing Ogorodnikov along, the men discussed what they were going to do with the body later on.

"Do we torture him first?" one of them asked.

"We'll start when we get there," said another.

"Where do you want to shoot him?" asked a third. Ogorodnikov stumbled on a bit farther, and then someone shouted, "Kneel!"

"I kneel only to God," Ogorodnikov answered.

The man discharged a few shots over his head, and he snarled, "We don't want any new martyrs!"

Suddenly, Ogorodnikov saw a side path and turned into it. The pulling and pushing of his assailants made it almost impossible for him to stand. The path led to the edge of the forest, from which he could make out the silhouette of a town. Managing to free himself from the men, he ran away as fast as he could, afraid once again of being shot. However, he reached the town uninjured; apparently his assailants didn't dare kill him.

When he got to the railway station, Ogorodnikov took the first train to Moscow, followed closely by the KGB agents, who jostled one another in order to sit right next to him. He could hardly move, and throughout the journey he could feel their hot breath on his neck — a tested intimidation technique of the KGB.

Alexander arrived in Moscow late in the evening, and as he walked he could hear the footsteps of his intimidators behind him echo through the silent streets. In his mind he went through the list of friends who could take him in. He decided to go to the apartment of Tatiana Chodorovich. She was a friend of dissident Andrei Sakharov and was well known to the Western journalists who were staying in Moscow. For those reasons the KGB agents would probably hesitate to use violence against her. Tatiana, along with Sergei Kovalyov and Tatiana Velikanova, was the driving force behind *Chronika tekuščich sobytiy* (the *Chronicle of Current Events*). She let Ogorodnikov in. The KGB agents following him tried to gain entrance by using force, but to no avail.

By morning, Tatiana's apartment was surrounded by KGB agents on all sides. Nonetheless, Ogorodnikov left the building — with a couple of agents close on his tail. In an attempt to shake them off, he hurried to the inner courtyard of a block of flats. Panicking, he pushed his shoulder against a door and, luckily, it opened. He ran up the stairs to the highest floor, expecting to be arrested at any moment. Out of breath, he opened the small New Testament he had with him. His eyes fell on verse 14 of the second chapter of the First Epistle of John: "I write to you, young men, because you are strong, and the word of God abides in you, and you have overcome the evil one."

A sense of peace suddenly fell over him. Ogorodnikov kissed the New Testament and returned it to his back pocket. The minutes ticked by, but there were no footsteps to be heard. He descended the stairs with caution, and once he got to the courtyard, there was no one to be seen. The agents had disappeared without a trace. He was free again — at least for now.

I

FROM COMMUNIST YOUTH TO RELIGIOUS DISSIDENT

CHAPTER ONE

Alexander Ogorodnikov's Russia

Russia in the Nineteenth Century

Russia, the most far-flung country in the world, had been ruled by the Romanov dynasty since 1613. The written history of the developments that took place during the nineteenth century expresses a number of stubborn biases. According to one such bias, the impoverished rural society was still based on a medieval model; it was not until 1861 that serfdom was abolished. Married women were not allowed to leave their marital home without their husband's permission. As a result of the high infant mortality rate, the average life expectancy was no more than thirty years. The average income was one-tenth that of the United States and one-fifth that of Britain. Only the big cities had a rising industrial sector. Under the authoritarian rule of the czar, the *Okhrana* (the secret police of the Russian Empire) followed a systematic policy of locking up opponents of the regime in camps. And the opposition to the czarist regimes in the Russian diaspora was hopelessly fragmented. In 1903, for example, the Russian Social Democratic Workers' Party split into two wings: the supporters of the hard-liner Vladimir Ulyanov, better known as Lenin, were in the majority and were called Bolsheviks; the minority were the more moderate followers of Julius Martov and were given the name *Mensheviks.*

The above picture, which was greatly distorted by Bolshevik propaganda, is in need of some adjustment. In fact, by the end of the nineteenth century, Russia had emerged as the fastest-growing economy of Europe, thanks to average annual growth figures of 10 percent, for which Sergei Witte, the minister of finance at the time, was responsible. The pearl in the Russian industrial crown was the Trans-Siberian Railroad: the longest railway line in the world, it covered a distance of 9,200 kilometers (5,700 miles) and connected the capital city of Moscow with the seaport of Vladivostok in the far southeastern part of Russia, on the Sea of Japan. The construction of the railroad brought a gradual expansion of economic activities into the Far East.

Russia did undergo an economic regression starting in 1905. Food prices dropped because of the importing of cheap grain from the United States and Canada. And the Russian urge for expansion to the east suffered a deep blow when they were defeated by the rapidly growing superpower Japan in the Russo-Japanese War. That war led to a revolution in 1905. On "Bloody Sunday," January 9, 1905, the army violently crushed a demonstration of striking workers in Saint Petersburg, resulting in a period of great social unrest. During this first Russian Revolution (1905-6), Czar Nicholas II was forced to forfeit some of his power in order to restore a sense of calm. In his *October Manifesto* (October 1905), he announced that Russia would become a constitutional monarchy with a bicameral parliament, which would consist of a lower house and an upper house. The lower house, the State Duma (or Duma for short), was established as the representative body and was given legislative power, written into the first Russian Constitution of 1906. The former State Council — the highest advisory organ for the czar in the Russian Empire — functioned as the upper house of parliament (sometimes nominally) from 1906 to 1917.

There were four Dumas during that 1906-1917 period, the first two of which were extremely short-lived. Shortly after the elections of March-April 1906, the czar dissolved the radical First Duma. Elections were held for the Second Duma in January-February 1907, but the second proved to be even more radical than the first, and it, too, was sent packing by the czar. After a change was made in the electoral law in June 1907, another round of elections was held on November 1, 1907, and conservative parties claimed a majority in the Third Duma. This assembly was able to complete its full term and governed Russia from 1907 to 1912 under the leadership of Prime Minister Pyotr Stolypin, who carried out large-scale agrarian reforms. The peasants were given the right to move out of their *mir*, their rural communities, and in June 1910 they were even obligated to do so. But this reform failed. The *kulaks*, the wealthy and independent peasants who bought land from the ruined farmers and the ever-powerful landowning nobility, laid the basis for a capitalistic agrarian sector.

Besides this cautious democratization, progressive judicial reform was also being implemented. The impact of the *Okhrana*, the secret police, which at one point numbered only fifty-seven employees, was negligible. Anyone could enter and leave Russia freely, and many young people were studying abroad. Paris, the fashionable French capital, was particularly popular with these Russian émigrés. But the number of opponents of the regime living abroad was small. Lenin, for example, lived in exile in Switzerland. Russia had no real concentration camps at the time, only prisons and places of exile, usually with a fairly lenient regimen. Prisoners repeatedly succeeded in escaping, among them Ioseb Jughashvili, better known by his moniker Stalin — "man of steel."

Tatarstan: Birthplace of the Ogorodnikov Family

The roots of the Ogorodnikov family lie in Tatarstan, a region in the east of European Russia. In 1878, in a village near the Tatar capital of Kazan, Maxim Ogorodnikov, the grandfather of Alexander Ogorodnikov, was born into a family of poor shepherds. When Maxim was at school, a local Russian Orthodox priest noticed that he was a talented boy and gave him permission to study in Kazan. Because of its favorable location on the border between Europe and Asia, this busy mercantile town had, by the beginning of the nineteenth century, developed into an important center for the translation and printing of Chinese, Japanese, and Arabic writings. The University of Kazan, founded in 1801, had played a crucial role in the development of the Tatar language and culture, which was previously based on oral tradition alone.

From Kazan, Maxim Ogorodnikov went to the University of Moscow, the most prestigious in the country, after which he began working as a surveyor in Siberia. Later he settled in Chistopol, a Tatarstan city of 16,000 inhabitants. This regional center for the grain trade, which had a daily market, enjoyed a flourishing social and cultural life. The seven libraries and numerous theaters attracted many visitors. The famous mathematician Nikolai Lobachevsky also lived in Chistopol, even though the city was rather remote. There was no train connection at the time, and the capital of Kazan, which was seventy-five miles away, could only be reached by crossing the Kama River, a tributary of the Volga.

Maxim Ogorodnikov became a member of the Socialist Revolutionary Party, a peasants' party that was opposed to the government of Pyotr Stolypin. Maxim's marriage to Anna Alexandrovna produced a son, Iol, in 1908. The family also raised an orphan girl, Barbara, whom Iol long thought to be his sister. Such a form of charity was not exceptional in nineteenth-century Russia: practicing the love of neighbor, *caritas,* was a moral duty. Businessmen who did not engage in acts of charity, or did not support any initiatives in the realm of art and culture, would find themselves socially isolated.

Cultural Renaissance

Riding the crest of an economic boom, the arts, culture, and science flourished in Russia at the beginning of the twentieth century as never before. The complex and highly advanced educational system provided a broad basis for this cultural renaissance. As a youngster, Alexander Ogorodnikov learned verses in Latin and French from Anna Alexandrovna, his paternal grandmother, who died in 1962.

Nowhere else in the world saw so many books printed during the nineteenth century. The works of Fyodor Dostoyevsky, Nikolai Berdyaev, and Leo Tolstoy, to name but three, became world classics. Russian companies in theater, dance, and the circus were among the best in the world. And in the development of abstract art, Russian artists played a key role. Following in the footsteps of Mikhail Larionov and Kazimir Malevich, Vladimir Tatlin developed constructivism, a school of art that would have a profound impact on the art and architecture of the twentieth century.

Russian cities were characterized by a lively intellectual life. Fiery debates were held in the *kruzhki,* small discussion groups of the intelligentsia. Some of the Russian intellectuals, the so-called *zadapniki,* held progressive ideas; under the influence of the nineteenth-century writers Pyotr Chaadayev, Vissarion Belinski, and Alexander Herzen, they called for a democracy based on the Western model.

Slavophiles and the "Russian Soul"

Then there were the Slavophiles, those who admired the Slavs and the Slavic culture and clung to the ideal of the morally unspoiled life of the peasants and their *mir* (peasant communities in which a sense of justice and warm human relationships were the principal features). Central to this idea was *sobornost* (solidarity). The peasants worked community lands together and shared their income according to unwritten laws. At the head of the *mir* was the *skhod,* the gathering of family elders, and the cornerstone of the *mir* was its mystical faith. After the conversion of Grand Prince Vladimir I of Kiev in 988, the Russian Orthodox Church had risen to great prominence.

The leading exponents of the "Russian soul" were the philosopher Nikolai Berdyaev and the writer Fyodor Dostoyevsky. In his book *Demons* (1872), Dostoyevsky says: "But there is only one truth, and therefore only a single one out of the nations can have the true God, even though other nations may have great gods of their own. Only one nation is 'god-bearing,' that's the Russian people." Dostoyevsky developed a messianic vision of "Holy Russia" that had maintained its ties with the earth. "From there the new empire of peace and brotherhood will spread across all of Europe."

During the period of Romanticism, the Western cultural movement that swept across Europe in the late eighteenth and early nineteenth centuries, the Russification policy of the czars was influenced by this prevailing Slavophilia. In 1894, after the death of his father, Czar Alexander III, Nicholas II even elevated the Russian Orthodox Church to the position of state religion. By 1914, the Orthodox Church had 54,000 houses of worship, 57,000 priests, 1,500 monasteries, 130 bishops, 58 seminaries, and four theological academies.

The Bolshevik Revolution of 1917

In terms of international politics, Russia sought to ally itself with Britain and France at the beginning of the twentieth century — against the rising superpower Germany. And in the Balkan powder keg, the czar supported Serbia, which was also Orthodox. After the murder of the heir to the Austrian-Hungarian throne, Archduke Franz Ferdinand, on June 28, 1914, Russia was drawn into World War I. For the poorly armed Russian army, military operations against the German and Austrian troops were disastrous. By the end of 1914 there were already a million dead and wounded, and that number shot up to about six million by early 1917. While lying in a field hospital, the wounded army officer Yemelian Firsov, the maternal grandfather of Alexander Ogorodnikov, decided to join a secret Protestant fellowship. It was his form of protest against the czar, who exerted great influence on the synod of the Russian Orthodox Church, and against the madness of the war.

Daily life in the hinterland was seriously disrupted in 1916 because of food shortages and skyrocketing inflation. Social unrest increased. In 1917, when the army refused to break a strike in Petrograd (the new name for Saint Petersburg since 1914), the dam broke. The resulting popular uprising, known as the February Revolution, forced the czar (who was then at the front) to abdicate, ending three centuries of Romanov rule.

The provisional government, which was supported by the bourgeoisie and the middle class, carried on with the war under international pressure, while in Petrograd and Moscow the *soviets* (local councils of workers, peasants, and soldiers) worked for the establishment of a socialist state. In April 1917, Lenin was smuggled back to Russia (from Switzerland) with the support of the German government. Still, at the first All-Russian Soviet Congress of June 1917, the Bolsheviks were in the minority. The moderate Social Revolutionaries and Mensheviks, who were five times more numerous, joined the provisional government, but they lost much of their credibility after the failure of a military offensive in Galicia.

The first armed Bolshevik uprising of July 1917 fizzled out when the provisional government proved that Lenin had received support from Germany. Lenin fled to Finland, where he lived in hiding, and the other leaders were sent to prison. At the end of August 1917, the provisional government managed to thwart another coup, this one led by Lavr Kornilov, the new supreme commander of the army, who wanted to establish a military dictatorship. But, in fact, the government was beginning to lose its grip on events. After the Bolsheviks won a majority of seats in the local soviets of Petrograd and Moscow in September 1917, Lenin returned from Finland and set up the Red Guard, a motley crew of armed workers, deserters, mutineers, and discharged soldiers. On October 25, 1917, during the second All Russian Soviet Congress, the Red Guard brought down the provisional government in Petrograd. This coup, the so-called October Revolution, was accomplished with almost no bloodshed. In the weeks that followed, the Bolsheviks seized power in Moscow and other cities of Russia.

In Chistopol, the marines of the Baltic fleet, who had reached the city by crossing the Kama River, seized power and executed the city's seven most prominent citizens by firing squad. The Bolsheviks then entered into a temporary alliance with the Socialist Revolutionary Party of Maxim Ogorodnikov, who became the commissar of economics.

Murderous Civil War between the Red and the White Armies

How could the new regime hold its ground with only a small number of supporters? News of the above events had barely reached the country-side, where almost no one had ever heard of the Bolsheviks. Lenin hoped to legitimate his takeover through the elections for a constituent assembly in November 1917. The Socialist Revolutionaries took 58 percent of the votes, however, with only 25 percent going for the Bolsheviks, and the Constituent Assembly was dissolved during its first session.

On March 3, 1918, the Bolsheviks signed a peace treaty with Germany — the Peace of Brest-Litovsk — that was detrimental to Russia. For Russia, the treaty meant the loss of Finland, Estonia, Latvia, Lithuania, Poland, Ukraine, and Bessarabia (or Moldavia). But the end of World War I brought no peace to Russia. A civil war broke out between the "Whites," the so-called White Army, and the "Reds," the so-called Red Army. The White Army, consisting of socialist revolutionaries and nationalists, among others, had been one of the contending parties in the October Revolution of 1917. The Whites wanted to overturn the Red regime, and they received support troops from France, Japan, the United States, and Britain at the end of World War I. Even with that support, the White military forces — ideologically divided, poorly organized, and fragmented — were forced to admit defeat after a bitter battle in 1921 against the Red Army, which had been thrown together in February 1918 by Lev Bronstein, better known as Leon Trotsky. This army managed to reincorporate Siberia, the Crimea, Azerbaijan, Armenia, Georgia, the Ukraine, and the autonomous regions of Central Asia and the Far East into one Russia. Only in Poland did the Red Army lose out. The Russian civil war took an estimated fifteen million lives.

A remarkable role was played at that time by the 60,000-strong Czech Legion. This legion, consisting of Czech and Slovak soldiers who had been a part of the Russian army, wanted to continue fighting on the western front in France after the Peace of Brest-Litovsk so that they could realize their dream of an independent Czechoslovakia. To reach that goal, they were forced to travel east via Siberia, because the western route was closed off by the advancing troops of the Central Powers, consisting of the German Reich, Austria-Hungary, the Ottoman Empire, and Bulgaria. On their way east, the Legion fought on the side of the White Army against the Bolsheviks in the fortified city of Samara, and they seized the Trans-Siberian Railroad.

In 1918 the Whites captured the Tatar city of Kazan, again with the help of the Czech Legion. The new capital city of Moscow was also being threatened by the Whites, and the Bolsheviks were at risk of losing control of western Siberia. Then, during the night of July 16-17, 1918, Czar Nicholas II and his family were murdered in Yekaterinburg by order of the local soviet to prevent them from being freed.

In Chistopol, the Czech Legion arrested the entire local government, which consisted of Bolsheviks and the Socialist Revolutionary Party. Anna Alexandrovna, wife of Commissar Maxim Ogorodnikov, immediately informed the leaders of the White Army, in which a couple of her family members were fighting. But the order to free the forty-year-old Maxim did not reach the unit of the Czech Legion that was holding him because they were traveling by boat. Maxim was thrown into the Kama River for dead, a bayonet already plunged into his body. As he attempted to swim away he was finished off by machine-gun fire. One way or the other, his fate had been sealed, for after the Bolsheviks recaptured Chistopol, they executed all the leaders of the Socialist Revolutionary Party, with whom they had entered into only a temporary alliance.

The Communist Party Rules with an Iron Fist

The Bolsheviks wanted to create a classless society, following the ideas of Karl Marx and Friedrich Engels. Because the bourgeois capitalistic "state" was doomed to disappear, according to Marxist doctrine, Lenin concentrated on building up the party. In 1917, the Bolsheviks, under Lenin's leadership, had sought to reconnect with the radical traditions of fifty years earlier by changing the name of their Russian Social Democratic Workers' Party to the Russian Communist Party (the term "communist" refers to the Paris *communards* in the Franco-Prussian War, 1870-71).

The party, which formed a parallel structure to the government institutions, prescribed every aspect of society. The president was the official head of state, but the actual leader was the party's general secretary. The party's executive body and most important organ was not the government but the *Politburo* (an abbreviation of Political Bureau), the Central Committee of the Communist Party, which charted the general course to be followed. The Supreme Soviet (the highest legislative power) and the People's Congress were subordinated to the Central Committee of the party and the Party Congress respectively. In all businesses, schools, hospitals, and armed services there was a *pervy otdel,* ("first department") of the secret service, to keep an eye on things and to make sure the party line was being followed. The undisguised ambition of the Bolsheviks to unleash a world revolution led to the founding of the Third International Comintern in March 1919, a worldwide cooperative of Communist parties under the leadership of the Russian Communist Party. This replaced the defunct Second International.

The Bolsheviks adopted an anti-Russian attitude right from the start. After all, the success of the revolution demanded the elimination of the old regime, which had been based on the landowning nobility and the Russian Orthodox Church from time immemorial. The first government consisted mainly of Jews and only one ethnic Russian. In December 1922, after the end of the Russian civil war, Lenin formed the Union of Soviet Socialist Republics (USSR, or the Soviet Union for short) as a multicultural state with fifteen Soviet republics, twenty autonomous regions, and ten national districts. The various peoples were given plenty of room to develop in terms of language and culture, with minimum representation at every level and a fixed quota of students at the universities. Yet that separate identity was merely a thin layer covering the Communist uniformity beneath. Russia, which contained 55 percent of the country's inhabitants and 76 percent of the land surface, was the largest Soviet republic by far; but it did not receive preferential treatment.

After the formation of the Soviet Union, the name of the party was changed to the Communist Party of the Soviet Union. Before long, the Bolsheviks had created a completely different society. Because of their draconian measures — the so-called Red Terror — the population became so frightened that it obeyed the regime blindly. "People's courts" replaced the existing courts of law. The touchstone for judicial decisions was no longer the law but revolutionary conscience. Wealthy citizens and the nobility were ordered to share their land and houses with their workers. On January 31, 1918, the Julian calendar was replaced by the Gregorian, which meant that the next day was February 14, as it was in the West. Thus, according to the new calendar, the October Revolution no longer had taken place on October 25-26, 1917, but on November 7-8, 1917.

The Communists built up a sophisticated control network that extended from cradle to grave. All branches of society played a role, from schools and clubs to the *babushkas* (old women), *upravdoms* (building caretakers), and funeral directors. Anyone who traveled, relocated, or registered his or her presence (which was mandatory if a person stayed in

a place longer than seventy-two hours) had to apply for an internal passport or risk arrest. A fourteen-page dossier was begun on anyone who obtained such a passport, and it was systematically updated and supple-
mented over the years.

If you wanted to move to a city, you needed a residence permit in addition to your passport. To secure this, you had to have a job, but you
could only get a job if you had a place to live or permission from the party,
the government, or the secret service. This stringent policy kept peasants
shackled to their land. They could only "escape" by marriage or by joining
the army or the secret service.

The capstone of the control network was the Extraordinary Commission for Combating Counter-Revolution, Speculation and Sabotage, or
Cheka, the first intelligence service of the Soviet Union and the Bolshevik
successor to *Okhrana.* The Cheka was chiefly manned by Latvians, and
the founder and first director of the service, Felix Dzerzhinsky, came
from Polish nobility. Hundreds of thousands of authentic, suspected, or
potential opponents of the regime were arrested and killed without trial
by Chinese assassins or hired killers. This fate befell mainly followers of
the czar and the landed nobility, who were first robbed of their power,
prestige, titles, possessions, and money. They were mercilessly elimi-
nated, not because they had done anything wrong but exclusively because
of their social origins and what they were thought to be capable of doing.
Others were labeled "enemies of the people" and were "re-educated" in
the notorious concentration camps that formed an essential part of the
Soviet system.

"Every Religious Idea Is . . . a Most Odious Blight"

The Bolsheviks immediately implemented a policy of separation of
church and state. Lenin had a deep aversion to anything that smelled of
religion. He said: "Every religious idea, even playing with the idea that
God exists, is an unspeakable horror and a most odious blight." Church
property was nationalized, schools were transferred to the Ministry of
Education, and Russian Orthodoxy lost its monopoly as the state religion.
Atheism became the state philosophy — indeed, the only philosophy of
life — that was taught. It was promoted by the Union of Militant Atheists,
which was created in 1925 and was responsible for the organization and
management of antireligious education.

Although the constitution of January 1924 guaranteed freedom of religion, the long list of restrictions imposed on it left nothing but a caricature. The *dvadtsatkas* (literally, "twenty") were boards of twenty people that were responsible for a parish or religious congregation, but they were given the churches only on loan. Their total dependence on the local soviets finally broke the power of the church hierarchy. Tichon of Moscow, who was chosen patriarch of the Russian Orthodox Church after the abdication of Czar Nicholas II in 1917, excommunicated the Bolsheviks and campaigned against the regime. During the famine of 1921, which claimed five million lives, the patriarch sold unconsecrated property to buy food, and the government responded by ordering the sale of all church property that was not immediately needed.

In 1922, Tichon landed in prison because of his opposition to the Communists, and during the wave of terror that followed there were between 1,400 and 1,800 victims (depending on the source) from among the clergy. A revolutionary court of law put God on trial — this was not a joke! — and condemned him to death. Christian holidays were replaced by Communist celebrations, such as International Women's Day on May 8, Labor Day on May 1, and the commemoration of the October Revolution on November 7. And because Christmas was forbidden by the Soviets, Ded Moroz, or Father Frost, became the proletarian counterpart to the Western Santa Claus.

From the New Economic Policy to a Planned Economy

After the economic experiment of worker self-management ended in total chaos in the latter days of the Russian Revolution, all businesses were nationalized. When the gross national product dropped to one-seventh of its prewar level, Lenin introduced the "New Economic Policy" in 1921. In this new "policy," private enterprises were permitted once again, but the government controlled all the banks, mines, and heavy industry. All land became state property, after which many peasants set up the centuries-old *mir* system. They had to turn over half their production to the government at fixed prices and were allowed to put the surplus on the free market, after paying a tax *in natura.* In 1924 the agrarian sector finally reached its prewar level, and industrial production reached half that level.

After the death of Lenin on January 21, 1924, Joseph Stalin defeated

Trotsky in the internal power struggle. Stalin quickly introduced free education and free health care and cheap public transportation. He also introduced rigorous inland economic reform, the so-called Five-Year Plan, to speed up the industrialization of the Soviet Union. In 1928 he put an end to Lenin's New Economic Policy and replaced it with a "planned economy." At the same time he pressed ahead with the forced collectivization of agriculture and cattle-breeding, using strong-arm tactics. In the first five-year plan (1928-32), fixed production figures were set for each industrial sector, which meant that within five years a certain quantity of goods had to be produced. The quality of those products, or the demand for them, was of no consequence. Quantity was the most important criterion. At the same time, agriculture was collectivized. To put this process in motion, the government set up 240,000 *kolkhozy* and *sovkhozy*, which were responsible for the production and the processing of agricultural products. Resistance to this forced collectivization by the "wealthier" independent peasants, whom Soviet propaganda unjustly called *kulaks* and who were often held in high esteem in the traditional communities, led to their mass imprisonment, deportation, and execution. After all, the agrarian class was the only group in society that was still potentially capable of organized revolt. Many peasants preferred to slaughter their animals and destroy their harvest rather than hand them over to the government.

In March 1930, when the fear arose that the peasants would refuse to plant their crops, Stalin approved the establishment of "auxiliary farms," which were private lands on which the peasants could grow vegetables and fruit and keep a few cattle for their private use. But the harshly enforced agricultural reform began under adverse conditions as a result of the failed harvests of 1931 and 1932. In the Ukraine there was a *holodomor,* a deliberate famine induced by Stalin to break that republic as a political factor; it took at least seven million lives. Stalin repeated this tactic later in a number of other regions.

The eventual agricultural surplus that collectivization produced after a few years laid the basis for the industrialization of the Soviet Union. The increased production of coal, steel, and electricity led to the development of the aeronautics and automobile industries, but that went hand in hand with absolutely rigid discipline and the limited production of consumer goods. The second five-year plan (1933-37), worked out by the Gosplan (the committee for economic planning in the Soviet Union), focused on heavy industry and introduced a number of material incentives, that is, in addition to coercion. Anyone who exceeded production targets would receive more wages, better housing, extra vacation, and access to more consumer goods. For example, Alexei Stakhanov, who mined 102 tons of coal in a single day, was made a national hero.

Yet terror remained the favorite means for reaching the desired goals. The number of prisoners in the concentration camps rose from 180,000 in 1930 to half a million in 1934. Since their beginnings in 1928, these camps also served an economic function: the prisoners were put to work mining the rich natural resources of Siberia, according to an ancient biblical principle: "He who will not work, neither shall he eat." Kolyma, rich in minerals and gold but the coldest and most desolate region of the Soviet Union, symbolized the greatest hardships of the Gulag. As a state within a state, each camp had its own hierarchy, rules, and customs. But in all the camps the prisoners were given insufficient food and threadbare clothing; ill treatment was common, and many were literally worked to death.

The Restrictions on the Russian Orthodox Church

After the death of Patriarch Tichon in 1925, the Russian Orthodox Church was not permitted to appoint a successor to him, despite the fact that "Acting Patriarch" Sergius pledged loyalty to the Communist regime in 1927. In 1929, the laws governing "religious societies," as the parishes were called from then on, came into effect, tightening the administrative restrictions for religious communities even further. Prayer meetings and gatherings for young people were forbidden, as were the establishment of libraries and the provision of organized aid for the sick. Work shifts with alternating days off were introduced, making it difficult to organize worship services on Sundays.

The local soviet could seize a church building at a moment's notice, and it was given veto rights in the election of the board of the *dvadtsatka* and the appointment of the clergy. The Kazan cathedral of Leningrad (as Saint Petersburg was renamed in 1924, after Lenin's death) was closed after the Russian Revolution; it was reopened in 1932 as the Museum for the History of Religion and Atheism. And in Moscow the demolition of Christ the Savior cathedral began in July 1932. This was Russian Orthodoxy's main church, as well as the largest church in the Soviet Union. In December 1932 the last remains were blown up along with a few priests who refused to leave. A megalomaniacal plan for the building of a 975-foot high "Palace of the Soviets" on the site, with a 325-foot statue of Lenin on the roof, consumed vast quantities of money over a number of years, but after Stalin's death it was filed away for good.

On January 1, 1938, rent for the use of church buildings was increased by 1200 percent. One year later there were only four active bishops left, and only two to three hundred churches were still open. According to the British expert William C. Fletcher, the Russian Orthodox Church found itself on the brink of oblivion during those years, and as a social institution it practically disappeared. Yet Stalin was still unable to wipe the church out entirely. It was too deeply anchored in the "Russian soul."

The "Great Purge" Eliminates Opponents and Rivals

The murder of Sergei Kirov, Leningrad's popular Communist Party secretary, on December 1, 1934, triggered the "Great Purge," a merciless witch-hunt that Stalin, who was sinking into paranoia, conducted on suspected opponents and rivals. Show trials were conducted for tried and true Bolsheviks who confessed to being spies, saboteurs, and agents of capitalist and imperialist powers. Of the 139 members of the Central Committee of the Communist Party of the Soviet Union, 110 were arrested and 98 were executed. Only 59 of the 1,196 delegates at the Party Congress in 1934, which was held every five years, were still there five years later. In the army, 78 of the 88 top military men and half of the 35,000 officers were executed. An estimated four million of the ten million who were arrested did not survive the Great Purge. Among those were 45,000 priests and others in religious orders. The population of the Gulag camps rose to 1.9 million.

In one village in Tatarstan, the name of the school director, Yemelian Firsov, was on the black list. This former army officer had remained secretly loyal to his Protestant faith after the war, but he had not told his children for fear of reprisals. An agent informed him that his arrest was imminent. When the secret service came to snatch him from his bed at the crack of dawn, he managed to escape through a secret hatch in the fence surrounding his house, and he ran into a nearby forest, where he lived in hiding for three years. On the pretext of gathering wood, his wife and twelve-year-old daughter, Margarita Firsova, who later became the mother of Alexander Ogorodnikov, provided him with food. The Russians' entrance into World War II in 1941 was what saved Yemelian. He moved to the city of Sormovo, on the other side of Tatarstan; his family gradually followed, and they built up a new life together.

Iol Ogorodnikov, son of Commissar Maxim Ogorodnikov (who was murdered in 1918), was a college student during the Great Purge. When a poem was found under his pillow that didn't square with the prescribed "socialist realism," Iol was successful in appealing to the status of his father as "victim of the Revolution."

From 1932 on, "socialist realism" was the only kind of artistic expression that was tolerated. "Our tanks are worthless," said Joseph Stalin, "if the souls that drive them are made of clay. So I say: the production of souls is more important than the production of tanks. Writers are the engineers of the human soul." Every book or work of art had to demonstrate reality in its revolutionary development; it had to radiate optimism, enthusiasm, and heroism; and it had to whip up the masses to exert themselves with even greater fervor. The Main Administration for the Protection of State Secrets in the Press (abbreviated as Glavlit), which employed 70,000 censors, put a code on every piece of printed matter (even including bus tickets), which consisted of a letter and five numbers. The writers Maxim Gorky, Konstantin Paustovsky, and Nikolai Ostrovski were the standard-bearers of "socialist realism," and millions of copies of their novels were printed.

The Second "Great Patriotic War" and Stalin's Revenge

At the end of the 1930s the Soviet Union was drawn into worldwide military escalation. During the Spanish civil war the country had supported the left-wing People's Front, but when it came to Adolf Hitler's Germany, a Soviet agreement with France and Britain on a common strategy was not forthcoming. So Stalin decided to make the best of a tough situation. The Molotov-Ribbentrop Pact, a nonaggression treaty signed on August 23, 1939, by the Soviet Union and Nazi Germany (named after the Soviet minister of foreign affairs, Vyacheslav Molotov, and his German counterpart, Joachim von Ribbentrop), marked off the spheres of influence between the two countries. The Soviet Union annexed the Baltic states of Finland, Estonia, Lithuania, and Latvia, a few parts of Romania, and part of Poland.

Despite warnings from Soviet diplomats, Joseph Stalin refused to believe that Germany would invade. But on June 22, 1941, along a 930-mile front, three and a half million German soldiers swept into the country. This campaign, whose code name was Operation Barbarossa, was the beginning of what the Soviet Union came to call the second "Great Patriotic War"; in the first "Great Patriotic War," the French emperor Napoleon Bonaparte had suffered a disastrous defeat at the hands of the Russians.

During their rapid advance, the Germans captured 70 percent of the iron and steel industry and 40 percent of the Soviet Union's "granary." About two million people died in the siege of Leningrad, which lasted from September 8, 1941, to January 27, 1944 — with the Germans still unable to take the city. Nor did Moscow or Stalingrad end up in German hands. Tatarstan grew into one of the most prosperous regions of Russia during World War II, not only because of its rich mineral resources (oil and gas) but also because high-quality industries were moved to Tatarstan to get them away from the front line. Therefore, in 1942, the Vostok Watch Factory of Chistopol was established when the Second Moscow Watch Factory was evacuated. Chistopol was not only the home of the Ogorodnikov family, but also of the writer Boris Pasternak, who lived there for a short time.

There was a temporary thaw in the relations between the Soviet government and the Russian Orthodox Church. Stalin, a former seminarian, had contact with the church leaders, and he eased the strict enforcement of antireligious legislation and reopened many church buildings. The reason for this was twofold. First, it was a reaction to the German policy of immediately opening all the churches in captured areas. Stalin wished to put an end to the secret sympathy that the populace felt for the formerly "friendly" Nazis — in the Ukraine they were greeted as liberators — and to elevate the low morale among civilians and troops. The government also adopted a more tolerant attitude toward Islam, which the Communists regarded as the most backward of religions. Stalin's desire was to mobilize all segments of society in the fight against Nazi Germany.

The fortunes of war turned after the surrender of the German general Friedrich Paulus at Stalingrad in February 1943. The Germans gradually retreated, and in June 1944 all of the Soviet Union was liberated. The Red Army advanced in triumph into Poland, Hungary, Austria, and Germany, and on April 25, 1945, in Torgau on the Elbe, they fell into the arms of the American soldiers. On May 2 the German capital of Berlin fell, and the Red Army was among the victors. But the war had taken a heavy toll in the Soviet Union: 27 million dead and 25 million homeless.

Stalin, who regarded himself as a genius, exacted horrific revenge on the Germans for having stabbed him in the back. The Soviet soldiers conducted a massive rape of German women, and of the 1.8 million Soviet soldiers who returned from captivity as German prisoners of war in 1945, more than 100,000 were executed or sent immediately to prison camps in the Gulag. In 1941, the Volga Germans were collectively deported to Kazakhstan on suspicion of collaboration, and their autonomous republic (established in 1924) was dissolved. The same fate befell the Crimean Tatars and the Turkish Meschetes. On May 18, 1944, the Crimean Tatars were moved to Uzbekistan in tightly sealed railroad cars. Half the women, children, and elderly died on the way (the men were conscripted into the army) or after they arrived in their new "homeland." And in September 1944, all the Meschetes were exiled to Uzbekistan. Of the 120,000 Meschetes deported in cattle cars, more than 10,000 died en route.

Stalin began a similar merciless witch-hunt against the Jews. For geopolitical reasons — the expansion of the sphere of influence in the Middle East — the Soviet Union supported the establishment of the state of Israel in May 1948. Before the Bolshevik Revolution of 1917, Russia had been the center of Jewish culture and the birthplace of Zionism, since half of all the Jews in the Diaspora lived in Russia at the time. Most of the leaders of the young state of Israel were born in the Soviet Union, and the Israeli army was formed under the leadership of a Soviet general. However, the new state's choosing to side with the United States led to Stalin's policy of anti-Semitism.

In the Grip of the Cold War

In the years following World War II, the Soviet Union emerged as the most influential country in Europe and — after the United States — the most powerful country in the world. In 1947-48, pro-Soviet regimes came to power in Poland, Czechoslovakia, Hungary, Yugoslavia, Romania, Albania, and Bulgaria. The zone of occupied Germany controlled by the Soviet Union, including part of the capital of Berlin, became the German Democratic Republic (GDR). In all those countries, Soviet experts had the last word.

The "Iron Curtain" (a term coined by British prime minister Winston Churchill) — a border running straight through Europe, from Stettin on the Baltic Sea to Trieste on the Adriatic — became a fact. The Communist International (also known as the Third International), which was dissolved in 1943 because of World War II, was replaced in 1947 by the Communist Information Bureau, Cominform, of which the French and Italian Communist parties were also members. Only the Yugoslavia of Josip Broz, better known as Tito, did not recognize the political dominance of the Soviet Union and set an autonomous course.

The polarization persisted during the Cold War. When the Americans came up with the Marshall Plan, which was meant to breathe new life into the economies of Western Europe, the USSR countered with the Council for Mutual Economic Assistance, or Comecon. And as an answer to the North Atlantic Treaty Organization (NATO), a military alliance consisting of the United States and a number of Western European countries, the Soviets formed the Warsaw Pact: a military alliance of Communist countries in Eastern Europe.

The scorched-earth policy that both Hitler and Stalin had followed during the war had left the Soviet Union in economic chaos by 1945. A new five-year plan became the basis for an economic kick-start. The prevailing rigid discipline, even harsher now than in the 1930s, finally began to yield fruit. In 1950 the Soviet Union produced one and a half times more coal and steel than it had before the war.

The return to the ideological hard line not only affected academics, writers, and artists; it also went hand in hand with the destruction of churches, the persecution of believers, and the imprisonment of priests, rabbis, and muftis. The Gulag camps held 2.5 million prisoners, more than ever before.

In the late 1930s, two children had been born to Iol Ogorodnikov and his first wife, Nadelia: Igor in 1936 and Ludmila in 1938. But while Iol was spending the entire "Second Great Patriotic War" in the Soviet army, Nadelia died of tuberculosis. After the war, Iol married Margarita Firsova in 1949, and together they had two more sons: Alexander in 1950 and Boris in 1951. A talented engineer, Iol Ogorodnikov was made the manager of a factory. But because he paid so much attention to improving the living conditions of the workers — which ran counter to the party line — he was fired. Iol then took a job at the Vostok Watch Factory in Chistopol.

The whole family — father Iol, mother Margarita, the four children, plus Iol's mother — lived in a one-room apartment. There was nothing unusual about this, since the Soviet leaders had not yet solved the housing shortage. The official norm of nine square meters of living space per inhabitant was never reached. As a result of the cramped living conditions, Iol's son Igor went to Kazan to live when he was twenty-five, and Ludmila moved to the Far East after her marriage. Since Boris often stayed with his grandfather, Yemelian Firsov, Alexander was usually the only child at home.

The First Wave of Liberalization under Nikita Khrushchev

After the death of Stalin on March 5, 1953, KGB boss Lavrenti Beria immediately released a million prisoners from the Gulag and put an end to compulsory forced labor. This decision was made mainly for financial reasons, since the camps were soaking up 16 percent of the national budget each year. But Beria's dynamic style quickly met with opposition, and in September 1953 the power struggle that ensued after Stalin's death was won by Nikita Khrushchev. On December 23, 1953, Beria was executed, and the members of his staff were sent to languish in the Perm-36 concentration camp.

As a faithful follower of Stalin — "his tongue was in Stalin's ass up to the tonsils" was a popular Russian expression — Khrushchev violently crushed the popular uprising that took place in East Germany in 1953. Yet the new Communist Party leader did not conduct a reign of terror like that of his predecessor. In fact, the relaxed atmosphere following the death of Stalin brought the first signs of a liberal tendency, which picked up speed when Khrushchev publicly denounced the former leader at the Twentieth Party Congress on February 23, 1956: "Stalin replaced the method of ideological struggle with violence, oppression and terror."

A shock wave could be felt throughout the country. Under Stalin's regime, at least 28.7 million people had been sent as forced laborers to 476 concentration camps, and 10 percent of them had died there. This minimal estimate reduces to an abstraction all the arbitrary executions and all those who died on the way to the camps, during their interrogation in prison, or a few days after being released. Writer Alexander Solzhenitsyn reported the figure of 50 million forced laborers, while some historians speak of between 60 and 70 million persons. An exact number of victims of this inconceivable human tragedy, unparalleled in human history up to the present day, can never be determined.

During that period, Khrushchev replaced the book that Stalin himself had written — *A Short Course on the History of the Communist Party of the Soviet Union,* an ideological tract that was meant to validate his power — with a revised *History of the Communist Party,* which greatly modified the titanic role Stalin had set aside for himself. The unmasking of Stalin led to a profound question: How could all this have happened? For the first time, Russian intellectuals were casting serious doubts on the Communist system, which until then had been beyond criticism. The progressive literary magazine *Novy Mir* (New World) published an influential essay by Vladimir Dudintsev, "On Sincerity in Literature," as well as his novel *Not by Bread Alone,* which was an indictment of the repression of the individual by the bureaucracy. Ilya Ehrenburg published his novella *The Thaw* in 1954, and poets read their own work on Mayakovsky Square in Moscow again, just as the futurist poet Vladimir Mayakovsky had done in the 1920s.

But after a few months the tide turned repressive again. The expressions of solidarity with the workers' uprising in the Polish city of Poznań led to an uprising in Hungary in 1956. When non-Communists also became part of the new Hungarian government of Imre Nagy, the troops of the Warsaw Pact stepped in to set things right by force. Thousands were killed in the weeks of street fighting in Budapest. In the Soviet Union, hundreds of protesting students were dismissed from the universities in Moscow and Leningrad. After Gosizdat, the state publishing company, signed a deal for the Italian publication of Boris Pasternak's novel *Doctor Zhivago* — a lament about the demise of the old intelligentsia that presents a less than flattering picture of the October Revolution of 1917 — the work was banned in Pasternak's own country. When Pasternak was awarded the Nobel Prize for Literature on October 23, 1958, he refused to accept it under pressure from the regime. Shortly thereafter, the first clandestine literary magazines appeared: *Syntax,* founded by twenty-four-year-old Alexander Ginsburg, and *Boomerang,* founded by twenty-one-year-old Vladimir Osipov. But both young men ended up behind bars, making them the first dissidents of the post-Stalin generation.

The summit conferences of the Communist world leaders of 1957 and 1960 confirmed the leading role of the Soviet Union as the "beacon of the international Communist movement." The encouraging economic figures made General Secretary Khrushchev overconfident. "Within seven years, we, the Russians, will have surpassed the Americans. Then we'll be on top, and we'll smile down and wave," he boasted to Vice President Richard Nixon in July 1959 at an exhibition of the achievements of the American consumer society that was held in Sokolniki Park in Moscow.

Intensified Antireligious Campaign

Nikita Khrushchev, portly and jovial but at the same time headstrong and impulsive, was notorious for his vulgar behavior. At a session of the United Nations in New York he pounded his shoe on the speaker's podium in protest against a remark by the Philippine representative, Lorenzo Sumulang. In 1959, Khrushchev, an ideological hard-liner, launched a new antireligious campaign. When Patriarch Alexei I protested against the wave of atheistic propaganda, he was forced to relinquish his official duties to his deputy, Pimen, and a committee was appointed for every parish to make sure that the legislation on religious cults was being properly observed.

The antireligious legislation of 1929 was intensified with the publication of the *Instruction on the Application of the Legislation on Religious Cults* in 1961. Those who did not raise their children according to the *Moral Code of a Builder of Communism* could be deprived of their parental rights. A priest was only to concern himself with the liturgy and was no longer allowed to participate in meetings of the parish council. No one under the age of eighteen was allowed to attend a religious service. Religious education was forbidden, and the minimum age for baptism was thirty years. Those who violated the regulations risked a three-year jail sentence.

This rigorous approach resulted in the deregistration of 44 percent of all churches. Fifty-three of the sixty-nine Orthodox monasteries were forced to close their doors. When the Russian Orthodox Church joined the World Council of Churches, Khrushchev tried to neutralize the international criticism of his antireligious campaign. "The atheistic regime feared the Bible and a dynamic religious community because Christianity was the most important alternative ideology to Marxism," concluded the Baptist leader Georgi Vins.

The new Russian Penal Code of 1960 officially put an end to the arbitrary rule of the Stalinist period. From then on, a suspect could only be convicted after having been found guilty of a crime by a court of law. A number of new sections of the law, however, imposed restrictions on freedom of speech. Article 70 punished "agitation" in small groups — as well as large-scale "propaganda" that undermined the Soviet regime — with a maximum of seven years of imprisonment and five years of exile. Recidivists risked ten years in jail and five years in exile. Those who had not intended to undermine the regime, however, could receive three years of imprisonment or one year of work in a re-education camp for "deliberately spreading deceitful fabrications" under Article 190.

Disturbing the peace and having contempt for society could result in a conviction of "hooliganism" under Article 206. Anyone who failed to perform any socially useful work for four months and did not live on his own income could be put behind bars for a year for "systematic vagrancy or mendicancy leading to a parasitic way of life." Often convicts lost their residence permits, so they couldn't return to their homes after being released. Those who tried to do so risked a new conviction for violating the passport law. In any case, arbitrary sentencing remained rife because the courts did not demand a burden of proof from the Public Prosecution Department.

CHAPTER TWO

From *Homo Sovieticus* to Samizdat

"I Want to Die for the Ideals of the Revolution"

Alexander Ogorodnikov grew up in the spirit of Communism. In 1957, when he was seven years old, he joined the Little Octobrists children's organization, and later the Young Pioneers. The hero of his youth was Pavlik Morozov, who was murdered in 1932 at the age of thirteen after having reported his father's "counterrevolutionary activities" to the authorities. At school Ogorodnikov rose to the position of chairman of his chapter of the Pioneers. This youth group helped young people with learning disabilities, collected old iron and paper, and visited elderly people who were sick. The Pioneers sang, danced, played, engaged in sports, cared for their bodies, and proudly wore their uniforms. When Alexander became ill with a rare disease, he had to undergo several blood transfusions and spend a great deal of time in the hospital, where he eagerly immersed himself in Pioneer literature.

Banners and signs with heroic statements and portraits of outstanding workers adorned the streets at that time. Ogorodnikov was brought up to love his homeland, his parents, and peace. He learned to be diligent, neat, and disciplined, to respect workers, and to be helpful wherever he could be. Communism's international character spoke to his imagination. At school there was a world map hanging on the wall with little flags indicating the Communist countries. He wished to die for the ideals of Communism, just as his grandfather Maxim had, and as a youngster he was fascinated by the Cuban Revolution. The way Fidel Castro had brought down the regime of General Fulgencio Batista seemed like child's play to him. Young Alexander detested the "pernicious cancer" of capitalism —

with its drug users, unemployment, crime, and the war in Vietnam. Were not the economy, social services, education, and health care of the Communist regime superior to those of the capitalist world? These sentiments and principles had been hammered into him since kindergarten. The lead that the Soviet Union had over the United States in the space race seemed the best proof. When Yuri Gagarin made the first manned journey into space aboard the Vostok 1 on April 12, 1961, the Soviet Union was wild with joy.

Ogorodnikov venerated Karl Marx, Friedrich Engels, and Vladimir Lenin, and was impressed by the military parades that marched on Moscow's Red Square every May 1st, when the regime showed off its power and prestige. Like every child of his generation, he firmly believed that the iron logic of worldwide Communism would banish slavery. He was eager to support that historic struggle and to convert the capitalist countries to Communism.

Ogorodnikov, an ethnic Russian, was barely aware that his best friends, including Nail Valeev, the current minister of education and science of the republic of Tatarstan, were Tatars. At school all the children were dealt with on equal terms. In its effort to preserve the Tatar identity, the government required Tatar youngsters to take lessons in their native language, literature, and history, though they themselves were somewhat indifferent to the subject. Like the rest of his generation, Alexander was given an atheist education. Later he learned that his grandmother, who had remained secretly loyal to her Orthodox beliefs after the Revolution of 1917, had had him baptized shortly after his birth. When the grandmother died, Alexander's mother inherited a number of icons, which she hid in a bookcase. Ogorodnikov pleaded with her to destroy the icons, but she never did.

Ivan Denisovich and the Second Wave of Liberalization

At the Twenty-first Party Congress of 1961, the supporters of liberalization were given more encouragement. "There are many things that need to be resolved, and we must communicate the truth to the Party and the people," announced General Secretary Khrushchev. "De-Stalinization must be carried on. The people have the right to know what happened in those dark years."

One result of this second wave of liberalization was the removal of the body of Stalin from the Lenin Mausoleum on Red Square in Moscow. And Stalingrad was to be called Volgograd from then on. Literary magazines, including the authoritative Soviet journal *Novy Mir,* opened their columns to articles that previously would never have withstood the scrutiny of the censor. The work of Boris Pasternak, Osip Mandelstam, and Anna Akhmatova, the real standard-bearers of twentieth-century Russian literature, was printed and distributed. Evenings of poetry readings were held at Lenin Stadium in Moscow, where poets read from their own work. In his poem "The Heirs of Stalin," which appeared in the Party newspaper *Pravda* on October 21, 1962, Yevgeni Yevtushenko warned of the power of the conservative wing: "They attack Stalin from the rostrum, but at night, deep within themselves, they nostalgically evoke the past." Composer Igor Stravinsky paved the way for the interpretation of modern music with his visit to the Soviet Union in 1962.

In his effort to cultivate a more voluntaristic attitude among the people, Khrushchev allowed the journal *Novy Mir* to publish the text of *One Day in the Life of Ivan Denisovich* on November 20, 1962, the first novel by Alexander Solzhenitsyn, a former prisoner who worked as a mathematics teacher in Ryazan. "No one has the right to change the author's version," said the general secretary, thereby putting the entire censorship structure at risk. For many, the book was a true revelation because Solzhenitsyn finally broke the taboo against revealing the true nature of the Gulag. The suffering of the protagonist, who was serving a ten-year prison sentence, was meaningless and hopeless. The difference between this candid approach and "socialist realism" was striking. Although Denisovich accepted his fate, the novel was a cutting indictment of the Gulag. The 94,900 copies of that issue of *Novy Mir* sold out in no time. Later, more works about the concentration camps appeared, including *Years off My Life* by Alexander Gorbatov and *Diary* by Nina Kosterina. The poet Anna Akhmatova was finally able to publish her masterpiece, "Requiem" (1935-40), and her last great work, "Poem without a Hero" (1940-65).

However, when Khrushchev attended an exhibition of abstract art in Moscow and allowed himself to be sucked into a discussion with sculptor Ernst Neizvestny, it was more than the conservative wing could take. The general secretary was forced to back off on his liberalization policy by issuing an attack on modern art: "A donkey could do better with his tail." Symphony no. 12 ("The Year 1917") by Dmitri Shostakovich, one of Russia's greatest twentieth-century composers, was banned from the concert halls, and the radio began broadcasting folk songs and military marches once again. When the second wave of liberalization came to an end, the first victim was twenty-year-old Vladimir Bukovsky, who worked on the staff of the clandestine literary magazine *Phoenix 61*. Bukovsky was put in a psychiatric hospital for fifteen months for possessing the book *The New Class: An Analysis of the Communist System*, by Milovan Djilas, the former vice president of Yugoslavia, who had fallen into disfavor.

A Return to the Hard Line under Leonid Brezhnev

In the autumn of 1962, the Cold War suddenly escalated. In September, photos taken from American spy planes had revealed that the Russians were deploying nuclear missiles on Cuba. On October 22, 1962, the crisis became public when President John F. Kennedy made a scathing speech in which he demanded the immediate dismantling of all Soviet missile bases on Cuba and announced a blockade of all munitions bound for the island. Two days later, on October 24, the day the blockade was to go into effect, the Soviet ships, with nuclear warheads on board, appeared to be close to entering the quarantine zone. On October 28 it became known that Khrushchev had decided to comply with U. S. demands and to have the ships make a U-turn. This became known as the "Cuban Missile Crisis," and the world narrowly escaped a nuclear war.

Khrushchev suffered even more loss of face when the country had disappointing agricultural yields and its relationship with China soured. For a number of members of the Communist Party's Politburo — the actual government — this was the last straw. Alexander Shelepin, head of the KGB, took the initiative of giving Khrushchev the boot after the latter's son-in-law, Alexei Adzubei, said in West Berlin that Moscow had no problem with possible German reunification. Shelepin hoped that he would be the next in line, but after Khrushchev disappeared in October 1964, a triumvirate consisting of General Secretary Leonid Brezhnev, President Nikolai Podgorny, and Premier Alexei Kosygin emerged.

The period of liberalization was history. Under the watchful eye of Party ideologue Mikhail Suslov, the clock was turned back. Solzhenitsyn's *One Day in the Life of Ivan Denisovich* was put on the blacklist, and on May 8, 1965, Leonid Brezhnev praised his predecessor Joseph Stalin as a strategist and victor over the fascist armed forces. When Stalin was officially rehabilitated during the Twenty-second Party Congress in 1966, twenty-five leading progressive artists and scientists protested, among them Andrei Sakharov. The restoration of order went hand in hand with the imprisonment of opponents of the regime, though there was no return to the Stalinist terror.

The antireligious policy remained unchanged as well. In 1964 the American professor Paul Anderson estimated that the number of religious believers in the Soviet Union was 64 million: 35 million Russian Orthodox, 15 million Muslims, 5 million Old Believers (or *Starovery*), 4 million Baptists, 3.5 million Catholics, 900,000 Lutherans, 500,000 religious Jews, 90,000 Calvinists, and 10,000 Mennonites. A report issued by the Institute for Marxism-Leninism of the Communist Party warned that the remnants of religious ideology, that is, prejudice and superstition, would continue to exist: "Because it will not die out by itself, a ceaseless struggle must be fought against it. The victory over religious prejudice remains an important part of a Communist upbringing."

In 1966 the power to set up and close houses of worship was taken from the local authorities and given to the Central Council for Religious Affairs (CRA). Within the Orthodox clergy there was considerable disagreement over what course to follow. Despite his many contacts with dissidents, Father Alexander Men could not reconcile open resistance with his priestly calling, while Father Sergei Zheludkov regarded dissent to be his sacred duty. Fathers Gleb Yakunin and Nikolai Eschliman lost their parishes after sending an open letter to Patriarch Alexei I, in 1965, in which they asked that the yoke of state control be removed.

Because of their fundamental anti-Soviet attitude, true Orthodox Christians, the true Orthodox Church, and, as the largest group, the *Starovery* ("Old Believers") were severely persecuted. (The *Starovery* had distanced themselves from the liturgical reforms adopted by Patriarch Nikon in 1666-67, which were meant to bring the Russian Orthodox Church into line with the Greek Orthodox rite.) The Protestant Pentecostal church and the Seventh-day Adventists, who were conscientious objectors, received even harsher treatment. In 1966 the well-organized but underground Baptists, the Initsiativniki, even held a prayer vigil in the street in front of the main office of the Central Committee of the Communist Party in Moscow. The Muslims of the Central Asian republics were also under continuous siege, as were the Catholics in the Ukraine and Lithuania, and the Buddhists in the Far East. After Israel won the "Six-Day War" in June 1967, anti-Semitism flared up again. In 1969 there were only fifty-nine open synagogues, compared to four hundred fifty in 1956. Two hundred thousand Jews, the so-called refuseniks, wanted nothing more than to be able to immigrate to Israel.

In Service to the Komsomol Youth Movement

In 1963, at the age of thirteen, Alexander Ogorodnikov became a member of the local chapter of Komsomol, the Communist youth movement — even though the official minimum age for membership was fourteen. The regime's young storm troops numbered twenty-three million at that time. During those years young people had practically no choice but to become members. The Komsomol was *the* stepping stone to the Communist Party and a springboard to a later career.

As a committed member, Ogorodnikov took the lead in an action against the only church left in Chistopol (all the other churches had been demolished after the Bolshevik Revolution). During an Easter celebration at the church, he violently barred a group of curious youngsters, who only wanted to take a peek inside, from entering the church. He also tried to persuade the *babushkas* (old women) to stop going to church. Like everyone else of his generation, Ogorodnikov was convinced that the church would become extinct when the last religious *babushkas* had died.

When Ogorodnikov read Dostoyevsky's novel *The Brothers Karamazov*, the chapter on the Grand Inquisitor of Seville, a high point in world literature, made a deep impression on him. In a long monologue, the Grand Inquisitor addresses Jesus Christ and defends the idea that only the principles of the devil can lead to the unity of all mankind: "Give a man bread, control his conscience and rule the world." But Ogorodnikov thought Dostoyevsky was writing about intangible things.

As a *"homo Sovieticus,"* Ogorodnikov had to admit, much to his regret, that the Komsomol's recruitment practice was faltering, despite the organization's elevated social position. Many regarded the Komsomol as a leisure-time organization for vacation camps and expeditions. As a newly chosen leader, he accepted only the most noble-minded and highly motivated young people. Alexander was so devoted that he seized alcoholic drinks during a school party and handed them over to the director, and he campaigned against long hair and listening to Western pop music.

At the age of fifteen, Alexander took the initiative to form a Komsomol commando group to crack down on a few of Chistopol's criminal gangs, because they had been given free rein without police interference.

There were forty young men in the commando group, and they operated in teams of five, systematically monitoring cafés and halls that were frequented by young people. The commandos took aside those who weren't behaving themselves, and if verbal persuasion didn't work, they beat them. At the age of sixteen, Ogorodnikov was appointed leader of the BKD, which was the Komsomol public fighting unit.

At that point Alexander was no longer bothered by the weak health that had been such a hindrance when he was younger. The commando raids could be so dangerous that, during one operation, two of his comrades were killed. Whenever Ogorodnikov returned home late at night, he never opened the front door of his apartment building without checking to see if someone was about to attack him. He was actually attacked several times, but as an experienced fighter, he always managed to rid himself of his assailants. Ogorodnikov rather liked the idea of pursuing a boxing career, a sport he enjoyed. His friend Anatoly Balagonov was his sparring partner, but because of Alexander's near-sightedness, this career was never a real option. Balagonov did continue with boxing and later became a boxing champion in Chistopol.

Che Guevara, who left Cuba in 1966 to spread the revolution in Africa and Latin America, was Ogorodnikov's icon. Ogorodnikov also had a soft spot in his heart for the *Niños de la Guerra* — the children of the Spanish Communists who had immigrated to the Soviet Union during the Spanish civil war.

Much as the ideals imprinted on his mind since childhood continued to influence the thoughts of his youth, Ogorodnikov had his first contact with a girl at this time. Disillusioned, she later wrote that he didn't attract her attention the way Pavel Kortshanin had done, the protagonist in the highly autobiographical socialist-realist Bildungsroman *How the Steel Was Tempered* (1932-34) by Nikolai Ostrovsky.

Samizdat: Critical but Not Anti-Soviet

Stalin had succeeded in keeping the Gulag hidden from the outside world. When Vice President Henry Wallace of the United States visited the Kolyma mining district in Siberia in May 1944, at the height of the friendship between the United States and the Soviet Union, he was shown no prisoners. Wallace had nothing but praise for "Uncle Joe," as Stalin was known in the American press at the time, and anyone who doubted the

Soviet Union's good intentions was given a good talking to: "Those who make that claim," said Wallace, "are itching for war, consciously or unconsciously, and I think that's a crime." Professor Owen Lattimore, who accompanied Wallace, wrote in the American magazine *National Geographic:* "There has probably never been more orderly pioneering work than the opening of the far north of Russia under the Soviets."

Twenty years later, a repetition of such a farce was inconceivable. After the outbreak of the Cold War, the British Broadcasting Corporation, the Deutsche Welle, the American broadcasting service Voice of America, and Radio Free Europe/Radio Liberty, a radio broadcaster financed by the Americans, made shortwave broadcasts in Russian day and night for listeners in the Soviet Union. Powerful jamming stations in the cities blocked the news broadcasts and current events programs, but the cultural programs were not censored. This was how Alexander Ogorodnikov became acquainted with American jazz music, which fascinated him.

New means of passing on information were also developed. The appeals for artistic freedom and the right to free speech, which could be spontaneously and publicly expressed during the second wave of liberalization (1961-64), found their way to the public through clandestine channels. In 1966 the word *samizdat* (underground press) suddenly cropped up, an acronym for "self-published" and a reference to *gosizdat,* the official state publishing house. The distribution of written material took place by means of manual transcription and the repeated typing of texts. Sometimes the rare, government-controlled photocopy machines were used, or texts were printed. Samizdat was particularly popular among young authors, who expected that their writings would never pass through the censors. Besides these literary works, there was also an increasing interest in the history of Stalinism and the gulag, and the voices of social criticism were growing louder and louder. The Communist Party had failed in the past. But was it going in the right direction now? And when mistakes were made, why were individual citizens not allowed to criticize so that corrections could be implemented?

The underground publications may have been critical, but they were by no means anti-Soviet. Valery Chalidze published his magazine *Obshchestvennye Problemy* (Social Problems), but the most important informative publication at the time was certainly *Chronika.* This bulletin began in 1968 and came out every month. It consisted of twenty to thirty wafer-thin pages containing detailed information on house searches, arrests, trials, and convictions; life in the Gulag; religious persecution; and the trials and tribulations of dissidents. The reporting was reliable (every mistake was corrected in the following issue) and without further comment. Other underground periodicals that came along later were the *Chronicle of the Catholic Church of Lithuania,* the Jewish magazine *Exodus,* the *Bulletin* of the Baptists, and *The True Witness,* the publishing organ of the Seventh-day Adventists. The Baptists' underground printing house was shut down five times.

The smuggling of copies of controversial literature to the West gave samizdat an international forum. Printed material that was published abroad but distributed illegally in the Soviet Union was called *tamizdat.* The terms *magitizdat* and *radizdat* refer to new reproduction techniques — the taping and clandestine distribution of audio recordings and the recording of foreign radio broadcasts, respectively. But the government was not to be fooled with. Samizdat publishers who got caught were invariably given maximum sentences. But once the genie was out of the bottle, there was no putting it back in. The more severe the repression, the more illegal publications appeared.

Literary Dissidents Sent to the Gulag . . .

When the twenty-four-year-old poet Joseph Brodsky was put on trial in Leningrad in 1964, the Russian intelligentsia, who had become frustrated with the end of the thaw, realized that from then on nonconformism would no longer be tolerated. Apparently there was no room for Brodsky's apolitical poetry, which created a dream world beyond the reaches of Soviet reality. Charged with "parasitism," he was sentenced to five years of hard labor. The response of the West to the trial made him the standard-bearer of Russian dissidents. On April 14, 1965, thirty-five years after the suicide of the futurist poet Vladimir Mayakovsky, the artists' association SMOG, which had a Christian basis, gathered on Pushkin Square in Moscow and demanded the release of the literary dissidents Alexander Ginsburg, Vladimir Osipov, and Joseph Brodsky.

In September 1965, the writers Andrei Sinyavsky and Yuli Daniel (for security reasons they had adopted the pseudonyms Abram Terts and Nikolai Arzhak, respectively) were sent to the Gulag for clandestinely publishing their books abroad (books that may have been too progressive). Although publishing abroad was not actually forbidden, the government wanted to make an example of this case in hopes of stanching the flow of publications to the West. During their trial, which was not open to foreign journalists or friends of the accused, both were convicted of "vagrancy" and sentenced to a prison camp, Sinyavsky for seven years and Daniel for five. In the storm of protest that followed, sixty-two members of the Writers' Union demanded their release.

But the trend was irreversible. One month later, in Kiev, twenty-four Ukrainian intellectuals were convicted. Article 190 of the Penal Code was amended to criminalize public protest; but because of growing polarization, the dissident movement became more and more political and ideological.

. . . or to Psychiatric Hospitals

The new generation of detainees, who called themselves "prisoners of conscience," were separated from the ordinary Gulag prisoners. Many were sent to the work camps of Mordovia or Perm. But beginning in 1971, some of them ended up in *psikhushkas* (psychiatric hospitals). The first to suffer this fate were Vladimir Bukovsky, who had already been interned in 1961, and the artist Viktor Kuznetsov. Not only did they lose their rights, but their internment discredited them in both their own country and in the West. After all, who could object to the confinement of lunatics?

Professors Andrei Snezhnevsky and Marat Vartanyan, psychiatrists at the Serbsky National Institute for Social and Forensic Psychiatry in Moscow, defined dissidence as "a progressive form of schizophrenia that leaves no traces in the intellect or outward behavior, but causes behavior that is anti-social or abnormal." After receiving a positive diagnosis at the Serbsky Institute, the interned dissidents were forced to undergo treatment involving powerful psychopharmaceuticals (tranquilizers) or antipsychotics. Those who resisted were given increasingly larger doses of insulin, which caused them to go into a hypoglycemic coma and shock. Others were restrained in bed or wrapped in wet sheets, which shrunk as they dried and caused terrific pain.

Stubborn dissidents such as Vladimir Bukovsky were diagnosed as "mentally disturbed" and were shut up in special psychiatric hospitals that were guarded by watchtowers and barbed wire. The psychiatric clinic in the city of Dnepropetrovsk was particularly notorious. Only those who renounced their beliefs and admitted that their criticism of the

Soviet system was the fault of mental illness could be declared cured. The KGB hoped that interned dissidents would receive less attention both within the country and abroad, but the opposite was true. The abuse of psychiatry for political purposes was first denounced in 1965 in Valery Tarsis's autobiography *Ward 7: An Autobiographical Novel.* And in 1971, Vladimir Bukovsky smuggled a 150-page memorandum out of the country describing abuses in psychiatric hospitals in the Soviet Union.

A Mishmash of Opposition Movements

As a matter of fact, there never was one single dissident movement in the Soviet Union. This collective term comprised a mishmash of opposition movements, all of them devoted to respect for human rights as set down in the Constitution of the Soviet Union of 1936 and the Universal Declaration of Human Rights of 1948. Woven into the fabric of all these movements were the threads of democratic, nationalistic, and religious motives.

The neo-Marxists appealed for a return to the uncorrupted principles of Marxism-Leninism. The leaders of the Union of Communards in Leningrad were given severe sentences in 1966, and in 1970 the Marxist study groups in the cities of Saratov and Ryazan were dismantled. In 1967 the All-Russian Social Christian Union for the Liberation of the People (VSChSON) was shut down. This was a utopian political organization of university intelligentsia with branches in five cities. The organization's aim was to seize power by force and to establish a theocratic society.

Besides the dissidents who were part of organized resistance groups, there were also many typical "lone wolves." The best known were the writer Alexander Solzhenitsyn, who carried on the Slavophile tradition, and Andrei Sakharov, the "father of the Russian hydrogen bomb," who received the Nobel Peace Prize, the Lenin Prize, the Stalin Prize, the State Prize, and the *Hero of Socialist Labor* award (three times).

The experiences of the dissidents, which are described in Anatoly Marchenko's book *My Testimony,* which he wrote after his release in November 1966, did move a small group of intellectuals in some of the Russian cities, but they were mainly consumed by the Western media, the foreign journalists living in the Soviet Union. However, none of this trickled down to Chistopol, the provincial town where Alexander Ogorodnikov grew up. Even samizdat was totally unknown there.

Because of the feature films that the government released, in which the KGB cunningly unmasked all the plots hatched against it, the public developed a positive impression and opinion of the secret service: the KGB seemed prepared for every challenge. When he was in his mid-teens, Ogorodnikov became aware slowly but surely, beginning in 1966-67, of the omnipresence of the KGB. During his last year at Secondary School No. 17 in Chistopol, he came into conflict with several teachers because of his critical questions. His questions were not anti-Soviet, but they did overstep the lines drawn by the regime.

Alexander's father, Iol Ogorodnikov, was not thriving under Communism. The technically skilled elder Ogorodnikov won a great deal of praise for his inventions and also received a couple of diplomas honoring his work. But to his chagrin, none of these ideas were given concrete applications, despite their practical usefulness. Frustrated, Iol sought consolation in drink.

Because of Alexander's resolute action as head of the local Komsomol unit, many of the residents of Chistopol began taking their problems directly to him instead of the police. Thanks to his involvement, some were able to avoid going to jail for minor offenses. When the Komsomol Public Fighting Unit, under Ogorodnikov's leadership, put an end to disturbances in Chistopol in 1967, he won praise from all sides. Shortly thereafter, he was warmly commended on the front page of the daily *Komsomolskaya Pravda,* which had a circulation of twenty million, in an article entitled "The Sentinel of Courage." After giving a speech at a Komsomol congress, he was approached by a few highly placed KGB agents, who told him, "We've been following you for a while. There's a brilliant future ahead of you if you do what we ask. You can study in Prague, and we'll give you the chance to live an interesting life as long as you don't tell anyone about this conversation." Ogorodnikov already imagined himself engaged in the worldwide struggle for Communist ideals, but at the same time he was troubled by doubts. In a second conversation with KGB agents, he revealed that he had informed his mother — which was actually a lie — and he heard nothing more from them. The secret service only wanted to work with people who were one hundred percent reliable.

Soon a second career possibility presented itself, this time in Naberezhnye Chelny, the second largest city in Tatarstan, 120 miles from Chistopol. Ogorodnikov was offered the leadership of the local unit of the Komsomol, which was about to move into a new headquarters. This meant not only the beginning of a career that would almost certainly prove successful, but as a member of the Komsomol *nomenklatura,* he would have the right to a car and other material perks.

But Ogorodnikov refused. He wanted to serve as a good example in Chistopol. This was why he decided to put into practice the ideals he had acquired since childhood by taking a job at the Vostok Watch Factory as an assembly-line worker in the summer of 1967. It was in this factory, however, that Ogorodnikov saw for the first time how Communism worked in real-life situations and heard workers asking critical questions, not openly but in the smoking rooms. That criticism went further than even George Orwell's book *1984,* which he was secretly reading at the time. He realized that his work booklet, which contained detailed information on his salary, job description, promotions, transfers, demotions, recommendations, reprimands, and disciplinary measures, was a powerful instrument of control. The representative of the KGB in the personnel department could damage one's future by making negative remarks in that booklet. This was used as a constant threat, since without a work booklet one could not get another job.

Ogorodnikov's faith in the Communist system was still not in serious doubt, but he began to question the economic policy. He also realized that the constantly promised "imminent" switch from a Socialist to a Communist society — when commerce, prices, and wages would disappear — was, in fact, a utopia. In addition, little was happening with the approved plan for the reform of 1965 based on the work of economics professor Evsei Liberman. The plan provided for more freedom for managers, a more flexible interpretation of plans, more demand-based production, and a fixed distribution of profits for workers. But the Gosplan state planning committee just went ahead with its centralized approach, so the reforms, half-heartedly implemented, did not result in higher work productivity, a better quality of goods, or less absenteeism and administrative red tape.

Besides that, the distribution system continued to function poorly. In Chistopol this was not so problematic, but in the larger cities residents had to stand in line every day to purchase the most elementary necessities of life. And in the service industries the theory of "full complement" was still being applied, so that only full trains went anywhere and only sold-out cinemas showed any films. Yet the Soviet Union at that time was going through a period of economic prosperity, with a rising standard of living and higher wages. These levels were admittedly lower than in the West, but everyone did have a job. A full workweek dropped during the 1960s to forty-one hours.

What really flourished in the Soviet Union, including in Chistopol, was the black market: the underground performance of odd jobs and the clandestine sale of food and scarce and desirable consumer products. Ogorodnikov eased his conscience with the thought that the ideas of Communism had not yet penetrated very deeply into the provinces: "The problem was with the local party bosses, not with the system."

Identity Crisis

When the fiftieth anniversary of the October Revolution was commemorated on November 7, 1967, the regime proudly showed off its achievements. According to government leaders, Communism was an indisputable and irreplaceable link in the geopolitical and social evolution of the twentieth century and was being successfully exported to Central and Eastern Europe, Africa, and Central America. In all the cities, Chistopol included, the event was celebrated with a parade and ended with a huge fireworks display. The Presidium of the Supreme Soviet of the USSR, the parliament's executive committee, ignored the call from thousands of intellectuals to declare amnesty for its political prisoners.

Alexander Ogorodnikov took his first journalistic steps at that time in a local newspaper. Under the all-seeing eye of agitprop (the "Agitation and Propaganda" section of the Central Committee of the Communist Party), any newspaper article or feature — even the crossword puzzle — was ideologically colored. As a fledgling journalist, Ogorodnikov had to exercise great self-control: he had to write articles from the point of view of Marxist-Leninist ideology. The Party and its general secretaries were beyond criticism. Only the Party decisions that had not yet been implemented were fair game.

In the summer of 1968, Ogorodnikov, at eighteen years of age, was "invited" to a new job. In the Soviet Union one did not apply for a job; one was "asked" to assume a responsible function. Ogorodnikov was given the leadership of the Chistopol athletics department. The whole department was in shambles because his predecessors in that leadership had let everything go. So Alexander organized sporting competitions and set a huge dynamic in motion. But he also was able to see what was really going on behind the Communist façade, and he realized that what he had witnessed at the Vostok Factory was not the exception but the rule.

As a member of the local *nomenklatura,* he became aware that the system was not sound in terms of practical conditions. The thoroughly honest Ogorodnikov, with his rock-solid faith in Communist ideals, found himself in an identity crisis. Was it coincidental that, during that very period, two of the idols of his youth should meet their deaths? On October 8, 1967, Che Guevara was shot and killed by the Bolivian army, and on March 27, 1968, Yuri Gagarin, the world's first man in space, was killed at the age of thirty-four in a MiG-15 jet fighter accident.

"Prague Spring" Violently Crushed

Fundamental social changes were under way in the Soviet Union at that time, but they were not much felt in the provincial town of Chistopol. In the January 1968 trial of the Phoenix Group — consisting of the writers Yuri Galanskov and Alexei Dobrovolsky, poet Alexander Ginsburg, and typist Vera Lashkova — the border between literary and political engagement was crossed for the first time. Unrest was growing in the Eastern Bloc. In Poland demonstrators demanded freedom of conscience, and in Czechoslovakia censorship was abolished by the moderate new Party leader, Alexander Dubček, advocate of "socialism with a human face."

In reaction, Communist officials tightened ideological control in the Soviet Union even more. Everyone who had protested against the internment of the poet and mathematician Alexander Esenin-Volpin lost his or her membership in the Communist Party. In Czechoslovakia, the writer and intellectual Ludvík Vaculík issued the manifesto *Two Thousand Words* (1968), in which he blamed the abuses in the country on the conservative wing of the Czechoslovak Communist Party and asked the progressive elements within the Party to support the implementation of reforms. Within ten days Vaculík had received 40,000 expressions of sympathy.

But on the night of August 20, 1968, Leonid Brezhnev, fearing the domino effect in other Eastern Bloc countries, abruptly put an end to the brief "Prague Spring." While protest demonstrations were taking place worldwide, he had the Czech leaders arrested and taken to the Kremlin in Moscow, the center of political power, immediately following the heavy-handed termination of a protest action by seven Russian dissidents on Red Square. Shortly thereafter, eighty-eight Russian literary men and women apologized to their Czech colleagues in an open letter. But the tide had turned. In Czechoslovakia, hard-liner Gustav Husák restored order, and in the Soviet Union repression went hand in hand with the boosting of national pride. The second "Great Patriotic War" and Joseph Stalin were dusted off once again.

Alexander Tchaikovsky's novel *Blockade,* which restored the old halo to the former Soviet leader, indirectly justified the exercise of more stringent authority. The arms race between the Soviet Union and the United States accelerated, and the Soviet government was quickly caught up in the production of intercontinental ballistic missiles. Defense spending in the Russian budget soared from 14.5 billion rubles in 1967 to 17.7 billion rubles in 1969 — in a budget of 133 billion rubles. According to international experts, however, the actual percentile rise was over 40 percent.

In the hot summer of 1968, Alexander Ogorodnikov took little notice of the unrest. Organizing the young people's summer camps took up all his time. No one around him was lying awake at night worrying about the dissidents, and most people thought that the Soviet Union's action in Czechoslovakia was completely normal. It was all part of the socialist struggle, wasn't it?

In Chistopol, Ogorodnikov did not meet a single inspiring figure who could kindle his inner doubts. He did read Solzhenitsyn's novel *One Day in the Life of Ivan Denisovich* — and with fascination. But it wasn't until months later that Ogorodnikov received details of the events in Czechoslovakia via a childhood friend, a young man who had taken part in the occupation of Prague as a Russian conscript. That could have been true of Ogorodnikov as well, except that he had been declared unfit for military service because of the health problems of his youth.

The flood of rumors about the power struggle in the Kremlin between General Secretary Leonid Brezhnev's "conservative wing" and the "reactionaries" of Premier Alexei Kosygin, who had not appeared in public for a very long time, gave rise to speculation in the Western press, but none of that reached isolated Chistopol. The media were equally silent about the incident on January 23, 1969, in which a young lieutenant fired at the car of General Secretary Brezhnev during the triumphal procession to the Kremlin of the Soviet cosmonauts of the manned Soyuz-3 spacecraft. And only careful readers of the obituaries knew about the mysterious deaths of ten Soviet generals in May 1969, and of the liquidation of a number of top functionaries from the Propaganda and Mass Media Service.

In the run-up to the summit conference of Communist leaders in Moscow on June 5, 1969 — the last gathering had been in 1960 — the Soviet Union was engaged in a bitter struggle with the People's Republic of China, both diplomatically and on the battlefield. On March 2, 1969, Chinese and Soviet troops clashed for the first time in the border region of the Ussuri River.

In May 1969, ten leaders of the Crimean Tatars were put on trial in Tashkent, the capital of Uzbekistan. The sixty-two-year-old Pyotr Grigorenko, a former army general who had been awarded the highest distinctions but had been initially confined to a psychiatric hospital in 1964 for protesting against the lawless and arbitrary treatment of citizens, was arrested once again on his way to Tashkent. That incident led to the establishment of the Initiative Group for the Defense of Human Rights, which promoted respect for the rule of law.

Consensus was rare at the Communist summit, at which seventy-five of the world's ninety Communist parties were represented. The Soviet Union could no longer project itself as the "beacon of world Communism." Foreign journalists who sought contact with dissidents during the summit were sent out of the country, and the six Crimean Tatars who unfurled banners on Mayakovsky Square demanding the release of General Grigorenko ended up behind bars. After the summit was over, all those who had made themselves heard were called to account. Among them were the fifty-five intellectuals who had signed a letter to the United Nations (intercepted by the regime) asking that the U.N. Human Rights Commission conduct an investigation of the increase in the number of dissidents being arrested.

The Party publication *Kommunist* appealed for a stricter application of criteria in the selection of professors and students: "Only Communists from industry, the agrarian sector and the army who are fully prepared should be allowed to enter the institutes of higher learning — and only on the recommendation of the Party organizations, the state and Komsomol." Anatoly Levitin-Krasnov, the most important religious author in the Soviet Union and one of the founders of the Initiative Group for the Defense of Human Rights, was sent to the Gulag in September 1969, and the writer Alexander Solzhenitsyn was expelled from the Soviet Writers' Union on November 4, 1969.

Startled by this wave of dissent, Yuri Andropov (since 1967 the new head of the KGB), at the behest of the Politburo of the Communist Party in 1969, established the Fifth Directorate within the KGB for combating and rooting out dissension and the dissident intelligentsia. Special subdepartments of the directorate were charged with investigating religious movements, ethnic minorities, citizens with family ties abroad, candidate emigrants, and dissident publications.

"The Soviet System Is One Big Lie"

Ogorodnikov, who by this time was hearing more and more snatches of the growing protest via Radio Liberty, decided to study philosophy. As an ethnic Russian, he could not be admitted to the University of Kazan, so he traveled to Moscow for the first time in August 1969. The admission criteria for the State University of Moscow, the largest and most prestigious school in the country, were extremely high, and without a Komsomol membership card one didn't stand a chance of being admitted. Because there were so few available places in the philosophy department, the candidates had to pass five consecutive selection tests.

Ogorodnikov got the highest scores, but he still was not admitted. Owing to the prevailing quota system for ethnic minorities, a less-qualified candidate from Kazakhstan was given priority.

"Try again next year," the professor said to cheer him up. "You're sure to be accepted."

Yet the one-month stay in Moscow had a deep impact on Alexander: he came into contact with young people from every corner of the Soviet Union, and he engaged in deep conversations for the first time, making him much more aware of what was going on around him.

Back in Chistopol, he could no longer repress his smoldering dissatisfaction with the policies of the city authorities. When an elderly couple was turned away from city hall, Ogorodnikov tried to help them, which some people interpreted as an anti-Soviet attitude — since he was supposed to be responsible only for sports. In a report to the higher government authorities on athletic activities in Chistopol, Ogorodnikov provided an overview of the actual situation. This was diametrically opposed to standard procedure: a bureaucrat was not supposed to write about what he did; he reported what he didn't do.

When the city council was reprimanded for this, the mayor summoned Ogorodnikov for a talk.

"Don't report the actual numbers, only the target figures," he said. "You must tell them that you made a mistake." Ogorodnikov now realized that the Soviet system was one big lie: all the figures were manipulated. In his view, this regime, with its crippling bureaucracy that suffocated every new initiative, no longer had an ethical basis. The "dictatorship of the proletariat" had apparently degenerated into a dictatorship of the Party and the Party elite, with the proletariat beneath them. Had he not seen with his own eyes in Moscow how the "guardians of the Revolution" generously helped themselves to food, clothing, and furniture in exclusive stores, while the population had to stand in line for hours at a time to get the basic necessities of life? An upper echelon of 225,000 *nomenklatura* (Party aristocrats) — who they were was a well-kept secret — were assured of receiving ample salaries, good medical care in special hospitals, the "Kremlin bonus" of sixteen to thirty-two "golden rubles," and preferential treatment in the allocation of the best apartments and vacation facilities — the dachas (country houses) outside Moscow, villas in the Caucasus, and hotels on the Black Sea. And with *bronyas* (reserved admission passes) these members could get their hands on last-minute theater or plane tickets. With such tickets they could travel to the *kapstrany* (capitalist countries) or the *sotsstrany* (socialist countries).

Party members with a lower rank received fewer privileges but lived in expectation of more. The same was true of the unwritten law concerning bribes: everyone grabbed a share, depending on his or her position. Hanging over the whole system was one big shadow: those who found themselves out of favor lost all their advantages in one fell swoop.

Harsh Treatment for Opponents

Suddenly, Ogorodnikov began looking at the world through totally different glasses; he could no longer reconcile his privileges with his conscience. This was not the kind of life he had in mind. He now saw that a great gulf existed between Communist ideals and practice, and it was getting larger. The silence of the intellectuals was illustrative of their fear — fear of losing their jobs or their homes, fear for their future or that of their children. They did not want to risk whatever they had.

Ogorodnikov learned from the American radio service Voice of America about the harsh treatment being meted out to dissidents and about the protests of Western sympathizers in the Soviet Union. On January 17, 1970, two Italians from the Italian group Europa Civiltà chained themselves to a fence in Moscow, and a Belgian attending an operetta in Moscow shouted, *"Svoboda Grigorenko!"* ("Freedom for Grigorenko!") during the performance and threw down pamphlets in the theater. The headquarters of the United Nations in New York received an open letter containing the names of sixty-two Russian dissidents who had been arrested in 1969. And on April 2, 1970, the psychiatric hospital in Kazan leaked an anonymous letter containing a detailed description of the isolation, the violent treatment, and the psychological pressure that Pyotr Grigorenko was suffering.

With the centennial of Lenin's birthday approaching on April 21, 1970, when once again a large number of Communist leaders from around the world would travel to Moscow, the KGB pulled out all the stops. They arrested one hundred sixty Crimea Tatar demonstrators; and after that they carried off the rebellious Moscow intellectuals Gorky and Charkov. On May 21 came the arrest of writer Andrei Amalrik. In his controversial essay "Will the Soviet Union Survive until 1984?" Amalrik predicted that the weakened Soviet regime would be an easy prey for China as a result of rigidity, dogmatism, and the centrifugal forces of the ethnic minorities. The internationally known biologist Zhores Medvedev was interned on June 1, 1970, for "slowly progressive schizophrenia" because he refused to limit his writings to scientific subjects. Psychiatrists diagnosed his condition as a "split personality." Scientists from both the East and the West who were attending an international symposium in Moscow urgently called for his release, and then something happened that had never happened before: on June 17, 1970, Medvedev was suddenly freed.

Two days earlier, the long, drawn-out question of the emigration of Soviet Jews had taken a dramatic turn when two groups of Jews who were trying to hijack a plane to Israel were arrested in Leningrad and Priozhorsk. Mark Dymshits and Eduard Kuznetsov were sentenced to death, and their accomplices — including Yuri Fedorov — were sentenced to a total of 101 years. After worldwide protest, the death sentences were commuted to fifteen years in prison camps.

CHAPTER THREE

Stalked by the KGB

I n 1970 the mayor of Chistopol refused to approve the request for a leave of absence for Alexander Ogorodnikov, who wanted to take the Moscow University entrance examination once more. So Ogorodnikov submitted a complaint to the public prosecutor; this had never before been done. As a result, many city officials refused to talk to him, or they openly turned against him. The mayor hesitated to dismiss him because there was really nothing to find fault with as far as his work was concerned. The athletic department was flourishing as never before, and appreciative articles about him were appearing in the local newspapers. Despite the opposition of his family and friends, Ogorodnikov tendered his resignation himself in July 1970. He could no longer function within the system. His mother understood his decision, but his father, a convinced Communist, was afraid of the consequences.

"You know how powerful the KGB is," he said. "They'll break you and discredit all the rest of us."

When he was registering at Moscow University, Alexander was taken aside by one of the professors, a member of the examination committee who had met him the year before. Not only had the professor been sent a negative report from the mayor of Chistopol, but he had also been tipped off by the KGB that Ogorodnikov had written a letter in which he had been critical of Lenin. Alexander was bewildered. He remembered that a couple of months earlier he had made a number of noncommittal comments about Lenin in a letter to a student he had met in Moscow the year before. Suddenly, he realized that the KGB must have been monitoring his correspondence for quite some time and was probably following his every move.

After the professor had made clear to him that there was no way he would be admitted to the University of Moscow, Ogorodnikov set off like a thief in the night for the city of Sverdlovsk, more than a thousand miles away. (In 1926, after the Russian Revolution, the historic city of Yekaterinburg had been given the name of the Bolshevik leader Yakov Sverdlov, who had ordered the murder of Czar Nicholas II and his family there in 1917.) The Ural A.M. Gorky State University in Sverdlovsk, named after the writer Maxim Gorky, also had a philosophy department. Ogorodnikov passed the university's entrance exam, and he thought he would be safe there for the time being.

According to tradition, students would help bring in the harvest at the beginning of the academic year. The one hundred fifty students from the philosophy department were given room and board in the homes of village families and got together each evening in the local culture house. Spontaneous discussions took place at these gatherings, and a poetry evening was held — at Ogorodnikov's suggestion. Without giving the poet's name, he recited a poem — which included a quote from Boris Pasternak — by the poet Alexander Galich, who was banned in 1970. The poem describes a multiplication of statues of Stalin, which take over a big city by night. The students were dumbfounded.

When Alexander Solzhenitsyn was awarded the Nobel Prize for Literature on October 8, 1970, Ogorodnikov was wildly enthusiastic. Solzhenitsyn accepted the honor, but he did not want to receive the prize himself for fear of not being allowed to return to the Soviet Union.

The climate at the time was still extremely hostile. On October 23, 1970, John Dornberg, the Moscow correspondent for the American weekly *Newsweek*, was expelled from the country for supposedly participating in "anti-Soviet propaganda." After Stanley Cloud of *Time* magazine and William Cole of the Columbia Broadcasting System (CBS), he was the third American in four months to be put out of the country. On November 4, 1970, Andrei Sakharov, Valery Chalidze, and Andrei Tverdokhlebov set up the Moscow Human Rights Committee. Like the Initiative Group for the Defense of Human Rights, this committee focused on the correct application of the law. The committee members provided free legal advice to any persons who felt that their rights were being threatened, and they urged the government to respect human rights.

Gennadi Burbulis, a final-year student at Gorky State University, who later served as state secretary to Boris Yeltsin in 1991-92 and became the number-two man in the Russian Federation, asked Ogorodnikov to run for the board of the university's Komsomol chapter. Ogorodnikov refused, but a few fellow students who were just as progressive as he was decided that they *would* run. Shortly thereafter, Ogorodnickov set up a clandestine seven-member discussion group whose purpose was to solve the unanswered questions of Marxist doctrine. One regular participant in these discussions was Alexander's roommate, Viktor Finkelstein. The group even pinned up newsletters on the university bulletin board, and those newsletters were not removed. The KGB ordered Burbulis to find out what was going on. As a result of Burbulis's investigation, Ogorodnikov was put on public trial in late November 1970, after which he was dismissed from the university.

With his dossier yet to be processed by the university administration, Alexander attended a meeting of the philosophy department's Komsomol chapter in Sverdlovsk a few weeks later. In that packed university auditorium, some students openly accused him of having an anti-Soviet attitude. When Ogorodnikov was given a chance to speak, he publicly confirmed that charge by denouncing the Soviet system for the first time — which was against the law. Despite warnings, two fellow students defended him, after which they, too, were dismissed. Other students remained silent out of fear that they would suffer the same fate. Ogorodnikov was then also thrown out of the Komsomol.

"From now on you'll go through life as an outlaw," Gennadi Burbulis warned him.

In late December 1970, Ogorodnikov returned to Chistopol, the city of his birth. The KGB conducted a search of his parents' house and seized a few samizdat publications. Ogorodnikov explained that they had come into his possession by chance during a book trade with an unknown individual at the unofficial book market in Sverdlovsk. At this point, he was not allowed to leave Chistopol and was ordered to work in a factory under strict supervision. Twice a week the KGB came to interrogate him. Then, six months later, in July 1971, aware that he was taking a huge risk, Alexander secretly fled to Moscow.

Studying at the Famous VGIK Institute of Cinematography

Once in Moscow, Ogorodnikov registered at the VGIK film academy, officially named the S.A. Gerasimov Russian National State Institute of

Cinematography. Since childhood he had been fascinated by this medium, which Lenin had regarded as the most important weapon for reunifying the country and bringing communist ideology to the illiterate masses in the countryside. Lenin's wife, Nadezhda Krupskaya, had laid the basis for a real film industry, which operated under the direction of the all-seeing eye of Goskino, the USSR State Committee for Cinematography. This body was responsible for approving work, granting subsidies, guaranteeing distribution, and monitoring censorship. In the film industry, too, creativity was in service to "socialist realism." With thirteen million people attending the cinemas each day, the impact of film on society was considerable. The Soviet Union even had a minister of film. Mosfilm, the Moscow film studio, made one-third of the two hundred films that were shown each year.

For every available place in the seven branches of the prestigious VGIK institute, an average of fifty candidates applied. After passing nine entrance examinations, Ogorodnikov, who ranked first in the screenwriting department, was accepted. One reason was that the KGB had not yet tracked him down. But, after registering officially as a student, Ogorodnikov had to return to Chistopol to have the information in his passport revised. The KGB agents were furious, but they didn't have anything against him. After all, he was already being threatened with punishment by the local branch of the secret service for having committed serious offenses.

Back in Moscow, Ogorodnikov at first tried his best to keep a low profile, becoming fully engrossed in his studies. In January 1971 his mother told him by telephone that the head of the KGB in Chistopol had been killed in an accident. But Alexander suspected that the secret service, which was very vindictive by nature, had murdered the man on account of Alexander's own unobserved escape from Chistopol. He immediately realized that returning to his hometown would mean certain death. His best life insurance for the time being was the VGIK, which was practically unassailable because of its international reputation and because of all the foreign students enrolled there.

Ogorodnikov shared a room with Adi Useldinger, the son of Arthur Useldinger, leader of the Communist Party of Luxembourg, and with a Bulgarian, Vlado Ganyev. Ogorodnikov tried to stay as inconspicuous as possible, but he wasn't able to keep silent during heated discussions. The KGB left him alone because of his popularity with the foreign students, and as a result Ogorodnikov developed into a man of irony and self-mockery.

Despite his intensive study, Ogorodnikov closely followed events in the dissident world, though he had yet to meet any dissidents in person. Such people were difficult to reach and usually worked underground. During the Twenty-Fourth Party Congress, which began on March 30, 1971, hundreds of Jews held a sit-down demonstration in the Kremlin for the right to emigrate, and a new series of books was published on the history of the Party. The fact that Leonid Brezhnev was the only Soviet leader present in a Party congress group photograph was an indication of his increasing authority. On the eve of the congress, Vladimir Bukovsky, who shortly before had been interviewed by William Cole of the U.S. television station CBS along with Andrei Almarik, was interned for the third time.

After gaining the approval of the Politburo, the Synod of the Russian Orthodox Church confirmed the appointment of Pimen as the new patriarch, replacing Alexei I, who had died. In his first speech, Pimen thanked Premier Alexei Kosygin "for his sympathetic attitude towards the needs of the Church." At the gathering of the 7,000-member Writers' Union in the Kremlin, Nobel Prize–winner Alexander Solzhenitsyn, whose latest book, *August 1914*, was circulating in samizdat, was fiercely attacked. The conservative hard-liner Grigory Markov denounced the West, which "labeled good-for-nothings and crackbrained writers as great, talented and prominent artists." The visit of President Richard Nixon to China (February 21-28, 1972), the crowning touch of America's "ping-pong diplomacy," showed to the rest of the world the increasing international isolation of the Soviet regime.

Andrei Tarkovsky's Film *The Mirror*

A few days after the Western broadcasting media announced the death of former General Secretary Nikita Khrushchev on September 12, 1971, his obituary appeared in the Party newspaper *Pravda*. And suddenly there was a breakthrough in the dossier of the Soviet Jews: following a secret accord between the Soviet Union and Israel, 14,000 of them were allowed to emigrate — more than all the Jewish emigrants during the past ten years combined.

In 1972, during his second year at the VGIK, Ogorodnikov was assigned to work on the film *The Mirror*, by filmmaker Andrei Tarkovsky, one of the great geniuses in film history. In 1962, during the second period of liberalization, he had made his debut film, *Ivan's Childhood*, which was honored with a Golden Lion at the Venice Film Festival. His second film, on the life of the medieval icon painter Andrei Rublev, was only given limited showing in 1966 because of its indirect criticism of the Soviet regime. A copy of this film was smuggled to the West in 1969, and was praised as one of the best films of all time at the Cannes Film Festival. Tarkovsky, who was reviled in his own country, needed foreign money to show his film *Solaris* in 1971. His fourth film, *The Mirror,* was his most original, most unconventional, and most difficult. Logical organization and plot development had been replaced by separate scenes that analyzed the psychology of the protagonist in an abstract way. Tarkovsky suffered terribly under the limitations and the badgering of the government. And in the end, *The Mirror* was not distributed in the Soviet Union.

Tarkovsky was very happy with his trainee Alexander Ogorodnikov. He wrote a favorable trainee report and asked the board of the VGIK to send Alexander to him after he had obtained his diploma.

The Campaign against "Internal Enemies"

In the spring of 1972, Ogorodnikov witnessed a new offensive against the dissidents. On January 6, Vladimir Bukovsky was sentenced to two years in prison. The publication of an article on the "pernicious activities of the dissidents" in *Pravda* on January 13, 1972, had given the green light to the massive hunt for "internal enemies." During house searches in Moscow, Leningrad, Kiev, and Lvov, which mainly targeted suspected contacts with the West, twenty-two dissidents were rounded up, and thousands of publications were seized. A house search was also conducted in the home of David Bonavia, Moscow correspondent for the *London Times,* and he was banished from the Soviet Union.

By shielding opponents from foreign public opinion, the KGB was trying to prevent recently announced new publications from reaching the West, including the memoirs of Pyotr Yakir on the Stalinist purges and the execution of his father. The wave of repression that took place in early 1972 did not keep the underground monthly *Chronika* from being distributed. During that period a 390-page issue appeared giving information on the most recent trials and reports of recent dissident actions in Moscow, Leningrad, and Riga. The KGB's heavy-handed approach was bound to give rise to a group of professional dissidents who could not be intimidated — and who became increasingly fanatical. Roy and Zhores Medvedev distributed the book *A Question of Madness*, an account of Zhores's internment in May 1970. The Ukrainian psychiatrist Semyon Gluzman, who wrote a negative psychiatric report on Pyotr Grigorenko, was sentenced to ten years in prison, and on October 30, 1972, thirty-three-year-old Yuri Galanskov of the Phoenix Group died in the camp in Mordovia.

Between January 1971 and October 1972, Vladimir Osipov, who with Alexander Ginsburg was among the first dissidents of the new generation, published six issues of the magazine *Vetsje*. And the April 7, 1972, issue of the ever-unassailable *Chronika* came out with the shocking story of fifteen prisoners in the Obuchovo prison camp near Leningrad who sewed their mouths closed with needle and thread to protest their living conditions. After the distribution of the twenty-seventh issue of *Chronika* in October 1972, the publication was not seen for a long time. This was an immediate consequence of a warning from the Fifth Directorate of the KGB, which stated that if one more issue of *Chronika* were to circulate by samizdat, a whole range of Soviet intellectuals would be arrested — even if they were innocent.

In the Baltic States, the protests against Russification and suppression of religion resulted in three self-immolations. Under pressure from Moscow, the Catholic bishops of Lithuania warned believers of the consequences of the protests, but many priests refused to read the letter aloud in church. Soon after the emigration of the badgered and battle-weary Valery Chalidze of the Moscow Human Right Committee in 1972, Andrei Sakharov, who until then had steered a cautious course within the legal framework, made contact with the Western media himself. He openly criticized the regime in the American magazine *Newsweek*. At the same time, the biologist Zhores Medvedev, who was allowed outside the country for a short time in 1972, was deprived of his Soviet passport.

In the meantime, Ogorodnikov witnessed the visit of President Richard Nixon on May 26, 1972, and the signing of the first SALT agreement (Strategic Arms Limitation Talks) on the limitation of long-distance missiles. To prevent demonstrations, the authorities again called up a number of dissidents for military service. In November 1972, Andrei Sakharov declared: "Since Nixon's visit things have gotten worse. The authorities in the Soviet Union have become more brazen. They sense that the state of international détente is making it possible for them to ignore Western public opinion, which does not meddle with our domestic security."

Due to a number of consecutive failed harvests, however, the food supply was seriously jeopardized. Butter and potatoes were rationed, and on December 20, 1972, on the eve of the celebration of the fiftieth anniversary of the Soviet Union, the first shipment of grain from the United States arrived in the port of Odessa. Fifty intellectuals — at the 1967 celebration of the 1917 Revolution there had been a thousand — asked the Presidium of the Supreme Soviet, the highest authority in parliament, to grant amnesty to political prisoners, but to no avail. The dissidence had lost its clout, but a persistent core fearlessly continued the struggle. In September 1973, Alexander Solzhenitsyn wrote the following prophetic words in his *Open Letter to the Soviet Leadership:* "Your greatest desire is that our state structure and our ideological system will never change. But that's not the way history works. Every system either finds a way to further develop itself, or collapses."

Pasolini Shows the Way to the Living Christ

In March 1973, during his third year at the VGIK, Alexander Ogorodnikov's life took a decisive turn. With his view of humanity and the world dashed to smithereens, Ogorodnikov began searching for the real meaning of his life, as an archaeologist would in trying to put together the shards of an antique pot. Through a contact person at the U.S. embassy in Moscow, he was able to obtain a copy of Boris Pasternak's novel *Doctor Zhivago* (1957). Also, the essay by the cultural and religious philosopher Nikolai Berdyaev about Alexei Chomyakov (1904) — philosopher, poet, and theoretician of the Slavophile movement — made a deep impression on him. The books *Crime and Punishment* (1866) and *The Idiot* (1869) by Fyodor Dostoyevsky introduced him to the notion of God. Ogorodnikov also became acquainted with the work of other Russian Slavophiles, such as Vladimir Soloviev, Sergei Bulgakov, and Georgi Florovsky, religiously inspired figures with close ties to the Russian Orthodox Church.

For the first time, Ogorodnikov had the feeling that God was present somewhere as an abstract fact, a creative power, a vessel full of ideas. When a fellow student loaned him a New Testament, Alexander at first did not dare touch this "dark book"; in fact, his Bulgarian roommate, Vlado Ganyev, even hid his money in it. But one day, as Ogorodnikov was traveling by train to the secret archive of the film academy in a forest in Belye Stolby, just outside Moscow, he began reading the New Testament he had brought along. He could not rationally understand the feeling of joy that overcame him. As a "protesting student" of the film academy, Ogorodnikov had not bought a train ticket as a matter of principle. But when the conductor came by to check his ticket, rather than argue with him (the customary student response), he paid for his own ticket plus those of six fellow students.

In the secret VGIK archive, the film students were studying the camera settings, photography, aesthetic design, and structure of the action scenes from the sensational 1964 film *Il Vangelo secondo Matteo (The Gospel According to St. Matthew)*, by the Italian director Pier Paolo Pasolini. What impressed Alexander most, however, were not the design and structural elements but the contents of the film. The basic idea alone was fascinating. That the notorious Marxist/Communist and atheist Pasolini, one of the most well-known filmmakers of his time, would put the Gospel of Matthew on the screen was strange enough. Yet there was perhaps nothing surprising about the story itself in the film, because the ancient Gospel from the New Testament simply served as the screenplay. Pasolini closely followed the chronology of the events and even used literal quotes from Matthew's Gospel.

The work breathed authenticity, and the dramatic staging — the rough character faces of the amateur actors and their shabby clothing — gave the inspiring wisdom of Jesus' words extra power. There was also something revolutionary about the film. Jesus was strict with his disciples, sometimes even rough. He attracted the multitudes but also drove them away. The lack of special effects in this black-and-white film reinforced its emotional and religious intensity. The music, from the *Missa Luba* — a unique version of the Latin Mass based on traditional Congolese melodies and performed by the combination of a choir, an improvisational singer, and a group of drummers — went straight to the heart. The film also featured renderings of Russian revolutionary songs. Ogorodnikov experienced all of this as completely true to life. Suddenly, he discovered what he had been searching for all those years. Pasolini showed him the way from an abstract notion of God to the living Christ.

After the film was over, Ogorodnikov delivered a spontaneous sermon to his surprised fellow students. They did not understand how this ironic man could promote Pasolini's film as the "real truth." Ogorodnikov felt like a believer for the first time: he was overcome by a feeling of vitality, energy, and freedom that he had long been searching for, even though he was still unable to put into words the sensation of the presence of God in his life.

After that experience Alexander listened regularly to the religious broadcasts on Voice of America radio: the daily readings from Scripture, the weekly commentary by Father Viktor Potapov, a priest in the Russian Orthodox Cathedral of St. John the Baptist in Washington, D.C., the broadcasts of the Sunday divine liturgy, and vespers from the same cathedral.

Meeting Vladimir Poresh in Leningrad

Like-minded people came to the film academy to see Ogorodnikov, so that by the spring of 1973 his room had become a place where young people carried on spontaneous discussions about religious matters. The first organized secret meeting took place in the apartment of a British student, Nathalie Ward, since the KGB were not allowed to barge in on foreign students without warning. But once, in August 1973, when the KGB had tracked Alexander to that apartment, he had to escape through the roof. Ten to fifteen young people got together either every two weeks or every month. Anonymity was of crucial importance, for as soon as an organization was formed, it was in danger of being shut down. In search of sympathizers, Ogorodnikov approached young people on the street whom he suspected of having similar ideas. That was how he bumped into Vladimir Poresh in Leningrad. Poresh had just finished his study of Romance philology and had already undergone his own long search.

"All too often I have been faced with questions for which I have no answer, but which keep returning, like an endlessly moving machine," Poresh wrote on December 24, 1969.

> But no one knows how the machine works, why it's there and why it was made. Everything is senseless from beginning to end. Yet most senseless things have more meaning than everything else. Senseless things like art, literature, the sciences, all sorts of interests and hobbies, seem more important than everything else. Every form of spiritual life seems senseless because it only causes suffering in man, but at the same time it's the most important thing. It is senseless to keep searching, but I shall go on searching for this very reason.

In December 1970, during an identity crisis in which he was considering suicide, Poresh had met his former teacher, Tatiana Shchipkova, nineteen years his senior, in his hometown of Smolensk. She had come to the same dead end. The two maintained contact, and one year later Poresh wrote to her: "I have come to the conclusion that God does indeed exist. It's not possible that he doesn't exist, because if that were true, then nothing would have any meaning."

There, on the streets of Leningrad, Vladimir Poresh and Alexander Ogorodnikov immediately hit it off. They spent the whole night talking in Poresh's apartment. For Poresh, this encounter triggered a deepening of his faith. "I have begun a new phase in my life," he reported to Tatiana. "I have met a certain Sasha Ogorodnikov. We have decided to create a new culture within the culture."

Ogorodnikov pointed the way to faith to other young people around him, including his own brother, Boris, a talented racing cyclist who had been the junior champion of Russia in 1968, but ended his career just before his first participation in an international competition. Boris had been in military service from 1969 to 1971, a third of which time he spent locked up for protesting the lawlessness and *dedovshtshina* (abuse) of young recruits by older army conscripts. After being dismissed from the Metallurgical Institute in Moscow as a student, Boris worked as a security guard. Key figures in his religious search, besides his brother, were the priests Nikolai Kuznetsov and Vsevolod Shpiller. When Boris registered for the entrance exam for the Moscow Theological Seminary in 1974, he had to go into hiding for fear of being forcibly admitted to a psychiatric hospital. But he succeeded in entering the monastery of Pskov-Pechory on the Estonian border and took the monastic name Raphael.

Alexander Ogorodnikov's religious journey also brought him in contact with the Soviet hippies, who distanced themselves from the Soviet system. The hippies lived together in poverty and solidarity, holding all property in common, and they wore their hair long. But that's where the similarity with Western hippies ended. Free love and drug use were strictly taboo in the Soviet Union at that time. The Soviet hippies drank tea and were engaged in endless discussions, and many of them had a strong interest in religion. Their meetings were held at differing locations that were kept secret until the last minute. But they were constantly being harassed and denounced — by the secret service, the police, and young members of the Komsomol, who attacked them on the streets and cut off their hair.

In 1973, Ogorodnikov came up with the daring plan to organize a mass meeting for young Christians, including a large number of Soviet hippies, and to make a film about that meeting called *Jesus People.* After a sham film scenario was approved by Goskino, Alexander was given the use of film material and equipment, as well as a cameraman, Viktor Abdalov of Turkmenistan. In the meantime Ogorodnikov worked secretly on the scenario of a gathering in Estonia. He labored under the illusion that because of Estonia's border with the West, the surveillance there would be less stringent.

In July 1973, two hundred young people from every corner of the Soviet Union hitchhiked to a clearing in a forest near the Estonian capital of Tallinn. But the plan was leaked. Hundreds of policemen surrounded the forest and formed a living chain through which no one could escape. All the participants were taken away for interrogation. To their amazement, the police discovered that Ogorodnikov had all the necessary documents for making a film, and because of the sluggish communication with Moscow, the deception had not immediately been discovered. Although Viktor Abdalov's camera was seized, he was able to hide the roll of film, which later reached the United States via the U.S. embassy. (Abdalov, who immigrated to the United States a couple years later, after his marriage to the American human-rights activist Catherine A. Fitzpatrick, made a television film in 1975 based on that shooting.)

Back in Moscow after the Estonian debacle, Ogorodnikov and Viktor Abdalov were interrogated at KGB headquarters on Dzerzhinsky Square, right next to the notorious Lubyanka Prison. Because members of the Central Committee — the "parliament" of the Communist Party — were eager to know why the Russian youths were so disillusioned, Ogorodnikov and Abdalov were given the chance to apologize.

In his answer to the Central Committee, Ogorodnikov wrote:

> Society in the Soviet Union deprives people of God and reduces them to an animal state. Atheism leads to the dehumanization of human beings. When God is fully banished from society, people live together like animals. All values, except for material gain, are eliminated. Because the Soviet regime only provides material rewards and is also the owner of all property, the people simply take what they think belongs to them. They begin to steal, a moment that even organized crime is waiting for.

The KGB was "not amused" by Ogorodnikov's response and began the procedure for having him dismissed from the film academy. It did not happen immediately; fellow students collected signatures and planned a demonstration. Nikolaevich Tretyakov, professor of art history, publicly shook Ogorodnikov's hand. Yet his fate was already sealed. After the campaigning students were also threatened with dismissal, the activism subsided. Tretyakov escaped sanction because of his reputation, but the director of the film academy was also forced to resign. And when Ogorodnikov left the VGIK in 1973, he also lost his Moscow residence permit. Because he definitely did not want to return to Chistopol, he tried to find temporary shelter with friends. But that was far from easy. Each apartment had its own *upravdom* (caretaker), a man or woman hired by the Communist Party, a kind of jack-of-all-trades for the residents who acted as janitor, porter, rent collector, manager, and inspector — but also as a spy for the Party. The *upravdom* reported all irregularities to the Party and registered all visitors who stayed longer than seventy-two hours.

Ogorodnikov continued to carry on his activities in the underground press, an environment in which he had come to feel at home. The rule of thumb of samizdat was: the more interesting the information, the faster and more widespread the distribution. At first Ogorodnikov signed his written material with his initials, but after a while he began using his full name, since the more he was talked about, the safer he was: that is, being widely known in the West was the best guarantee against being arrested, given the fact that the Soviet government was afraid of negative publicity. Yet writing in samizdat publications was no picnic; the government put restraints on all reproduction techniques, and typewriters and carbon paper were systemically confiscated during house arrests.

The "Official" Church Collaborates with the Power Elite

When Ogorodnikov paid a visit to a church in the center of Moscow one day, he was surprised that there were so many people attending the divine liturgy. Among the believers standing there he recognized a few intellectuals. Many of those intellectuals were moved by the way the liturgy was celebrated by Metropolitan Anthony (Bloom) of Sourozh, the Russian Orthodox bishop of London who was temporarily staying in Moscow. When Communion was distributed, an indefinable power pushed Ogorodnikov forward. A few *babushkas* responded with deep emotion, and some of them even began to shout, perhaps shocked that a young person would go forward to receive Communion. This is not common practice in the Orthodox tradition, but Ogorodnikov did not know that at the time. A believer often first goes to his *starets* (spiritual father) for confession — in many cases not a priest but an old monk — after which the *starets* decides whether the person is ready to receive Communion. The person should also fast a few hours beforehand.

Some time later, when Ogorodnikov was regularly attending liturgy with a few friends, the *babushkas* thanked and kissed him because they were seeing a new generation of believers coming to church. Yet the suspicion was great. One day when Ogorodnikov went to church, an old woman tried to push him outside. She thought he had come to provoke the believers. At that time there were only fifty churches in Moscow, a city of eight million residents.

In a letter that reached the West via samizdat, Ogorodnikov wrote:

It was at this point that a revision of our moral values became necessary, and we began to strive openly for self-realization within the flow of history and thought. Expelled from academic circles by the will of history, driven off the pages of books by censorship, expelled to the night-watchman's room, aspiring Russian thought matured in agonizing disputes (sometimes lasting for weeks), which opened up to us the truth of Russian religious philosophy. Khomyakov, Dostoyevsky, Soloviev, Bulgakov, and Florovsky brought us up to the threshold of the Church, and set us before its doors.

Bursting out of the solitary cell of one's own soul, overcoming the temptation of modern culture, we came to the firm conclusion that only the Orthodox Church and roots in the national communality of the Church body can save a man, confirm him in the Truth and bestow meaning and purpose on his personal and social life.

Ogorodnikov wanted to live as a Christian, and he searched for a place in the Orthodox Church with the Bible in hand, but he was constantly confronted by the schizophrenic situation in which the church found itself. It was not a living community, because the only thing that was permitted was attending the liturgy. In the official Orthodox Church, which collaborated with the men of power in the Soviet Union, Ogorodnikov did not find the religious life he was seeking. Only here and there in the countryside, where belief was still deeply rooted, did he encounter an authentic experience of faith.

It occurred to him how much the secret service had paralyzed the work of the church. As his brother, Boris, had discovered, the only candidates for the theological seminary who stood a chance of being admitted were those who had been given a positive evaluation by the Council for Religious Affairs and the KGB. The priests who cooperated with the secret service were quickly promoted, but those who didn't were sent to remote parishes with paltry salaries. In fact, the Russian Orthodox Church was a bureaucratic agency infiltrated by agents of the secret service. The Department of Foreign Affairs of the Moscow Patriarchate served as a branch of the Fifth Department of the KGB. The church leaders enjoyed the same facilities as did the regime elite. "That the Church is run in a dictatorial way by atheists is a spectacle that hasn't been seen in two thousand years," Alexander Solzhenitsyn wrote bitterly.

Yet not every priest was a wolf in sheep's clothing. In a secret report for the Central Committee of the Communist Party that was leaked via samizdat, Vice Chairman Furov of the Council for Religious Affairs divided the episcopate into three groups. Besides the "loyal" bishops who indoctrinated their believers with a pro-Soviet spirit, there were others who adopted a loyal position with regard to the state but also fostered the spirituality and further growth of the church. A third group tried to evade religious legislation altogether.

The Inspiring "Saturday Evening Talks" of Dmitri Dudko

Ogorodnikov's life took a new turn after his meeting with Father Dmitri Dudko, with whom he immediately established a very close bond. Dudko had already had an eventful life. In 1948, while studying at the Moscow Theological Academy in the town of Zagorsk (now Sergiev Posad, a suburb of Moscow), he was sentenced to more than eight years in the Gulag for writing a religious poem. In the early 1970s, Dudko served as priest in the church on Preobrazhensky Square in Moscow, where the young people were greatly attracted to him. Every Saturday evening about 150 young people came to the church for confession and vespers, and in December 1973 he began his inspiring "Saturday evening talks," in which he answered all questions openly and honestly, without avoiding any controversial issues. After the Sunday morning liturgy there was still plenty of time to sit around a table and engage in deep discussions.

Dudko was not a man with philosophical or literary inclinations, but he was extremely engaged, combative, and eloquent. His sermons were what made the biggest impression, and they could often be heard on Western radio stations. His listeners valued his unvarnished attacks on atheism and the official church. Soon after they met, Dudko invited Ogorodnikov to help him prepare answers for the more thorny questions.

What was happening in the meantime in Soviet society? In 1973, General Secretary Leonid Brezhnev strengthened his position by dismissing Pyotr Shelest and Gennadi Voronov from the Politburo and appointing three of his supporters: Andrei Grechko, the minister of defense; Andrei Gromyko, the minister of foreign affairs; and Yuri Andropov, the chairman of the secret service. Brezhnev polished his own prestige even further with official visits to East Germany, West Germany, and the United States, and he increased the military power and efforts of the Soviet Union. The country at that time had twice as many fighter planes as did NATO, the second largest fleet in the world; and it had the largest fleet of submarines. Brezhnev's autobiography (written by a ghostwriter), entitled *The Promised Land,* bursting with heroic deeds that never happened, was given the highest literary award.

During that period Ogorodnikov was emerging as the most important underground "newsmaker" in the realm of religion. He wrote biting articles against Marxism and pressed for the reconstruction of Russia based on Christian values. Many of those pieces were read aloud on foreign radio broadcasting services, such as Voice of America and Radio Liberty.

Leading Role for Andrei Sakharov

In dissident circles, the fifty-two-year-old Andrei Sakharov was playing an increasingly prominent role. After a television interview in a June 1973 broadcast on a Norwegian channel, he was severely reprimanded by First Deputy Prosecutor Malyarov. But a couple of months later, on August 21, Sakharov held a press conference for foreign journalists in his home. "The Soviet Union is a totalitarian society," he said, "a country wearing a mask, and its deeds can be unexpected and extremely dangerous." After the publication of an article entitled "The Supplier of Slander" in *Pravda,* in which forty academic members called Sakharov's behavior "unbefitting a Soviet scholar," hundreds of orchestrated protest letters against Sakharov appeared in the media, supposedly written by academic scholars, doctors, war veterans, mineworkers, writers' unions, and artists' societies.

Nevertheless, during a press conference on September 7, 1973,

Sakharov denounced the abuse of psychiatry for political purposes and demanded that the International Red Cross come and inspect Soviet prisons, prison camps, and special psychiatric hospitals. The response to that appeal — unprecedented in Soviet history and thus absolutely new — resulted in a visit by a group of foreign psychiatrists to the Serbsky Institute for Social and Forensic Psychiatry in Moscow. The visiting psychiatrists concluded that the diagnosis of schizophrenia in detainees was based on a "rather broad" interpretation. The independent psychiatric investigation proposed by dissident Pyotr Grigorenko was not carried out, however, because the interpreter recommended by Grigorenko's wife was not accepted by the staff of the institute.

In the meantime, the dissidents Pyotr Yakir and Viktor Krasin, who had been arrested and deprived of visitation rights or legal support, broke down during the preliminary inquest. The KGB managed to "zero in" on their weak spots. In Yakir's case, it was his alcoholism. He must have expected that things would go wrong, because he had given his last will and testament to a foreign journalist before his arrest. Yakir and Krasin were given light sentences, and both made televised "confessions." On September 30, 1973, the court of appeals reduced their sentences, enabling them both to leave the Gulag a few months later. Two months later, the Ukrainian author Ivan Dziuba was also freed after making a statement of self-criticism.

In Search of Kindred Spirits

As a result of the rising turmoil caused by Father Dmitri Dudko's "Saturday evening talks," the patriarch issued a silencing order on May 4, 1974, and he had Dudko transferred to a rural parish. When Dudko protested a few days later, he was stripped of his priestly function. After a show of remorse, he was appointed to the rural parish of Kabanovo.

Ogorodnikov was working at the time as an assistant in a canteen; but when the KGB found that out, he was immediately dismissed. He then traveled to Novosibirsk in Siberia, and to the cities of Smolensk, Tallinn, Riga, Vilnius, and Kaliningrad, making his way by plane and hitchhiking as he searched for new kindred spirits. Living a frugal life, he paid for these trips with the remaining funds from his scholarship to the film academy and money that he occasionally received from his father. Plane tickets were cheap at the time, and Ogorodnikov, who still had his student pass, got a discount on fares. But the improper use of that pass would result in severe punishment, so it was highly risky. During a flight from the Georgian capital of Tbilisi to Moscow, Ogorodnikov became aware that he was being shadowed. So he tore up his student pass and flushed it down the airplane's toilet — just in time, as it turned out, because, on leaving the plane, he was body-searched by KGB agents. They were unable to find anything illegal on him, much to their chagrin.

During his odyssey through the Soviet Union, Ogorodnikov entered into the same kinds of spontaneous discussions with young people that he had had earlier in Moscow and Leningrad — young people whose appearance, glance, posture, and clothing were a subtle hint that they were searching for something. That was how he happened to come in contact with Tatiana Shchipkova, the former teacher of Vladimir Poresh, in Smolensk.

In 1974, Ogorodnikov presented his plan for the creation of an informal study and discussion group to deal with religious, theological, and philosophical questions to a few influential spiritual leaders. The first one was the writer Anatoly Levitin-Krasnov, follower of a schismatic movement within Orthodoxy called the "Living Church," which was aimed at reconciling socialism with Christianity. After his confinement in the Gulag — from 1949 to 1956 — Levitin-Krasnov was one of the few intellectuals to oppose the antireligious policies of Nikita Khrushchev. Because he was an activist with the Initiative Group for the Defense of Human Rights, Levitin-Krasnov was sent back to the Gulag in 1969 and 1971. When the KGB continued to pursue him after his release in the autumn of 1974, he was able to immigrate to Switzerland on the basis of his Jewish origins, and he continued the struggle from the city of Lucerne. After years of being hounded, he just wanted to work in peace on the publications he had planned.

Although Ogorodnikov had his doubts about Levitin-Krasnov's "Christian socialism," he had a great deal of respect for this talented man. Levitin-Krasnov regarded Ogorodnikov as his spiritual son, and before he left for Switzerland he gave him all the books he was not able to take along with him, instructing him to distribute them as widely as possible. In the years that followed, Ogorodnikov exchanged messages with him regularly via Swiss tourists visiting the Soviet Union.

Levitin-Krasnov put Ogorodnikov in contact with Alexander Men, an eminent theologian and biblical scholar who, despite his close ties with the underground church, had never been arrested because he did not openly campaign against the official Orthodox Church. Temperamentally the very opposite of the "chatterbox" Dmitri Dudko, Men worked mostly in secret and published his books under a pseudonym. His magnum opus, *Heaven on Earth* (1969), made church doctrine accessible to the public at large and taught thousands of Russians the basic principles of Christian doctrine and Orthodoxy. The book was published abroad and circulated in the Soviet Union via samizdat. Alexander Men baptized thousands of believers, mostly intellectuals, and mainly in secret, since the registration of passports was required for every baptism. Alexander Men's parish in Pushkino became a veritable pilgrimage site, especially on Sundays. He inspired his numerous followers with his spiritual dissidence, by which he also built bridges to religious and philosophical thinkers from the beginning of the twentieth century.

Dissidents always responded to personal contacts with reticence and suspicion, but Ogorodnikov and Alexander Men hit it off immediately, thanks to the mediation of Levitin-Krasnov. Father Alexander was very interested in Ogorodnikov's plans for the creation of a Christian Seminar, and he came to their first talk armed with ideas about strategy for reaching even more young people. They continued to maintain regular contact, and when Ogorodnikov failed to show up on one occasion, Men sent a messenger to find out if he was all right. Men also referred to Ogorodnikov people he thought might be interested in the future Christian Seminar. Most of them were highly educated and made an enormous contribution in terms of content, which was extremely important because there was no form of religious education in the Soviet Union at that time. Alexander Men never actually attended a meeting of the seminar himself — for reasons of safety.

Ogorodnikov also made contact with Father Ioann Krestiankin, a well-known *starets* (spiritual leader) who became another spiritual father for him. Father Ioann had spent seven years in the Gulag during the 1950s for "anti-Soviet agitation." To keep him from attracting too many followers with his charismatic personality, the church authorities had sent Father Ioann to a different parish every year until he withdrew to the monastery of Pskov-Pechory, where the monk Raphael, Ogorodnikov's younger brother, was also living. Orthodoxy has always embraced a monastic ideal that is aimed at meditation and spiritual exercises, and everything that Father Ioann thought and did was permeated by the spirit of Orthodoxy. He did not play an active role in the Christian Seminar, because he never left the monastery; but Ogorodnikov did visit Father Ioann regularly to consult with him on thorny questions.

CHAPTER FOUR

The Christian Seminar

I n 1974 Ogorodnikov began showing up regularly at the press conferences that Andrei Sakharov held in his home for foreign journalists. As
a specialist in human rights cases in the Soviet Union, the atheist
Sakharov felt less at home in religious affairs, though he had great respect
for them. So it was Ogorodnikov who presented a picture of recent developments in the religious realm based on material provided by his information network in the Orthodox, Protestant, and Catholic communities.
The refuseniks, Soviet citizens (mostly Jewish) who had been denied permission by the authorities to emigrate, were also usually represented
there to report on Soviet Jewish emigration.

In August 1974, with Sakharov's help, Ogorodnikov got a job as a janitor at Tuberculosis Clinic 11, an out-patient facility in the Dzerzhinsky
district of Moscow. His days of seeking temporary shelter with friends
were finally over, since he was also given the use of the porter's quarters at
the clinic. This former carpenter's shop consisted of two rooms, a hallway
and a kitchen. In time it became the meeting place of the Moscow branch
of the Christian Seminar. A Jewish man named Abraham was the head of
the clinic, but he lent his tacit cooperation in allowing Ogorodnikov's visitors to stay overnight in hospital beds until daybreak.

Vladimir Poresh wrote:

We loved that little flat for the spirit of freedom that filled it. It was
there that we held our seminars on religion and philosophy — in other
words, where we discussed the questions that were most important for
us: questions of religion and life. The door of that house was open to
all, and anyone could take part and speak. Newcomers were struck by

the variety there: they might meet old men or sixteen-year-old hippies, scholars or seekers. Those conversations, that way of life, took hold of me completely: it was all so sound, so full of meaning and depth, so full of the warmth and genuine feeling that you cannot confuse with anything else. It was so different from vulgar Soviet life that I always hurried to Moscow, to Alexander, to that flat, with my whole being. It had become palpably obvious to us that it is very easy to live according to the truth. You just have to make a determined stand against the pressure of the frantic world, and God will help you and strengthen your convictions.

Many members regarded the apartment as a free state entirely separate from the territory of the Soviet Union. The twenty-five participants who came to the first meeting were not only from Moscow but also from Chistopol, Kazan, Smolensk, Minsk, Riga, Kiev, and Leningrad. Sometimes there would be twenty people attending the monthly meetings, sometimes thirty, with a maximum of forty.

With the help of Poresh, Ogorodnikov also set up a branch of the Christian Seminar in Leningrad in the autumn of 1974. And the driving forces behind the Smolensk branch were Viktor Popkov and Tatiana Shchipkova, the only participating leader older than thirty-five. Sergei Shuvalov and Boris Razveyev were key figures in the Ufa branch. In 1975 and 1976 the network widened to include new centers in the cities of Odessa, Chistopol, Kazan, Minsk, Riga, Pskov, and Novosibirsk.

The KGB: Powerless in the Face of the New Movement

How did Alexander Ogorodnikov succeed in building up a network that reached a few thousand individuals — at least three hundred of whom regularly attended the meetings — in a country where gatherings of even three persons were suspect and closely monitored by the KGB? The Seminar was not an organized association. As its driving force, Ogorodnikov alone was the unofficial leader, and growth took place in total silence. The members did not carry on a campaign for more religious freedom. And the branches did not accept outsiders; they only accepted interested people who were introduced and recommended by trusted members.

Yet, after a while, as the success of the Christian Seminar increased, it became clear that this way of working was not watertight. The first phase consisted of KGB infiltration in the new movement. Moles tried to win members' trust in an attempt to expose the Seminar's strength and to identify the leaders. But that proved relatively unsuccessful. The movement was based on an authentic experience of faith and close friendships, and various levels formed spontaneously within the movement that were not accessible to outsiders. Not a single mole was able get through to the top of the organization. As a result, the Christian Seminar remained elusive for a long time, and the secret service simply didn't know what to do about the rapidly growing base of support within the population.

Despite the limitations on communication and mobility, the Seminar expanded steadily. Each new branch could count on the sympathy, respect, and support of a small segment of the community. That factor was unprecedented in the KGB's experience, given the fact that most dissident movements consisted of isolated groups of intellectuals who had almost no contact with the population for whom they wished to obtain more rights and freedoms.

The Seminar did not proclaim its ideas from the top down, but took root from below, finding a rich breeding ground in the "Russian soul" and the principles of Slavophilism — a humus that had not entirely disappeared despite fifty years of religious persecution and atheist propaganda. This also explained the unusually cautious approach of the secret service, which contrasted sharply with the aggressive way they had dealt with other dissident movements. The success of the Christian Seminar was all the more remarkable because there were no means available for openly circulating its aims and ideas. Religious literature was scarce in the Soviet Union at that time. It amounted to samizdat publications and books, most of them dating back to before 1917, that members exchanged among themselves. The rare copies of more recent works all came from abroad.

The key to the success of the new Seminar was the inner strength emanating from the meetings. The participants discovered a world that was totally unknown to them: the rich tradition of Orthodoxy and the ascetic life of the Orthodox monks and church fathers. Many experienced the faith as a gift and an experience of great freedom. What connected them was not only their aversion to the Soviet way of life but also, to a great extent, the desire to create a new society based on a contemporary interpretation of that age-old tradition.

The topics discussed by the Seminar members included the work of the French-Jewish philosopher Henri Bergson, the sermons of the American Baptist preacher Billy Graham, and the ideas of Vladimir Soloviev, a Russian philosopher, mystic, writer, and poet who had played an important role in the spiritual renaissance of Russia at the end of the nineteenth century. Soloviev's thought had deeply influenced the work of writers such as Fyodor Dostoyevsky and Leo Tolstoy. Other favorite themes were the relationship between church and state, the history of the Russian Orthodox Church, the creation of an Orthodox world vision, popular culture, and the Russian response to the question "What is truth?" On the list of discussion topics at the Moscow branch of the Christian Seminar during the period 1974-76, the name of Vladimir Soloviev appears four times and that of Alexei Khomyakov three times. Khomyakov was one of the religious poets who helped lay the groundwork for Slavophilism in the nineteenth century.

The methodology of the Christian Seminar was based on the "Saturday evening talks" given by Dmitri Dudko. The frank and lively discussions, in which arguments were constantly being bounced back and forth — something that never happened at that time, not even among friends — made the participants wildly enthusiastic. The issue that was most important to the Christian Seminar led to the formulation and publication of two texts: *The Missionary Duty* and the *Declaration of the Principles of the Seminar.* The thread running through the first work, a theological tract, was the input of the laity in the revitalization of the Russian Orthodox Church. In the idealistic *Declaration,* which took for granted the imminent collapse of the Communist regime, all Seminar attendees were called on to devote themselves to and contribute toward a new era in which the Russian Orthodox Church, free of all state interference, would be able to concentrate on meeting the deepest human longings. This approach profoundly influenced the lifestyle of the participants. Tatiana Shchipkova wrote:

> These meetings of young Orthodox believers, their discussions, lectures and arguments, gave me what I had been unable to find either at academic conferences or in the company of my respectable friends — warm Christian fellowship, completely untrammeled thinking, and total immersion in the spiritual realm. Social questions were discussed only in connection with religious ones.

Other members' responses were more like that of Yelena K.: "I was accustomed to going to church, but recently the celebration of the worship services had struck me as uninspired and wooden. When I found the Seminar I was supported, I learned to take courage and I found inner peace." Vladimir Blagovestov put it this way: "Only in the Seminar did I find God." Andrei Yevgeni said: "In the Church it was impossible to meet other young people and to have free and open discussions about Christianity." Alexander Shchipkov wrote that he was moved by "the presence of Christians together, without a single atheist." Another participant noted: "For the first time we didn't have to invest any time defending our faith, but we could devote ourselves fully to the study and the deepening of our faith."

Striving for Ecumenical East-West Dialogue

Another part of what was innovative was the ecumenical approach. Although most of the participants in the Seminar were Orthodox Christians, the group deliberately portrayed itself as simply Christian, with the focus on the preservation of Christian identity, and Catholics and Protestants also attended the meetings.

There was also a great longing for contacts with Western Christians. In 1975 the student Leonardo Paleari, of the Italian Catholic movement Comunione e Liberazione, attended a meeting of the Moscow branch of the Seminar. Ogorodnikov also made contact with young French and Czechoslovakian Christians who were studying in the Soviet Union, and he asked the exiled writer Alexander Solzhenitsyn to put him in touch with young American Christians. In a letter to the Americans, Ogorodnikov wrote:

> The time has come for many of us, living as we do on different continents and raised in different historical traditions, to open our hearts to each other and unite our efforts in creative searching. We feel your influence around us at every step. We are grateful to you for the spirit of liberation, which has filtered through the customs barrier and the infernal wailings of the radio-jammers. We turn to other people with our souls laid open. Open your hearts to us, as we are opening our own to you.

It is not known whether that appeal was ever answered; in any event, no answer ever reached the members of the Seminar. The "water" between the United States and the Soviet Union was still too deep — ideologically, linguistically, and politically.

The success of the Christian Seminar illustrated the increasing interest in religion in Soviet society, though it never grew into a mass movement. The converts remained small in terms of numbers, but they did break with their upbringing and the prevailing cultural climate. In 1974, for the first time, *Pravda* devoted an entire article to the "remarkable growth" of interest in religion and the increasing ideological apathy. The journal *Science and Religion,* the organ of the popular scientific society Knowledge (successor to the Union of Militant Atheists), reported that, in a number of regions of the Soviet Union, one out of every two couples was choosing to marry in the church, and more than half of the newborn babies were being baptized.

Solzhenitsyn's *Gulag Archipelago*

In the meantime, the publication of Alexander Solzhenitsyn's *The Gulag Archipelago* on December 31, 1973, in Paris held the whole world spellbound for months. The author had decided to have the book published in the West after the suicide of the librarian Elizabeta Voronyanskaya, to whom he had given a copy for safekeeping. This woman had been interrogated by the KGB for five days, after which she finally handed them her copy. In this vast and magisterial work, Solzhenitsyn provides an almost encyclopedic analysis of the Great Terror under Lenin and Stalin and the system of repression as it functioned in the Soviet Union between 1917 and 1956. The work is based on his own personal experiences in Stalin's camps and the testimony of 227 other prisoners. What was new about his work was that he pinned the responsibility for the terror not only on Joseph Stalin but also on Lenin and the Communist ideology, which left no leeway for any departure from the norm.

While *The Gulag Archipelago* was being read in its entirety on Radio Liberty and Deutsche Welle, *Pravda* called the book "a cynical falsification resulting from a sick imagination." Lydia Chukovskaya was thrown out of the Writers' Union in 1974 — thereby simultaneously losing her job — because she had given shelter in her dacha to Solzhenitsyn, who had no residence permit for Moscow. The same fate befell Vladimir Voinovich because he had defended the author.

After Solzhenitsyn refused to answer a summons, he was flown to

West Germany on February 12, 1974, and stripped of his citizenship, thus becoming the first Soviet citizen since Trotsky to be forced into exile. That same day, all the librarians of the Soviet Union were ordered to remove the five existing works by Solzhenitsyn from their libraries and to destroy them. Razor blades in hand, librarians also cut the novel *One Day in the Life of Ivan Denisovich* out of all the bound copies of the cultural monthly *Novy Mir.* The meeting between Solzhenitsyn and Alexander Ogorodnikov, which the latter had long awaited and which had been planned for mid-February 1974, never took place.

On March 14, 1974, the fervent dissident Pavel Litvinov — the grandson of Maxim Litvinov, whom Stalin had dismissed as minister of foreign affairs in 1941 — was arrested and flown to Vienna. While the expulsion of Solzhenitsyn and Litvinov may have increased the popularity of the dissidents in the West, dissidents were forced to take an even more defensive posture in their own country. Dissension grew within the depleted dissident groups, and the struggle to improve the physical conditions of prisoners attracted more attention than did their political demands. The *Chronicle of Current Events* dropped out of sight, a further indication of how much the strength of the dissidents had been diminished.

On June 26, 1974, the eve of the visit of President Richard Nixon to Moscow, Pyotr Grigorenko (who had become very ill) was released. At the same time, however, a number of Jewish activists were arrested. Andrei Sakharov went on a hunger strike to draw attention to the fate of political prisoners in the camps and psychiatric hospitals. The government also came down hard on the Soviet branch of Amnesty International only a few months after it had been established in Moscow (in September 1974). Shortly after Sergei Kovalyov was arrested in December 1974, Secretary Andrei Tverdokhlebov was put behind bars (March 1975). His successor, Vladimir Albrecht, lost his job and afterwards was constantly harassed by the KGB.

On October 30, 1974, the first "Day of the Political Prisoners," all the prisoners of conscience in the Soviet Union went on a hunger strike. Vladimir Osipov was interned that November. As the former publisher of the magazines *Boomerang* (1960) and *Vetsje* (1971-72), he was one of the dissidents with the longest history of service. The world-famous cellist and conductor Mstislav Rostropovich, who had been given permission to leave the Soviet Union temporarily, decided not to return.

On December 18, 1974, copies of *A Manual on Psychiatry for Dissidents,* by Semyon Gluzman and Vladimir Bukovsky, began to circulate in samizdat. This book contained tips on how detainees could convince psychiatrists of their mental health, for example: "Tell them you have no interest in philosophy, psychiatry, parapsychology, mathematics, or modern art, and say that your political activities were due to ignorance and the desire to be famous." As soon as they were admitted to the hospital, the dissidents were to use tactical tricks to convince the psychiatrists that they had given up their earlier "sick ideas."

After laborious negotiations, the U.S. Congress passed the American Trade Act on December 20, 1974, which included the Jackson-Vanik amendment sponsored by Senator Henry Jackson and Congressman Charles Vanik, both Democrats. In this amendment, the granting of "most favored nation" status to the USSR would thenceforth be linked to the right of Jews to emigrate from the Soviet Union. A few weeks later, on January 15, 1975, Moscow unilaterally revoked the trade agreement between the United States and the Soviet Union because of increased international tension. That decision had ideological motives but also material consequences: as a result of two consecutive failed harvests, more and more articles were difficult to obtain in the Soviet Union. "Meatless Thursday" was introduced, and butter, sugar, sausages, and chicken were rationed as well. The population had to stand in line for mineral water, canned fruit, raincoats, women's clothing, stockings, shirts, and fabrics. There was a shortage of chairs in the furniture stores, one reason for which was inefficient industrial production. Quality control officials rejected 11 percent of the monitored fabrics and shoes as "unusable"; the same applied to 13 percent of the knitwear.

The Helsinki Accords: Theory, Practice, and Enforcement

The passing of the Helsinki Accords on August 1, 1975, gave the human rights movement a new impulse. In the Finnish capital, thirty-five countries — including the Soviet Union — signed the final act of the Conference on Security and Cooperation in Europe (CSCE). Part of this declaration had to do with human rights and the freedom of thought, conscience, and religion. Other parts had to do with cooperation in the areas of technology, the environment, economics, science, security questions, humanitarian issues, and the inviolability of European borders.

Yet there was a wide gap between theory and practice. When Andrei Sakharov received the Nobel Peace Prize on October 9, 1975, he was firmly denounced in his own country. But the propaganda machine worked both ways. The first session of the Sakharov hearing on the violation of human rights in the Soviet Union was held on October 20 in Copenhagen. On December 10, 1975, the day before Yelena Bonner, Sakharov's wife, was to accept the Nobel Prize for her husband in Oslo, Sakharov's good friend Sergei Kovalyov was sentenced in Vilnius to seven years in a labor camp and three years of internal exile. Kovalyov was one of the founders of the Initiative Group for the Defense of Human Rights (1969) and the Soviet branch of Amnesty International (1974). He also wrote many articles for *Chronika* and *Chronicle of the Catholic Church of Lithuania.*

Religious persecution in the Soviet Union became the focus of international attention when Lev Regelson and Father Gleb Yakunin wrote a letter to the fifth assembly of the World Council of Churches, which met in the Kenyan capital of Nairobi, November 23 to December 10, 1975. The Regelson and Yakunin letter sparked a debate at that WCC meeting between Western church leaders and the Russian Orthodox delegation (led by Metropolitan Nikodim of Leningrad and Novgorod) that degenerated into a shouting match. Finally, the Keston Institute of Oxford, England, was asked to draw up a report on religious freedom in the thirty-five countries that had signed the Helsinki Accords.

After the texts of Father Dmitri Dudko's "Saturday evening talks" were published in the samizdat magazine *Zemija* and collected in a book entitled *Our Hope* (first published in French and later in eight other languages), Dudko was punished by being forced to leave his parish of Kabanovo on December 21, 1975. A few months later, he was the victim of a car accident staged by the secret service. Father Dudko survived the crash but broke both legs. An ambulance brought him to a remote hospital, where plainclothes KGB agents posted a permanent guard outside his room. A short time later, a number of members of the Christian Seminar, including Alexander Ogorodnikov, abducted Father Dudko from the hospital after a scuffle with the agents, and brought him to a place where he was able to convalesce under optimal conditions. Dudko was later sent to serve in a church in Grebnevo, far from Moscow.

On May 12, 1976, Yuri Orlov and Andrei Almarik formed a work group in Moscow to monitor the USSR's observance of the Helsinki Accords. Other founders of that group included Yelena Bonner, Pyotr Grigorenko, Anatoly Sharansky, and Alexander Ginsburg (one of the early dissidents). This initiative was imitated in the Ukraine, Lithuania,

Georgia, and Armenia. In Czechoslovakia, Charta 77 was set up in January 1977 — on the initiative of the writer Václav Havel — as a movement for the defense of human rights in that country. All these groups targeted the government and foreign public opinion, and they gave a new impulse to the defense of human rights. Yet their ideals and activities made little headway in their own country. The populace, which had been rendered apathetic for more than fifty years, distrusted intellectuals and saw nothing to embrace in political upheaval — despite their own latent dissatisfaction with the government.

Introduction to an Underground Church

To escape the delusions of the day, the members of the Christian Seminar made imaginary journeys to the city of Kitezh, a legendary place, swallowed up by the waters of Lake Svetloyar, where daily life and worship continued without pause. In 1903 the Russian composer Nikolai Rimsky-Korsakov devoted an opera to this theme: *The Legend of the Invisible City of Kitezh and the Maiden Fevroniya.* For the Seminar members, this mental journey functioned as a metaphor for their search for the true spiritual life: a hidden world that was only opening little by little for the participants of the Seminar gatherings.

At that time Ogorodnikov became acquainted with an underground church, whose very existence was a revelation to him. The underground church in the Soviet Union consisted of between one and two hundred centers. These centers represented a whole spectrum of different currents, but their activities were carried out by small groups of insiders. It was almost impossible for outsiders to gain access to these groups. But in 1976, Ogorodnikov came in contact with a priest (whose name is no longer known) who was the head of a community of six elderly nuns; these members of religious orders made absolutely no concessions to the regime, nor did they have passports. The priest, who himself lived a double life, asked Ogorodnikov to launch a campaign for the release of a number of community members who had been locked up, including a priest who had been in the Gulag for thirty years. Ogorodnikov made the contacts, but indirectly. He knew that the KGB was monitoring him day and night, and he didn't want the priest or the nuns to be endangered.

Fearing problems, more and more priests urgently appealed to Ogorodnikov to stop coming to their churches. Meanwhile, he was continuing to carry on the activities of the Christian Seminar — but with great difficulty. The dynamic of the various branches was entirely dependent on the efforts of the leaders and the local situation. Because the KGB was particularly annoyed by the group's strong community structure, which was entirely alien to atheistic Communism, they began to subject the leaders and participants in the Seminar to systematic intimidation beginning in mid-1976. This was the government's unequivocal response to the call for more religious freedom made in 1976 to the Presidium of the Supreme Soviet by twenty-eight Christians from six different denominations.

First in line was Boris Razveyev of Ufa, a brilliant student whose university career was sabotaged. Valentin Serov of Moscow was brutally beaten and kicked, leaving him with a broken arm. After having earned his diploma as a cameraman at the VGIK film academy in Moscow, Serov was not allowed to take the state examination. As a result, he was not able to get a job in his field; a short time later he was also stripped of his diploma.

On June 15, 1976, two police lieutenants broke into Ogorodnikov's home at 25 Mira Prospekt, just when seven leaders of the Seminar were meeting there. The agents searched the apartment, threatened those present, and demanded that they show their documents. A second break-in took place later that evening — again without the required court order — this time by eight police officers, three of whom were in plain clothes. The visitors were taken to the police station for questioning, and all the books, typed papers, manuscripts, notebooks, and telephone indexes were seized, as well as some money.

After the house search, Ogorodnikov was also taken to Police Station 22. The detainees were insulted and ridiculed, and those with long hair and beards (which at that time was a symbol of protest against the regime) were threatened with having their heads shaved. A police major gave them a menacing reprimand: "All the priests were shot in the twenties, and the churches were closed; that's where you nits have crawled out from, and that's where your road leads, too."

The double house search served as an official warning. The KGB started up a dossier for each of the participants, which meant that the secret service could interrogate and arrest them at any time. The next day, Ogorodnikov was fired as janitor at the tuberculosis clinic on police orders; and in the aftermath of the case, Abraham, the clinic's director, was also fired. On July 13, 1976, Ogorodnikov's home was searched by the police a third time — this time during his absence. In the meantime, KGB inspector S. Pavlenko, in a search for Ogorodnikov's manuscripts, illegally broke into the apartment of Andrei Yevgeny, a friend of Ogorodnikov and member of the Christian Seminar. In his interrogation at KGB headquarters on Dzerzhinsky Square, Yevgeny was told to turn over the manuscripts, which he had been keeping for Ogorodnikov. One day later, Pavlenko and his crew returned to Yevgeny's apartment, where they blackmailed his mother, who was critically ill. This second illegal house search was also futile, and shortly thereafter a summons was issued.

On the same day, a twenty-one-year-old woman who regularly attended the Christian Seminar meetings was harassed by two plainclothes KGB agents on her way home. The men followed her into the subway and onto the bus. They leaned against her, pushed her, and stepped on her toes — while she shouted, "Why are you stepping on people's toes?!" When she got off the bus, her attackers followed her and started breathing down her neck. As she tried to get into her apartment, the agents acted as though they were going to force themselves in. At that point the woman fled to her neighbors' apartment.

Argentov and Fedotov Interned and Released

The most tragic fate befell Alexander Argentov. After receiving a summons to appear before the military committee of the Tushinsky district, he was referred to Moscow for a psychological examination. The Moscow psychiatrists interned Argentov, announcing that they were going to "knock all that religious nonsense out of him." Two orderlies took him to the third section of the psychiatric clinic in Moscow. On July 21, 1976, a week after his internment, Argentov, in a letter that was smuggled out and soon began to circulate in samizdat, pleaded with Patriarch Pimen to intervene.

> According to the doctors treating me, the only reason for my being interned is my belief in God and my devotion to the Orthodox Church. I am being forced to take aminazine, a powerful neuroleptic drug, with the threat that if I refuse to take it orally it will be given to me by injection. The extremely ill patients with whom I am confined are tied to their beds because of their aggressive behavior, while I am forced to listen to their wild ravings. The worst are the doctors, who know nothing about religion. They try to convince me that my religious feelings are the result of a mental illness. My parents, who are militant atheists,

have repeatedly appealed for my release, but this has been refused because according to the doctors I need intensive care on account of my mental condition.

On July 27, 1976, Ogorodnikov sent a letter to Philip Potter, the general secretary of the World Council of Churches, a letter that contained a review of the harassment to which the members of the Christian Seminar were being subjected. The final sentence of this letter was: "I particularly beg Christians of the whole world to make every effort to obtain the immediate release of Alexander Argentov." In an accompanying statement, seven prominent Orthodox priests and laypeople expressed their respect for Ogorodnikov and supported his appeal. The letter reached Potter's desk via a secret route, and it received an international response from the WCC. The KGB was furious, and on August 10, 1976, they arrested Ogorodnikov on the street. During a twenty-four-hour cross-examination at KGB headquarters, he was subjected to severe psychological pressure. He was told that he would be locked up in the adjacent prison if he refused to make a statement. Finally, Ogorodnikov was released after being told once again to stop his activities immediately. In 1976, during the annual meeting of the Central Committee of the World Council of Churches in Geneva, Philip Potter announced that an advisory committee would be set up to investigate religious freedom in the Soviet Union and Eastern Europe.

Nevertheless, the persecution of the Seminar members continued. The next victim was Eduard Fedotov. At the Serbski Institute, Dr. (Col.) Daniel Loents diagnosed "schizophrenia," after which Fedotov was permitted no contact with his family and was put in a room with people who were dangerously mentally ill. When Ogorodnikov went to visit him, he got no further than the lobby. Only after much insistence on Ogorodnikov's part did Dr. Levitsky agree to see him. The psychiatrist took the Bible and prayer book that Ogorodnikov had brought for Fedotov and said:

I'm not against belief. Belief is a matter for a man's conscience. But you're talking about Fedotov as if he were a healthy person, and I find that he's ill. Religion for him is an obsessional *idée fixe*. Your Eduard is living in a world of illusions, and I want to bring him back to real life. Belief isn't helping him. It's undermining his health. He's isolated from life. But he's a fine lad — capable. You can go into a church, pray, take communion — but why preach? We only want what's best for him.

Thanks to the publicity that this case received in the West, Alexander Argentov and Eduard Fedotov were both soon released.

But the KGB began to close in on Alexander Ogorodnikov. To avoid being accused of "parasitism," he was feverishly searching for a job. But wherever he applied he was rejected, due to the intervention of the secret service. He was able to find a few minor jobs through friends — as a stable boy at the Moscow racetrack, for instance — but was immediately dismissed as soon as the KGB would contact his employer. The KGB used the same tactics when it came to housing. The friends who had given him temporary shelter were told to stop doing so — first gently, then with harsh threats. For five months the secret service approached thirty-two people from Ogorodnikov's circle of friends before they found Sergei Shuvalov of Ufa willing to refute Ogorodnikov's accusations in his December 10, 1975, letter to Philip Potter. Shuvalov declared:

I became convinced that Ogorodnikov does not believe in God nor the devil and is morally a completely dissolute person. He doesn't work anywhere and leads, I would say, a parasitical way of life. Speaking bluntly, he is a swine, if I can't put it more rudely. Last autumn the Voice of America broadcast a letter of his, in which I heard a reference to myself. He says that I was expelled from the Bashkir University for my "religious convictions." I was outraged at his base action. You know, we haven't seen each other for more than a year, so where did he get all that from?

The harassment aimed at Christian Seminar participants continued unabated. From September 1976 to April 1977, thirty-one members were picked up and interrogated. A number of those dropped out of the Seminar, and a few cooperated with the secret service, but most refused to be intimidated. The oppression did make them more cautious, but at the same time it deepened their solidarity and sense of community. In the fall of 1976, three Seminar meetings took place in Moscow, with new members reporting each time. Starting in 1977, Lev Regelson, author of the book *The Tragedy of the Russian Church: 1917-53*, and a prominent defender of human rights and religious freedom, regularly attended the meetings.

Ogorodnikov explored new ways to establish contact with foreigners. Because Western journalists and embassies in Moscow were always closely watched, he made skillful use of his contacts with the alternative art world. One woman in Moscow made her apartment available for the exhibition of abstract modern art, and numerous foreign diplomats secretly visited these exhibitions, which were difficult for the KGB to track. Ogorodnikov was able to go there unnoticed and make contact with those diplomats.

The Seminar took the initiative to set up a solidarity fund for victims of the repression. Seminar members voluntarily contributed part of their salary so that the families of the detainees could be given material and financial support in order to attend trials and visit the prison or the psychiatric hospital where their loved ones were being held. Needy family members of ordinary prisoners were also given assistance when it was financially possible.

The Seminar was not the only group to suffer hardships. On October 20, 1976, Vladimir Albrecht, secretary of the Moscow branch of Amnesty International, received several death threats. The refuseniks — Soviet Jews who hoped to emigrate to Israel — made themselves heard once again. On October 21, 1976, fifty-one Jews wearing yellow stars of David on their clothing demonstrated in the center of Moscow, after which they continued their sit-down strike in a government building. During the annual silent demonstration that was held every December 5th at the Pushkin statue in Moscow to commemorate Stalin's new Constitution of December 5, 1936, the KGB provoked a fight in which the dissidents present ended up covered with snow and mud.

Two weeks later, in the Swiss city of Zürich, the dissident Vladimir Bukovsky was exchanged for the Chilean Communist leader Luis Corvalán. After his release, Corvalán immediately flew to Moscow to attend, as guest of honor, the seventieth birthday party of General Secretary Leonid Brezhnev. Brezhnev was awarded the Order of Lenin for the fifth time, and for the second time he received the Gold Star Medal, which bore the inscription "Hero of the Soviet Union."

New Dissident Movements

In the autumn of 1976 two new groups joined the dissident movement: the unofficial Working Commission to Investigate the Use of Psychiatry for Political Purposes, set up by psychiatrist Anatoly Koryagin, and the Christian Committee for the Defense of the Rights of Believers in the USSR, an initiative established by Father Gleb Yakunin, Hierodeacon

Varsonofy Khaibulin, and Viktor Kapitanchuk. The latter two had worked on Vladimir Osipov's magazine *Vetsia* in 1971-72.

Alexander Ogorodnikov was also one of the initiators of the Working Commission, but he pulled out just before the actual founding because he could not get along with Yakunin. The latter demanded all the attention and wanted to portray himself, via the committee, as the leader of religious dissidents. In addition, the activities of the Working Commission were focused especially on respect for human rights, an activity that had actually been the work of the members of the Christian Seminar since its founding, though that was not part of its core mission. During its four-year existence, the Commission distributed 423 appeals, petitions, and open letters — a total of three thousand pages. The Commission was never openly attacked by the patriarchate of the Russian Orthodox Church, and Father Vassily Fontchenkov, who joined later, continued as professor at the Moscow Theological Academy.

Because Yakunin and his co-workers only knew about what was happening in Moscow, most of the necessary information was provided by the Christian Seminar network. Yet relations remained tense because Yakunin constantly trivialized the role of the Seminar and claimed all the honor for himself.

After the bombing of the Moscow metro on January 8, 1977, which left seven people dead, the KGB seized the opportunity for a provocation by leaking a report that the bombing was the work of dissidents. The dissidents set up a great hue and cry over the report, but the tone had been set. House searches soon followed, for example, at the home of Yuri Orlov and other members of the Moscow Helsinki Group. Then the KGB seized the money in Alexander Solzhenitsyn's Support Fund for political prisoners and their families, which the author had set up and financed from the proceeds of his world-famous *The Gulag Archipelago*.

In this bitter climate, Jimmy Carter, who had been elected president of the United States in 1976, announced that the focus of his policy would be respect for human rights. His intentions were sincere, but there was a gulf between word and deed: Carter's policy was neither consistent nor bold. In February 1977, he wrote a personal letter to Andrei Sakharov; but he did not react when a search was conducted at the home of Vladimir Slepak, to whom he had sent a telegram during his election campaign, nor when the leaders of the Moscow Helsinki Group were brutally dealt with one by one. On February 3, 1977, Alexander Ginsburg, administrator of Solzhenitsyn's Support Fund, was accused of currency smuggling. Yuri

Orlov was arrested on February 10, and Anatoly Sharansky was sent to the Gulag on March 5. Vladimir Borisov and Natalia Kazarinova were also arrested. The expanding wave of arrests included members of the Helsinki Groups in Georgia, Armenia, the Baltic states, and the Ukraine, where, as usual, the reprisals were the most severe. All of those arrested received maximum sentences at their trials — without exception.

George Krimski, correspondent for the Associated Press (AP), was forced to leave the country on February 7, and correspondent Charles Wallace of the United Press International (UPI) was arrested and beaten on May 1. Mikhail Stern, the Ukrainian endocrinologist who had been forced to perform heavy physical labor in a prison camp for three years and who was quite ill — he was one of the best-known victims of the Soviet campaign of anti-Semitism — was freed in 1977 in response to an international petition signed by fifty Nobel Prize winners, after which he immigrated to the Netherlands. The government's standard approach, which was to send leaders of the resistance either to the Gulag or to a psychiatric hospital — or to exile them from the country — appeared to have been successful, as it usually was. Once again, the dissident movement had been dealt a heavy blow.

When U.S. Secretary of State Cyrus Vance visited Moscow in March 1977, he signaled that the Carter administration was backing off even further. Vance announced that, as a gesture of good will, he was not going to meet with any dissidents. But General Secretary Brezhnev and Minister of Foreign Affairs Gromyko rejected the American disarmament plans that he proposed at the negotiating table anyway. And that diplomatic failure set the tone for disarmament talks between East and West for years to come.

First Issue of *Obshchina* Intercepted

On April 13 and 20, 1977, Boris Roshchin published a two-part article entitled "Religious Freedom and Its Slanderers" in the popular cultural and political weekly *Literaturnaya Gazeta*. The article was an attack on Lev Regelson, Alexander Ogorodnikov, and Fathers Dmitri Dudko and Gleb Yakunin. Ogorodnikov refuted Roshchin's allegations one by one in an open letter that began to circulate in samizdat on April 27, indicating that the Christian Seminar was still active in the underground press.

Indeed, one of the most important accomplishments of the Seminar was the publication of the underground magazine *Obshchina* (Community). For years Ogorodnikov had dreamed of an uncensored religious-philosophical magazine that would not only be written for members of the Seminar but would also serve as a model for the religious revival of the Soviet Union. The name of the publication emphasized the importance of community formation. Putting the magazine together was no easy matter: ink and paper were hard to come by — even on the black market — and the texts of articles had to be typed on a typewriter.

Ogorodnikov and Vladimir Poresh worked on editing the first issue for months. Finally, in May 1977, the work was almost finished when Ogorodnikov, through the kind auspices of a friendly doctor, was rushed to one of the best-known hospitals in Moscow. The KGB was able to track him down by shadowing his friends, though one Seminar member secretly brought him two hundred pages of copy for the first issue so that he could complete the final editing. Ogorodnikov hid that copy in his hospital room. But during his absence from his home, his roommates were sent away, and the KGB conducted a search. When Ogorodnikov returned home, he noticed to his bewilderment that not only was his religious literature gone but so was the original copy for the first issue of *Obshchina.* He and his co-workers had apparently greatly underestimated the power of the secret service.

Shortly thereafter, the *Chronicle of Current Events,* which was circulating again in samizdat, published an overview of all the stolen documents: "The story of the founding of the Seminar and the history of its persecution; an article by Boris Roshchin in *Literaturnaya Gazeta* and the reactions from those who were disgracefully maligned in that article; articles on the activities of the Seminar and the Christian Committee for the Defense of the Rights of Believers in the USSR; an Easter sermon by Dmitri Dudko; and an appeal for support."

All of this was taking place just when the power struggle in the Kremlin, which had lasted many years, finally reached a climax with the dismissal of President Nikolai Podgorny. This removed the last obstacle to the approval of a new constitution, which made it possible to combine the mandates of the Communist Party general secretary and the president. On June 16, 1977, Leonid Brezhnev was unanimously elected president by the Supreme Soviet.

At the Belgrade Conference, which was called to review compliance with the Helsinki Accords, the United States once again took a hard line. The case of Anatoly Sharansky, in particular, aroused strong feelings:

Sharansky had been accused of high treason and collaboration with the American CIA, which President Jimmy Carter promptly denied. Carter decided to increase by 50 percent the capacity of the American radio stations broadcasting to Eastern Europe in order to expand American influence in the East. Now light amusement programs, backed by music from the Swedish group ABBA and other Western popular artists, alternated with serious news broadcasts.

On August 31, 1977, four thousand psychiatrists from sixty different countries met in Honolulu for the international congress of the World Psychiatric Association (WPA), an event that was held every six years. Great Britain, Australia, Canada, and the United States threatened to withdraw from the association if the group failed to condemn the Soviet Union for abuse of psychiatry for political purposes. Marina Voikhanskaya, a psychiatrist who had emigrated from the Soviet Union to the West, said that between 700 and 1,100 dissidents were being detained in psychiatric hospitals in the USSR. According to her colleague, Avtandil Papiashvili, another émigré, the abuse was increasing. Former detainee Leonid Plutsch gave a personal testimony during the congress. Two professors, the Australian Sidney Bloch and the American Peter Reddaway, declared that in the Soviet Union at least 365 "normal people" were being detained in hospitals for "political insanity." While the Soviet Union was being condemned by a narrow majority of the congress attendees, and an official research commission was set up, the Orthodox monk Mikhail Gertchev, one of the leaders of the underground Russian Orthodox Church, died in a psychiatric hospital in Kazan after forty years of detention.

How many prisoners of conscience were in the Gulag at the end of the 1970s? No exact numbers have ever been released. Amnesty International, Andrei Sakharov, and Andrei Sinyavsky believed that there were about 10,000 in a prison population of one million. But Andrei Almarik estimated the number to be 25,000 to 30,000.

Ogorodnikov Marries Yelena Levashova

Alexander Ogorodnikov's own personal circumstances changed abruptly on March 30, 1977, when Yelena Levashova, with whom he was having a relationship, gave birth to their son, Dima. Yelena had grown up in a "closed" suburb of Moscow (a district not open to outsiders because it was the home of the city's aerospace industry and advanced military technology). Her father was an army colonel in a secret research institute that designed rockets for eliminating satellites, and her mother was a medical assistant. As true-blue Communists, both parents had looked on with anguish as one of their two daughters became a member of the Christian Seminar. That meant that, right from the start, the relationship between Alexander and Yelena and her parents would be filled with tension. Her parents despised him and regarded their daughter's planned marriage to him as a great tragedy.

Ogorodnikov and Levashova did not want a civil wedding because they refused to recognize the Soviet system. In November 1977, they had a secret church wedding, which was conducted by Father Dmitri Dudko. Because Ogorodnikov and Levashova were not registered parishioners, the ceremony was not conducted in Dudko's own parish but in a private hall in Moscow in the presence of a large number of Christian Seminar members.

While Levashova and young Dima stayed in Moscow, Ogorodnikov continued with his activities. Contacts with the monks of the ancient Pechersk Lavra, or Monastery of the Caves, in the Ukraine — the first contact had been in 1975 — became more intense. Despite regular raids by the KGB, and the fact that the former church had been forcibly turned into a Museum of Atheism in 1920, this monastery, which at the time was under the leadership of Anatoly Shchur (or Brother Andrei), was an important spiritual center for the underground church.

The Seminar Gets Its Own Building in Redkino

In 1977 the monks gave Ogorodnikov some money to buy a house in which the Seminar could develop independently. Since it was impossible to buy a house in Moscow, Ogorodnikov decided to search in a nearby town within easy reach of Moscow. Finally, the choice came down to a house with a large garden in Redkino, a village of 10,000 inhabitants that was about one hundred miles from Moscow and had a good railroad connection with the capital. To avoid possible problems that might come with registering the purchase, Alexander bought the building in the name of his father, Iol Ogorodnikov. Ten members of the Seminar made plans to live and work in Redkino, the new home base of the Moscow branch, and in this way to realize the dream of a Christian community. They would support themselves with the produce from the vegetable garden.

With a nod to the nineteenth-century Slavophiles, they changed the name of the organization to the Christian Seminar for Solving the Problems of the Religious Renaissance in the Soviet Union — thereby hoping to contribute to the spiritual revival of Russia. The deep discussions among the members led not only to strong mutual ties but also to serious differences of opinion. And some of these differences resulted in Ogorodnikov's breaking with Father Dmitri Dudko in 1977.

On October 14, 1977, Valentin Turchin, the battle-weary chairman of the Moscow branch of Amnesty International, was finally given an exit visa. The celebrated mathematician had not only lost his job but was also continuously being harassed, falsely accused, arrested, and even imprisoned. Georgi Vladimov was the next to go. Just as the dissident Pyotr Grigorenko was leaving the Soviet Union on November 30, 1977, a rift developed between the Russian Communist Party and the Communist parties of Western Europe. The Italian Communist Party distanced itself from Marxism-Leninism, and Santiago Carillo, the secretary-general of the Communist Party of Spain, was not permitted to give a speech on November 7, 1977, during the celebration of the sixtieth anniversary of the Russian Revolution in Moscow. At that event, an impressive military parade was held at which the public got to see the new T-72 tank. And Dmitri Ustinov, the minister of defense, announced that the Soviet Union would soon expand its military potential even further.

At the 1977 Venice Biennale in Italy the theme was "Dissidents in Eastern Europe," and nonofficial Soviet art, Czechoslovakian graphics, and prohibited samizdat literature from the Soviet Union were shown. The Soviet authorities were even more offended by the second international Sakharov Tribunal on Human Rights in the Soviet Union, which was held November 26-29, 1977, in Rome, and chaired by the well-known Nazi hunter Simon Wiesenthal.

In 1978 several autonomous labor organizations were created in the Soviet Union. This initiative was the most far-reaching and most visible expression of collective labor protest in the Soviet Union up to that time. The foundation for the first independent trade union was laid in 1977 by the unemployed Ukrainian miner Vladimir Klebanov, who had already spent a few years in prisons and psychiatric hospitals for openly criticizing violations of workers' rights. After being released in 1973, he was unable to find another job because the words "dismissed in connection with arrest" had been entered into his work booklet. Over the course of 1977, Klebanov published various open letters and collective appeals that were signed by a number of workers who had suffered the same fate in different parts of the Soviet Union. These open letters were addressed to the editors of a few large Russian newspapers, including *Izvetsiya* and *Pravda,* to various state organs, and to "world opinion" in general.

During a Moscow press conference for foreign journalists on November 25, 1977, the "Klebanov Group" announced its plan to set up an independent trade union. Second and third press conferences were held in January and February 1978, and the group published another open letter, this one signed by forty-three workers. On February 1, 1978, the group also published the statutes of the Association of Free Trade Unions of Workers in the USSR (AFTU), which had been founded a week earlier, a list with the names of a hundred candidate members, and a letter to the International Labor Organization (ILO) in Geneva, a specialized section of the United Nations, requesting that they be recognized as an official labor organization. But all this led to nothing. Shortly after the founding of the so-called Free Trade Union, the authorities arrested most of its members. A relatively large number of them, including Vladimir Klebanov himself, were locked up in psychiatric hospitals.

A few months later, the lawyer Vsevolod Kuvakin, a specialist in labor law, formed the Work Group in Defense of Labor, Economic and Social Rights. And in October 1978, the AFTU (which had been terminated) was followed by the Free Interprofessional Association of Workers (SMOT), which consisted of technicians and mechanics. By the end of 1978, however, most of the leaders of the new trade unions were behind bars. The monopoly of the single, all-encompassing Communist trade union could not be broken. The vigorous government action against the new trade unions prevented — at least for now — the combining of dissident forces, which was a potential danger for the regime. In fact, Ogorodnikov had already been in contact with the trade union leader Klebanov, who was arrested in February 1978.

Just how dangerous to the regime an independent trade union could be was demonstrated a few years later by Lech Wałęsa, who was then working as an electrical fitter at the Lenin Shipyard in the Polish city of Gdańsk. With his independent trade union *Solidarność,* which he formed in September 1980, he sent shock waves through the Communist regime, after which General Wojciech Jeruzelski, commander-in-chief of the Polish army, staged a coup in December 1981.

In the fall of 1978, the problem of the Crimean Tatars arose once again. After Resolution No. 700 ("Concerning additional measures for stricter passport controls in the Crimea oblast") of October 15, 1978, was approved by the council of ministers of the USSR, the Russian Ministry of Foreign Affairs was given a free hand to take harsh action against the Crimean Tatars, who had tried to settle in Crimea once again. Homes were demolished, and people were forcibly removed. A few months earlier, the carpenter Musa Mamut had been threatened with expulsion from the village of Besh-Terek in the Crimean Autonomous Socialist Soviet Republic. Mamut set himself on fire, but this apparently made no impression on the Soviet regime either.

Another thorny case during the period when the government was taking harsh action had to do with exit visas. After more than 130,000 Jews and 40,000 Soviet Germans had left the Soviet Union between 1972 and 1977, the criteria for obtaining exit visas were tightened even further, and the administrative procedure was lengthened. Anyone who applied for emigration had to hand in his passport, even though a person caught without a passport could be convicted of "maliciously violating the passport regulations."

On March 14, 1978, in the Uzbek capital of Tashkent, five Seventh-day Adventists went on trial, among them the eighty-three-year-old clergyman Vladimir Shchelkov, who had already spent twenty-three years in the Gulag. He was sentenced to five years in prison with a strict regimen, and he died in custody two years later. A little while later, Arkady Shevchenko, a top Soviet diplomat at the United Nations, caused an uproar when he asked the United States for political asylum on April 11, 1978. It was the most spectacular defection by a Soviet functionary. One month later, his wife, who did return to the Soviet Union, committed suicide.

In the meantime, plans for a new issue of the magazine *Obshchina* began to take shape. Because so much original material had been lost when the first edition was seized, the editors decided to start again right from the beginning. Ogorodnikov collected information on the Seminar, and Vladimir Poresh selected contributions on theology, history, and literature. Poet Oleg Ochapkin took charge of the literary section. As a precautionary measure, they did not allow anyone else to be involved in these preparations.

Nonetheless, not everything ran smoothly. Unbeknownst to the Seminar leaders, their phone had been tapped, and on April 21, 1978, staff members of the Smolensk *procuratura,* after forcing the front door, burst into the home of Tatiana Shchipkova and spent six hours searching the apartment. This raid resulted in the confiscation of seven copies of the brand-new issue of *Obshchina,* plus about eighty books. Ogorodnikov and Viktor

Popkov were also present when the raid occurred, and Sergei Yermolaev was taken to the Smolensk station and put back on the train to Moscow.

Despite the legal action, the distribution of that issue of *Obshchina* went ahead unimpeded. As announced earlier in the underground press, nineteen "original" copies of *Obshchina* began circulating in samizdat on April 28, 1978. A few copies found their way to the West. In the years that followed, the KGB managed to confiscate about six hundred copies.

This double issue (283 pages all told) opened with the "Declaration of the Principles of the Seminar," followed by the features "On Striving toward a Theological Culture" and "Missionary Service and the Orthodox Community." The literary part contained two poems by Oleg Ochapkin, a poetic anthology, and the poem "The Apocalypse of Leningrad," by the mystic Daniil Andreev. In the essay "The Culture of the Catacombs: The Experiences of Our Generation," Ogorodnikov explained what the group's ideal quest was all about. The issue also contained a number of valuable texts that had fallen into oblivion: the correspondence between Konstantin Kavelin, spiritual father of liberalism, and the Russian czar Alexander II, in which Kavelin puts the success of the nihilists in perspective; an article by the artist Vasilii Chekrygin (1897-1922); an excerpt from the "Reminiscences" of Andrei Bely (1880-1934), the theoretician of Symbolism; and letters from the Russian philosopher, theologian, and economist Sergei Bulgakov (1871-1944). The issue also contained the article "To Interconfessional Unity," a prayer for Russia written by a Catholic, and a number of essays and documents discussing the current condition of the Orthodox Church in the Soviet Union and the persecution of those in the Christian Seminar. Two other pages appeared separately. They contained recollections — photocopies of source material that had never been published before — of the murder of Czar Nicholas II and his family in 1918, written by an anonymous "red guard."

For Tatiana Shchipkova, her distribution of *Obshchina* meant the end of her teaching career. On June 7, 1978, she told her students the truth: "I explained that Christianity had always been a living faith — it was the first time the students had ever heard anything like this before — and was exercising a strong attraction on more and more educated people. I told them what it meant to be a Christian and how I myself had become a Christian." After her dismissal for "unscientific behavior," she lost her diploma as candidate in the political sciences and her title of doctor of philology, which she had been awarded summa cum laude several years earlier.

Ogorodnikov Goes into Hiding

On April 30, 1978, two days after *Obshchina* went into circulation, the Moscow members of the Seminar got together in the Seminar house in Redkino. They were planning to attend the Easter vigil that night in the local church. True to custom, this service was to begin at eleven o'clock and to last until five in the morning. Their plan was foiled, however, by thirty KGB agents, who had surrounded the house. So they decided to hold an improvised prayer service where they were.

It was then that Ogorodnikov decided to go into hiding. Because the KGB could not initially trace him, they circulated a description of him throughout the entire Soviet Union. He was first in Kiev, where he stayed for a few weeks in the basement of the home of Georgi Vins, a Baptist leader who was in the Gulag at that time. The deep discussions he had with Vins's son Pyotr resulted in the latter's conversion to Orthodoxy. Alexander then stayed in hiding places in the Caucasus and in the Pechersk Lavra, Monastery of the Caves, in Kiev. A visit to the monastery of Pskov-Pechory, near the Estonian border, home of his spiritual father, Father Ioann, and his brother, Raphael, was out of the question because the director of that monastery, Abbot Gabriel (Stebluchenko), was known to be a secret agent of the KGB.

Ogorodnikov's possible hiding places were shrinking in number because the KGB agents were carefully tightening their net. They were even watching people whom he hadn't seen in ten years. Ogorodnikov was discovering for himself what means, manpower, and potential the KGB had at its disposal. All during his hiding he kept in contact with his parents and his wife by letter. On July 7, 1978, the house in Redkino was searched, and a short time later the secret police set up a permanent observation post in the neighborhood. Meanwhile, Ogorodnikov was spending his time editing the book *The Culture of the Catacombs: The Experiences of Our Generation,* part of which had already been published in *Obshchina.*

Leaders of the Helsinki Groups Convicted

At that time, the trials of the leaders of the Helsinki Groups in the Soviet Union were receiving worldwide attention. Yuri Orlov, chairman of the Moscow Helsinki Group, was sentenced to seven years in a labor camp and five years internal exile on May 18, 1978, for distributing "counterrevolutionary material." The French Communist daily *L'Humanité* called that verdict "inadmissible" and "unjust." And on June 21, 1978, Vladimir Slepak, the well-known Jewish refusenik, was given the maximum sentence.

In 1978, seven Pentecostals (known as "the Siberian Seven"), members of the Vashchenko and Chmykhalov families, sought asylum in the American embassy in Moscow, fearing that they would soon be sent back to Siberia following the government's refusal to issue them emigration visas. Another indication of the level of tension between the United States and the Soviet Union at the time was the fact that the American journalists Craig Whitney of *The New York Times* and Harold Piper of *The Baltimore Sun* were convicted of slander by a Moscow court in July 1978.

On July 10, 1978, Anatoly Sharansky, who had been charged with high treason and espionage, was sentenced to thirteen years of hard labor. The international outcry over his arrest in March 1977 had led to the founding of the human rights committee Scientists for Orlov and Sharansky in June 1978 in the United States (SOS, later renamed Scientists for Sakharov, Orlov and Sharansky). And President Jimmy Carter promptly cancelled the contract for the sale of computers to the Russian news agency TASS.

With the intention of splitting the opposition, the Soviets started two trials at the same time, on July 14, 1978. The "veteran" Alexander Ginsburg, who had already been sentenced once in 1961, was summoned to appear in court in Kaluga. Then in Vilnius, the capital of Lithuania, Viktor Piatkus, the cofounder of the Lithuanian Helsinki Group, was sentenced to fifteen years in prison at hard labor. He was the seventeenth member of one of the five Helsinki Groups in the Soviet Union to be convicted. According to the American historian Jane Ellis, the Helsinki Groups in the Soviet Union were treated more harshly than those in the Christian Seminar because the former were seen to constitute a greater threat to the Soviet regime.

The dissident movements were being successfully decapitated, but the physicist Sergei Polikanov simply went ahead with the activities of the Moscow Helsinki Group anyway. Shortly before this, physicist Yuri Karimangayev had replaced Alexander Pordrabinek in the Working Commission to Investigate the Use of Psychiatry for Political Purposes after Pordrabinek had been arrested in May 1978 at the opening of the Yuri Orlov trial. Astrophysicist Lev Ulanovski and engineer Pavel Abramovich took over the role of the convicted Anatoly Sharansky.

After the 1977 conviction of the dissidents Merab Kostava and Zviad Gamsachurdia of the Georgian Helsinki Group, both were nominated by the American Congress for the Nobel Peace Prize in 1978. Gamsachurdia "confessed" when he was first taken into custody. He said on television that he had acted wrongfully, and he was given an early release in June 1979 (he had been sentenced to three years of hard labor and three years of exile) — after which he immediately resumed his activities.

"You Have One Month to Leave the Soviet Union"

In early September 1978, Ogorodnikov suddenly appeared in public, in Moscow during a press conference for foreign correspondents, an event at which Andrei Sakharov was also present. Ogorodnikov gave the journalists detailed information about the perils involved in the reopening of the church of the Pechersk Lavra, the Ukrainian Monastery of the Caves, the persecution of the underground church in the Soviet Union, and the situation of the Roman Catholic Church in Lithuania.

After the press conference he was picked up by the KGB and taken to KGB headquarters.

"It's high time you stop acting like a hero," a man in uniform told him. "You have one month to leave the Soviet Union."

"Why should I leave my country?" Ogorodnikov protested. "I was born here, and I don't want to leave. *You* are the foreign elements who are tearing this country apart. It's not I but you who should leave, since you're the ones who are occupying our country. You're only sowing fear, cynicism, and hate."

The KGB agents became enraged.

"Did you understand what we said?" shouted one of them. "You have one month. If you haven't emigrated by then, we're going to arrest you, and you'll never get out of jail. You'll die there, forgotten and abandoned by everyone."

Ogorodnikov asked his friends for advice. A few urged him to accept the KGB's offer.

"Don't go to prison," they said. "You can accomplish much more by continuing the struggle from abroad."

He received a written invitation from Anatoly Levitin-Krasnov to go to Switzerland and another from Father Alexander Schmemann, dean of

Saint Vladimir's Orthodox Theological Seminary in New York, to go to America. But Ogorodnikov refuted his friends' arguments.

> A new generation of believers is rising in Russia, and they have been given the mission to witness to their belief, not only with words but also with deeds. Great deeds begin with the making of victims. We must show, with our flesh and blood, that our words are not empty. It is a great privilege to suffer for Jesus Christ. Forgive me these high-flown words, but I cannot refuse that privilege.

Some began to weep, but they did not ask him to change his mind. Other Seminar members announced that they, too, would let themselves be arrested.

"Without suffering, our faith doesn't make sense," Ogorodnikov continued. "True religious work simply demands a sacrifice." By announcing his arrest, he wanted to be a living witness to the religious persecution in the USSR, and to prove that Christianity was not an abstract idea.

In the little time left to him, Ogorodnikov made sure that the activities of the Christian Seminar would proceed as usual after his arrest. A monk from the Pechersk Lavra gave him money so he could visit all the branches of the Seminar in order to improve their approach and policy and to build up an information network.

Because the KGB was constantly shadowing the leaders of the movement and listening in on their conversations, secret communication was of great importance. Ogorodnikov knew all kinds of clever tricks for passing messages that would be unnoticed. During one seemingly innocent conversation, for example, he passed a note under the cushion of a chair. The group developed its own language, with code words and code names: their intercepted letters were impossible to decipher, and they also started a special system for hiding letters in secret locations. An envelope symbol with a diagonal stripe through it drawn on the wall, for example, meant that a letter was to be collected somewhere.

In the meantime, Ogorodnikov prepared himself for his stay in prison. He prayed a great deal and fasted regularly. Nevertheless, it was very difficult for him to get used to the idea. At one point he was afraid he would never become accustomed to the prison regimen because of his attachment to freedom. He was also afraid that a life behind bars would be completely lacking in dignity, the vile reputation of the custodial personnel filled him with anxiety.

On September 9, 1978, in his capacity as representative of the Orthodox youth, Ogorodnikov went to the home of Leo Tolstoy on the Yasnaya Polyana estate, near the city of Tula, to take part in the commemoration of the 150th birthday of the author of *War and Peace* and *Anna Karenina.* There he met young people who had enormous spiritual hunger, and he told them all about the Christian Seminar.

While his wife and son remained in Moscow, Ogorodnikov supported himself in Redkino by selling apples from the orchard and assisting in the restoration of a few churches. His request to become registered as a farmer — to avoid being charged with parasitism — was refused in early November 1978. In Chistopol, the police detained Iol Ogorodnikov for six hours in an attempt to convince him to sell the house in Redkino.

After a charge of parasitism was officially brought against him, Alexander Ogorodnikov was told to report to the police on November 22, 1978, with documented proof that he had a job. On Friday, November 17, Ogorodnikov was apprehended just as he was about to get on a train to look for work and was detained for sixteen hours at the Redkino station. When he tried to look for work once again on Monday morning, November 20, he was arrested at the Redkino station and taken to the prison in Kalinin, the historic city of Tver that had been renamed after the Soviet hero Mikhail Kalinin, the first president of the Soviet Union.

II

SURVIVING IN THE GULAG

CHAPTER FIVE

The Soviet Union's Inhumane Detention System

A lexander Ogorodnikov entered the Gulag with a deep faith and the firm conviction that he would be able to withstand the trials that awaited him. "He alone is worthy of life and freedom who each day fights for them anew," wrote Johann Wolfgang von Goethe in his masterpiece *Faust* (1806-32). To protest his arrest, however, Ogorodnikov began a hunger strike as soon as he arrived at the prison in Kalinin. This was a favorite form of protest among dissidents, and they used it frequently. But a newcomer refusing all food on the very first day was something prison directors had never seen before.

Ogorodnikov became acquainted with the true nature of the Soviet Union's detention system right from the start. Four to five prisoners were packed into each of the cells in the nineteenth-century Kalinin prison. Due to a lack of ventilation, an unbearable stench permeated the building. Many security measures had been taken to prevent prisoners from escaping: peepholes were in the cell doors so the detainees could be spied on every few minutes by the guards; the small cell window was covered with a roll-down shutter, preventing any daylight from shining in and the prisoners from looking out; the cells were lit by artificial light day and night; prisoners were required to sleep with their heads pointed toward the cell door and their hands outside the covers.

Discipline was extremely harsh, and possession of money and valuables was forbidden. Prisoners could be frisked at any time, and their cells could also be searched without warning. During the preliminary investigation, the detainees were given no bedding and were not permitted to write letters. Hygiene was poor, and there was an absence of even the most elementary medical care. Every ten days they were given five books or magazines from the prison library, which consisted of boring Soviet literature imbued with the ideal of "socialist realism."

Days in the prison followed a strict schedule, with fixed hours for getting up, eating, and getting fresh air (one hour a day). Talking in the hallways was strictly forbidden. Prisoners who were let out for fresh air or for interrogation were required to walk in front of the guards with their hands behind their backs. When two groups of prisoners passed each other in the hall, one group had to face the wall in order to prevent any form of contact from taking place between fellow prisoners. Because of its inhumane character, the detention system was a permanent source of conflict.

Whenever a member of the prison management passed prisoners, the latter were required to state their last names, first names, and sections of the law with which they had been charged. Ogorodnikov consistently refused to provide this information. This was his way of protesting the hatred and contempt that the superiors exhibited and the humiliating treatment he had to endure.

Ogorodnikov was persuaded to end his hunger strike on December 6, 1978, after which he was introduced to prison fare. The meager rations were allocated in accordance with the regime under which the prisoner had been convicted, the nature and place of the work he did, and his sentence. There were thirteen norms in use. Ogorodnikov, who before his trial was still regarded as a common prisoner, was initially fed under norm number one, the highest category.

According to prison regulations, this daily ration consisted of 2,500 calories and 65 grams of protein, and was made up of 650 grams of black bread, 10 grams of wheat flour, 110 grams of groats, 20 grams of macaroni, 50 grams of meat, 85 grams of fish, 10 grams of fat, 15 grams of vegetable oil, 20 grams of sugar, 450 grams of potatoes, 200 grams of cabbage or some other vegetable, and 5 grams of tomato puree. In actual practice, however, the kitchen and prison personnel kept the most nutritious ingredients for themselves — when they were available. Meat, fish, and fats almost never ended up on the prisoners' plates. The food that was served was chronically deficient in vitamins and never fulfilled the calorie requirement. In addition, the food was so poorly prepared that at first Ogorodnikov ate only bread. But after a few days, his raging hunger gave him no choice but to eat the slop that was being served.

Keeping Silent during the Preliminary Investigation

Within twenty-four hours, the Public Prosecution Service informed Ogorodnikov of the reason for his imprisonment: leading a parasitic lifestyle. Under the watchful eye of the KGB, who constantly monitored the activity of all dissidents at the time, the Ministry of the Interior (MVD) investigated the charge. From the very first interrogation session, Ogorodnikov refused to answer the barrage of questions he was asked. The main purpose of this questioning was to extract confessions from the imprisoned, to get him to acknowledge that the activities with which he was being charged were "criminal," and to obtain information about other dissidents.

Because Ogorodnikov stubbornly remained silent, the prison management decided to get tough. He was put in a cell with several violent criminals whom the management had set against him. Now Ogorodnikov ran the risk of being molested or of never waking up in the morning. But that's not how things turned out. Because he was not easily frightened and would not let himself be intimidated, he quickly established good communications with his cellmates.

Ogorodnikov's constant movement from cell to cell meant that he became more and more influential among his fellow prisoners. Of course, he fully realized that in such an environment, which was crawling with anonymous informers, one could never trust anyone. But this did not make him any more talkative with his interrogators. The MVD investigation was fruitless as well. Ogorodnikov opened his mouth only to denounce the violation of human rights and to criticize the show trial that was awaiting him.

Because Ogorodnikov was not allowed to receive any visits from family members or friends during his pretrial detention, or to consult with a lawyer, he had no idea what was going on in the outside world. Gleb Yakunin's Christian Committee protested against Ogorodnikov's detainment: "This arrest, which is based on religious beliefs, must be regarded as discrimination. Because Ogorodnikov's name is widely known, his trial will undoubtedly lead to mass protests by religiously inspired young people in both our country and in the West." Yet only scattered protest was heard at that time.

Signatures were collected in Lithuania demanding his release. Because of the delicate issue of nationality in the Soviet Union, Ogorodnikov was the first Russian for whom something like this had been done in Lithuania. But it was no accident. He had repeatedly defended the Catholic Church in Lithuania in the past, and the meetings of the Christian Seminar were regularly attended by Lithuanian Catholics. Adi Useldinger, Ogorodnikov's former roommate at the Moscow film academy, was so moved by his arrest that he decided to become a monk.

In the meantime, the struggle for more religious freedom continued unabated. In November 1978, the Catholic Committee for the Defense of the Rights of Believers, a sister organization of the Christian Committee, began to concern itself with the fate of Roman Catholics in the Soviet Union. Russia had relatively few Catholics, but in the Ukraine there were between 3.5 and 5 million. Their interests were promoted by the Initiative Group for the Defense of Believers and Church, founded in 1982 by Jozef Terelya, which saw itself as part of the Ukrainian Helsinki Group that had been formed in 1976.

In the fall of 1978, Vladimir Poresh began editing a new issue of *Obshchina,* the periodical issued by the Christian Seminar, but he was unable to finish it. At the end of 1978, Seminar members Alexander Kuzkin and Sergei Yermolaev were both arrested in the Moscow subway for openly protesting Ogorodnikov's arrest. Kuzkin ended up in a psychiatric hospital, and Yermolaev and his friend Igor Polyakov (who was not a member of the Seminar) were charged with "hooliganism." Yermolaev was referred to the Serbsky National Institute for Social and Forensic Psychiatry in Moscow, and Polyakov was locked up in jail.

After the preliminary investigation was finished and the charge had been formulated, preparations began for the trial of Ogorodnikov. He was about to protest the entire procedure by beginning another hunger strike when he finally succeeded in gaining access to his dossier. He discussed his case with his lawyer, Galina Reznikova, who had provided legal assistance to other dissidents. In the weeks that followed, the indictment was drawn up by the investigating officer, after which the public prosecutor provided written confirmation that the preliminary investigation had been "thorough, complete and objective." Then the indictment was forwarded to the court of law, which assigned the dossier to a judge and accepted the lawyer of the accused. Accepting the lawyer was not a mere formality, since the bar was under the strict supervision of the Ministry of Justice. In addition, all lawyers had to be members of the College of Lawyers, which could accept them or expel them if "misconduct" or "incompetence" could be established.

The court also decided on a trial in open hearing and drew up the list of witnesses. Two weeks later, the trial finally began. No matter what Galina

Reznikova did, her impact was limited because the Soviet Union did not have a normal judicial system. Anyone who appeared before a judge was always automatically convicted. During the trial, the most one could hope for was a mitigation of the charge, which could lead to a somewhat lighter sentence. One advantage was that Galina Reznikova could pass on information to Ogorodnikov's family and friends, and vice versa, though guards were always present at the discussions between her and Ogorodnikov.

On January 8, 1979, Ogorodnikov was moved from Kalinin to the prison of the people's court in Konakovo, a city of 40,000 inhabitants and the administrative center of the Konakovski district, where the village of Redkino, Ogorodnikov's place of residence, was located. This worked out very well for the KGB. Konakovo was remote and difficult to reach, and as a "closed city" it was off-limits to foreigners, making it impossible for Western journalists to attend the trial.

Ogorodnikov was transferred to Konakovo in a *voronok* ("black raven"), a special bus used to transport prisoners over short distances. This vehicle contained two benches and two small cells for "dangerous" prisoners. Most of the roads to Konakovo were very poor, and the risk of physical injury was great because of the *voronok*'s metal interior. An additional inconvenience in the summer was the total lack of ventilation. In Kazan, seventeen prisoners had suffocated in a *voronok* (the official maximum capacity was eleven) that had stood a few hours in the burning sun. But this occasion was in the dead of winter, and Ogorodnikov was the only passenger. He was actually given a jacket because the KGB did not want him to catch cold in his thin cotton garments.

"You Really Don't Scare Me. The Struggle Goes On."

The trial began on January 9, 1979. Family and friends, who had not been informed of the date and location of the trial until the last moment, showed up in large numbers anyway; however, not one of them was able to secure a seat in the public gallery of the courtroom. These had all been reserved for "listeners" who had been specially selected by the KGB before the hearing began, and who had been given special entrance passes. Ogorodnikov's sympathizers were forced to wait outside in the hall, while the secret service made sure that as little information as possible leaked out of the courtroom during the trial.

Before entering the courtroom, Ogorodnikov made a quick visit to the restroom, and on the way he looked through one of the windows in the stairwell of the courthouse and saw a large number of members of the Christian Seminar standing outside in the square. Afterwards, in the courtroom, he immediately recognized the KGB agents sitting in the audience. In the meantime, there was an uproar out in the hallway because Ogorodnikov's parents and his wife, Yelena, had not been allowed to enter the courtroom. They were serving as witnesses, and, according to the law, witnesses had to wait to be admitted until they were summoned — in order to guarantee the objectivity of the judicial process. After Ogorodnikov threatened to walk out on the trial, his parents and his wife were allowed to take a seat in the courtroom.

The court consisted of a presiding judge, who chaired the hearing, and two lay judges. Also present were a clerk, who took minutes of all the proceedings; a public prosecutor, who, as a representative of the Public Prosecution Service, was responsible for the "public monitoring of the administration of justice"; defense lawyer Galina Reznikova; and the armed police escort who was accompanying Ogorodnikov. Although the judge was Jewish, Ogorodnikov did not think that fact would be to his advantage. In order to save his own skin, the judge had to pretend that the matter at hand was an extremely serious crime. Therefore, whenever Galina Reznikova got up to speak, the judge interrupted her systematically. He also treated Ogorodnikov with inordinate hostility, over and over again, and people in the audience kept heckling Ogorodnikov as well.

Iol Ogorodnikov, a Communist of the old school, gave his testimony: "My son has not harmed anyone. He shared his possessions with others and has always worked hard. People love him. Can you explain to me, as a member of the Communist Party, exactly why he is being tried?" But the judge would not allow him to finish his passionate argument. Others also testified in Ogorodnikov's defense and were likewise abruptly interrupted.

The trial, therefore, was mainly a formality. Most of the attention was focused on the reading of the indictment, the closing argument by the defense, the closing speech by the public prosecutor, the last words by the defendant, and the reading of the verdict. Hardly any attention was paid to the judicial investigation or to the proof of the charges being brought against the defendant. After all, Ogorodnikov was not being convicted on the basis of his religious convictions but for the civil offense of "leading a parasitic lifestyle," which was almost impossible to demonstrate.

The judge would not allow anyone to challenge the criminal file, which was a compilation of absurd accusations. He also refused to grant the request of Reznikova and Ogorodnikov to call up new witnesses or to add extra facts to the dossier. The defense lawyer also asked that Ogorodnikov be examined to see if he was fit enough to perform hard labor — he had always suffered from a blood disorder resulting from the removal of his spleen — but that request was also denied.

On the last day of the trial, January 11, 1979, Reznikova presented her closing argument, followed by the closing speech by the public prosecutor. Then Ogorodnikov was given the last word. His statement, which was continuously interrupted by both the judge and the audience in the public gallery, was inspired by *J'accuse,* the open letter that the writer Émile Zola had written to the French president, Félix Fauré, in 1898. With that letter Zola had given a decisive turn to the notorious Dreyfus affair in France by establishing the innocence of the Jewish-French army captain Alfred Dreyfus, who had been accused of spying for the German army in 1894.

For his part, Ogorodnikov lashed out fiercely against the regime that had victimized him: "Since infancy I have been spoon-fed Communist ideas. I grew up in the Soviet system and was a leader of the Komsomol youth movement. But now I denounce all of this." He told the KGB agents in the courtroom what he thought Communism had become, and he emphasized that he was being persecuted exclusively for his religious beliefs. Ogorodnikov refused to show any remorse or to confess to any of the charges, and he concluded belligerently: "You really don't scare me. The struggle goes on!"

Surprisingly, the court did not impose the expected maximum sentence. The secret service decided that one year in the prison camp in the city of Komsomolsk-na-Amur in the Far East would be enough to change Ogorodnikov's mind. But behind this relatively "light" sentence was a cunning plan. The KGB wanted to avoid a fierce international response to the trial and to gain time to see whether the Christian Seminar would remain active now that Ogorodnikov, the driving force behind the organization, was temporarily out of action. If it did, then there would be plenty of time to prepare new sentences that would keep Ogorodnikov in prison for as long as the secret service deemed necessary.

Starvation as Punishment

When Ogorodnikov left the courtroom, the guards demanded that he hand over his notes. Thinking he might need them later to appeal the sentence, he refused. So a group of policemen followed him into the stair-well and began beating him with rubber truncheons before the eyes of the astonished public, tearing the papers from his hands. That same evening, Ogorodnikov was taken back to the Kalinin prison in the *voronok*. But this time, despite the extreme cold, he sat in the unheated transport bus in only his cotton garments. Ogorodnikov was freezing, and his great fear was that he would become ill.

Back in prison, he immediately began a new hunger strike to protest his conviction and rough treatment; but for punishment he was locked up for ten days in the *kartser* (punishment cell). In Kalinin this was a stone dungeon that was cold, damp, and filled with an almost unbearable stench. But he got used to even that after a while. It was a tiny cell, barely three paces across. It had no table or chair, only a concrete cylinder about half a meter high and 25 centimeters across with an iron ring around it; the cylinder was impossible to sit on. The cell was lit by a weak bulb that was too faint for reading or writing. During his isolation in the *kartser*, Ogorodnikov was given no books, pen, or paper — not even toilet paper. When he returned, he had to exchange his clothes for thin cotton prison garments. There were no bed linens, and at night he slept on a plank fit-ted with iron springs that had to be hung on the wall during the day.

Apart from the incredible cold, staying in this isolation cell was mainly psychological torture. One sat there, without any contact with the outside world or any notion of time, in a maddening silence that was in-terrupted only occasionally by the rattling of the keys when the guards came to bring one's daily portion of food. The maximum length of deten-tion was fifteen days, but under the MVD Guideline 37 of March 1978, that detention could be extended by additional consecutive terms of fif-teen days each. The food norm applied in the *kartser* was the lowest: 9B, which in theory consisted of 1,300 calories and 38 grams of protein, less than half the minimum norm set by the World Health Organization. In practice there were two "menus" that were served on alternate days. One day the prisoner was given a piece of bread and a serving of borscht, pota-toes, and sauerkraut, but without the usual beef. The next day — the "hunger day" — he was given only 450 grams of black bread, hot water, and some salt. The borscht was barely edible, and the bread was not fully baked. When a fish or meat dish was served, the fish or meat was invari-ably frozen. Systematic starvation was an essential part of prison punish-ment in the Soviet Union.

After his release from the *kartser*, Ogorodnikov was put back in a cell with violent criminals, all of whom had been convicted of murder. At first, these men threatened him physically, having been goaded by the prison management. But after a number of conversations, the hatred turned to sympathy once again. Most of them thought Ogorodnikov was a priest.

The reactions to his conviction never made their way inside the doors of the Kalinin prison. On January 12, 1979, Ogorodnikov's sentence and violent treatment in the courthouse were condemned in a press communiqué issued by Gleb Yakunin's Christian Committee. The Moscow Helsinki Group also protested. But the expected commotion in the foreign press never materialized. The only protest came from the ROCOR, the Russian Orthodox Church Outside of Russia, which did not recognize the authority of the Moscow Patriarchate.

In a Stolypin Car to the Far East

In February 1979, after the deadline for appealing his sentence had expired (Ogorodnikov deliberately did not file an appeal), he was put on the next transport to the Far East, where he was to sit out his punishment.

"Ogorodnikov," he was ordered one day, "get your stuff!" And when one of the wardens gave him a piece of bread, he knew he would be going on a "trip."

Alexander was taken in a *voronok* to the Kalinin railway station, where a few hundred prisoners were crowded together on the platform. He was then pushed into a special steel prison carriage, the so-called Stolypin car, named after Pyotr Stolypin, the prime minister under Czar Nicholas II, who used strong-arm tactics to suppress revolutionary groups in the former Russian Empire. The Stolypin was a windowless, benchless railroad car that consisted primarily of cells. Ogorodnikov was locked into a tiny one-man cell in which he could hardly move. Hours later, the packed train, composed entirely of Stolypin cars, pulled out of the station.

Ogorodnikov's first experience — spending days in cramped quarters with a pestilential stench — confirmed the baleful reputation of this degrading form of transport. He had heard horror stories from fellow prisoners about the violent behavior of the guards and the rape of male and female detainees. Twice a day everyone was let out in turn to go to the toilet — hands behind their backs and in the presence of guards. Those who urgently had to go to the toilet more often had to have special permission. Prisoners were totally dependent on the whims of the guards, who for security reasons were always accompanied by huge guard dogs.

In principle, the prisoners were to be given water every four hours, but that happened at irregular intervals and often after long periods of waiting. When Ogorodnikov pointed out to the guards that this was fully in breach of basic human rights, he was beaten. But the most complaints had to do with the food: the portions were undersized, and the food was often spoiled.

After two days, the train stopped in the historic city of Ryazan, 120 miles southeast of Moscow, about 250 miles from Kalinin as the crow flies. Actually the train traveled many more miles because the route ran around the urban agglomeration, not through it. In addition, the journey proceeded by fits and starts because the Stolypin train cars could only use the tracks when the regular rail traffic was finished with them.

Finally, in the dead of night, the carriage doors were opened and the prisoners were led to an open area by soldiers. There everyone had to squat in the snow, despite the freezing cold, with their hands on their heads. This was a terrible ordeal, particularly for the elderly and the sick. However, Ogorodnikov refused to squat and remained standing, provoking the guards to fire a few shots over his head.

The detainees were then taken in *voronoks* to the prison in Ryazan. There Ogorodnikov came in contact with a political prisoner who was unknown to him, Vetyeslav Bepko. Ogorodnikov took down Bepko's personal information and managed to send it secretly to friends in Moscow, via the ordinary criminal network, so that it could be published in the *Chronicle of Current Events.* Publishing this information was of vital importance to Bepko, a timid man who had hardly any contact with his fellow prisoners. His timidity contrasted sharply with the resolute approach of Ogorodnikov, who would not be intimidated and knew how to forge a close bond with the other inmates by showing interest and engaging in deep conversations. They left him alone out of respect. Because of his tolerance and open mind, Alexander was told a great deal of secret information, including facts about an unknown prison uprising; he also sent this report to Moscow for publication.

After a week, Ogorodnikov and a number of his fellow prisoners were told to pack their things again for the next leg of the trip — again in the familiar Stolypin cars. This time their route turned north to the historic city of Yaroslavl, which has been on the UNESCO World Heritage

List since 2005. Once again, the distance was 250 miles as the crow flies, but the train journey took a long time because the route circumvented the Moscow agglomeration. Yaroslavl is a beautiful city, but Ogorodnikov and his companions were bound for a less idyllic spot: its dilapidated nineteenth-century prison, with crowded and filthy cells that swarmed with vermin. The mattresses were dirty and foul-smelling. When Ogorodnikov asked if he could speak with a priest, he was beaten by a guard.

After seven days the journey continued, now in the direction of Kuybyshev, a city with over a million inhabitants located about 620 miles east of Moscow. In 1935 the city had been renamed after the Soviet statesman Valerian Kuybyshev, former commandant of the Red Army and chairman of Gosplan (in 1991 it got its original name back — Samara). In this city, the sixth most populous in the Soviet Union, there was a large prison complex. There Ogorodnikov was put in a punishment cell on February 13, 1979. He was beaten by guards because he had spoken up in defense of a *zek* (ordinary criminal). Here, too, Ogorodnikov managed to win the trust of the criminals by being calm and candid and by communicating with them. They listened to his stories for hours and asked all sorts of questions. Ogorodnikov gathered a great deal of information there, which he passed on to his network in Moscow.

During the next stage of the journey, the prisoners were served salted fish, which made them all extremely thirsty. When the guards refused to give them any extra water, the prisoners joined forces and started shaking the Stolypin car; eventually the carriage began rocking back and forth so forcefully that there was an increased risk of derailment. Because of faulty communication, however, the train did not come to a halt until several miles further on. When the prisoners threatened to repeat their dangerous action, they finally got their way.

In the city of Chelyabinsk, 460 miles further east, the "leaders" of the train revolt — which included Ogorodnikov — were locked into a *kartser* for punishment. Chelyabinsk, another city with a population of almost a million, was known locally as *Tankograd*, or Tank City, because it was a center for the production of T34 tanks and Katyusha antiaircraft missiles. Owing to the presence of the war industry, the city was off-limits to foreigners.

The next phase of the journey took them 120 miles further north to the city of Sverdlovsk, the former Yekaterinburg, where Ogorodnikov had studied in 1970. From there the long train traveled 870 miles via the

Trans-Siberian Railroad line to Novosibirsk, the third largest city in the Soviet Union. A few inmates in the Novosibirsk prison recognized Ogorodnikov immediately; he had visited this Siberian city several times in the past when setting up a new branch of the Christian Seminar.

The next stop was 400 miles further on: Krasnoyarsk. After a brief stay, the prisoners traveled another 620 miles, to the city of Irkutsk on Lake Baikal, and then continued eastward in the direction of Chita, a distance of more than 500 miles.

The Miracle of the Cigarettes

The last leg of the journey took the longest and was also the farthest. The train ran for days, covering a distance of roughly 1,500 miles, and finally stopped in Khabarovsk, a city in the easternmost reaches of Russia, on the Chinese border. This was the penultimate stop. There Ogorodnikov was taken to a large, fully-packed cell. When the door slammed behind him, he saw about forty half-naked men, most of them tattooed, sitting on the floor in the dim light. Ogorodnikov greeted them cheerfully with the words "Peace be with you." The prisoners looked up in astonishment. Because Ogorodnikov was still not wearing prison clothing, one of them shouted, "Take off your clothes!" He threw Ogorodnikov several threadbare garments and ordered him to put them on.

"I only give my own clothes away to people who really need them," Ogorodnikov answered, "but not under coercion." Half jokingly, he added that they would probably be spending a lot of time together in that cell. This unexpected answer made some of the prisoners angry. They began shouting, and a few of them tried to grab him. Then the leader of the group stepped in and announced:

"Tonight you sleep next to the latrine." That was the traditional sleeping place for newcomers and the "worst" category of detainees — pedophiles and rapists — who were often punished by being sexually assaulted themselves by their fellow inmates.

The leader of the group then said: "You just said to us, 'Peace be with you!' Are you a Christian by any chance?" Ogorodnikov nodded.

"Seems to me that a miracle always takes place whenever a Christian prays to God," the leader said. "Prove to us that you're really a Christian and not just somebody who's trying to make an impression on us."

Another prisoner picked up on the idea: "We're the scum of the earth. We don't have anything, not even cigarettes. We were just trans-ferred here, and we don't know anybody. We haven't had a smoke for days and we're dying for a cigarette. If you're really a Christian, pray to that God of yours to bring us cigarettes and make it snappy. Then we'll believe in him, too."

"Smoking poisons the body," Ogorodnikov responded, "and I'm sure the Lord thinks so, too. But I also think that the Lord will answer your ap-peal out of love and have mercy on you because of your dreadful living conditions. I'm sure a miracle will take place, but to beg for that to hap-pen we all have to pray together first."

Ogorodnikov stepped into the middle of the cell and asked all the prisoners to stand up, the customary sign of respect for God in the Or-thodox tradition. Some of the prisoners stood up. This was followed by howls of derision, and everyone looked on in disbelief. A few of them wanted to attack Ogorodnikov again, but he begged them:

"Please listen carefully to the words of the prayer. And I ask all those who are able: repeat these words after me. The rest of you, just listen carefully. If we pray together with total devotion, the Lord will certainly hear our prayer."

As he prayed, Alexander took from his pocket a small prayer card that had on it a print of an icon from the abbey of Chevetogne in Belgium. He had the feeling that something was going to happen, because it be-came eerily silent in the cell. Fifteen minutes after his prayer, most of the prisoners were no longer sneering. As Ogorodnikov gave them a sign to sit down, the cell door suddenly opened and a handful of cigarettes were thrown inside. Some of the prisoners caught them before they even hit the ground. Tears came to Ogorodnikov's eyes: God had manifested him-self through these cigarettes! He realized that God loves even the worst outcasts. "There is a God!" the prisoners shouted in unison,

Ogorodnikov understood that his stay in prison was not a punish-ment but a mission.

Malignancies during a Six-Thousand-Mile Odyssey

From Khabarovsk, Ogorodnikov was taken another 220 miles to the la-bor camp in Komsomolsk-na-Amur, his final destination. This city on the Amur River, which took its name from Komsomol, the Communist youth organization, had been thrown up practically overnight in 1932 as part of the industrialization of the Far East. It was a showpiece of the Russian So-viet Republic, built partly by Komsomol volunteers who had been re-cruited from all over the country, but mainly by convicts. The Stalin re-gime chose this extremely desolate place, which was closed to foreigners until 1992, to build more than forty concentration camps.

During his exhausting two-month odyssey by Stolypin, Ogorodnikov had covered more than six thousand miles. Throughout this appalling journey it became clear to him that the Soviet prison regime was far harsher than the prescribed norm, and that prisoners of conscience, as "ideologically hostile elements," were often the targets of serious abuse. But he also learned that every prison had its own pattern of norms and values. In many places he had seen the malignancies brought on by this policy: the widespread problem of tuberculosis and the many cases of self-mutilation, which prisoners resorted to in order to induce the au-thorities to transfer them to a hospital section, where they would escape forced labor and be given better rations. Homosexuals were the target of severe discrimination, and informers or inmates who lost at cards were sometimes forced to "bend over" or to "do it" like a woman.

To his frustration, Ogorodnikov learned about the recent declaration concerning freedom of religion in the Soviet Union by Patriarch Pimen I of Moscow, head of the Russian Orthodox Church, while he himself — as a religious dissident — had received no support at all from the church. But his daily worry was about how his comrades in the Christian Seminar were faring.

Despite the skepticism of the KGB, the Christian Seminar remained active, and a number of branches were steadily growing in numbers. On February 10, 1979, one month after Ogorodnikov's conviction, the police of District 60 of Moscow forced their way into an apartment where a meeting of the Seminar was taking place. In the official report, this raid had taken place "on suspicion that a gang of thieves were gathering there." All those present at the meeting were taken to the police station for interrogation. The police searched the apartment and seized a Bible, a few religious and philosophical works dating from before the Russian Revolution, and six copies of the Seminar's magazine, *Obshchina*. During the search, Tatiana Shchipkova struck a policeman who had demanded that she turn over her notes; she was later charged with "hooliganism."

On February 26, 1979, members of the Christian Seminar appealed to the Council for Religious Affairs to stop the persecution, and once again they protested Ogorodnikov's conviction. Andrei Sakharov also championed his case, but the government responded with a new wave of arrests, dismissals, and interrogations.

The publication of the article "Why Does Ogorodnikov Need His Bit of Land?" in the July 1979 issue of the magazine *Kalinskaya Pravda* brought new accusations against Ogorodnikov and the Seminar, and provoked a new series of arrests. The first, which took place on August 1, 1979, was of Vladimir Poresh, the leader of the Leningrad branch of the Seminar. After his apartment was searched and a large number of religious and philosophical books and articles were seized, the Public Prosecution Service elevated the severity of the original charge from "slander" to "anti-Soviet agitation and propaganda," the notorious Article 70 of the Penal Code. Raids took place on August 1, 1979, in the homes of seven other members of the Seminar — four in Leningrad and three in Moscow.

Shortly after that, the KGB arrested six members of two other groups in the Soviet Union who were advocating compliance with the Helsinki Accords. As usual, the Ukrainian group was hardest hit, with five arrests.

In a *Shizo* Full of Excrement

When Ogorodnikov arrived at the camp in Komsomolsk-na-Amur, where 2,000 to 3,000 prisoners were being held, he discovered to his surprise that the persistent rumors about him had already made their way to this remote place. His fellow inmates respected him, though they hardly knew who he was. On April 7, 1979, Ogorodnikov was condemned to a "strict regime" for confessing just before Easter. This meant that he was locked up for fifteen days in the *shtrafnoi izoliator,* otherwise known as the *shizo* (the camp isolation cell). As in the notorious prison *kartser,* a whole range of additional restrictions were imposed there.

While Alexander was on his knees praying in the *shizo,* a guard came in and commanded him to stand up. Ogorodnikov quietly kept on praying. After this "serious" breach of prison regulations, the guards used artificial air pressure in the sewer system to pump raw sewage into his cell, leaving a layer of muck almost ten inches deep. In the middle of this tiny cell, barely three paces across, there was a concrete post about ten inches wide, on which he could not sit; there was only room for one of his feet. For two days Ogorodnikov stood straight up in that stinking pool as the water subsided with exasperating slowness.

"I'm going to lodge a complaint against you for this outrage," he shouted at the guards when he was finally allowed to leave the *shizo* after two weeks.

Most of the wardens followed the guidelines strictly and applied their authority in a heavy-handed way. By wringing respect from the prisoners, they were venting their frustrations and compensating for a sense of inferiority that was mainly due to the lack of social prestige that came with their job. Most of them harbored a deep hatred toward the prisoners of conscience. Although beatings by guards were an everyday occurrence in the prison camps, the wardens often did not step in to deal with irregularities in the cells. This wasn't only to save their own skins; it was also out of respect for the balance of power among the inmates.

But not all the wardens were cruel disciplinarians. Some exhibited interest in the prisoners and listened to Western shortwave radio stations. One of them, Boris Chaplain, who worked in the Komsomolsk-na-Amur prison in 1979, later converted to the Protestant Evangelical Church and is still active in prison ministry.

The concentration camps were no longer part of the planned economy as they had been when Stalin was alive, but forced labor was still a compulsory part of daily life in the Gulag. It was justified by the importance that was attached to the notion of labor in Marxist-Leninist doctrine. According to this doctrine, labor contributed to the "improvement and re-education of prisoners," which would keep them from repeating their offense. But there was a world of difference between theory and practice. In forced labor, the main consideration was always economic results, because each month official production norms were imposed on every camp by the government. The camp management had no choice but to economize as much as they could on financial outlays, housing, food, and medical care. Management also ignored safety regulations completely, resulting in many unnecessary work-related accidents, partly due to the fact that the prisoners were chronically underfed. The compulsory labor was exhausting, monotonous, and pointless: combined with the high quota of work required, it reduced the prisoners to glassy-eyed machines. Anyone who left his post momentarily or failed to meet the daily quota ran the risk of being locked up in the dreaded *shizo*. Often sick or elderly prisoners of conscience were given heavy tasks, while the lighter work was assigned to informers or to prisoners who "had chosen the path of re-education."

Each year, a medical commission from the Ministry of the Interior determined which prisoners were able to work; exemptions were extremely rare. Men of retirement age were required to work as well, and the sick could be punished for "feigning" illness. The forced labor was imposed eight hours a day, six days a week, and was so exhausting that, after returning to the camp, no prisoners had the desire or the energy to do anything, though they were expected to keep their cells and barracks clean on top of everything else.

Officially, the prisoners were given a salary, but after living costs were deducted there was very little left over. With this bit of money, which was entered into the prisoner's record, he could go to the prison shop and buy food, toiletries, writing utensils, and tobacco — for a maximum of three rubles a month — provided he wasn't being punished. But there was very little for sale in the shop. Meat, dairy products, sugar, honey, chocolate, oil, and margarine were all taboo. The other goods were offered in limited quantities, if they were available at all. The most popular was bread. Black bread cost .15 rubles a kilo, and white bread was .22 rubles for 800 grams (a prisoner could not buy more than four kilos of bread per month). Apple jam cost .60 rubles a half-kilo jar, and the price of cheese was 1.60 to 3.60 rubles per kilo, depending on the kind. Naturally, only prisoners with a credit balance in their account could make any purchases.

Moral Support to Fellow Prisoners

One invariable part of re-education was political instructions, which were imposed for two hours each week. This was especially meant to instill "a suitable work attitude" as well as "strict obedience of the law, respect for the rules of socialist community life, and the will to protect socialist property." After a while, Ogorodnikov, who had become thoroughly annoyed with these gatherings, which were of dubious value and which everyone in the camp hated with a passion, decided to abandon them. The camp administration reluctantly agreed because the teachers were often at an utter loss as to how to answer his cutting questions and comments, which also influenced the other prisoners.

During his stay in Komsomolsk-na-Amur, writing letters was about the only meaningful activity open to him. For the prisoners, mail from the outside world was of great psychological importance. The family was given precise information about the place where a person was being held, since that was required by law. However, all the incoming and outgoing mail was subject to extremely strict censorship. Moreover, Ogorodnikov was not permitted any visitors.

He spoke with his fellow prisoners about freedom and about the true nature of the Soviet system, answering their often penetrating questions. Ogorodnikov gave them good advice and also provided spiritual support and pastoral care. He would write down a prayer for someone, for example, or listen to another man's confession, and he baptized a few of his cellmates at their request. But he gave most of his attention to the weakest prisoners, who often became the playthings of the "gangs." He also gave moral support to the prisoners who had been sentenced to death.

Soon Ogorodnikov was asked to provide support to those sentenced to death in other barracks. He managed to do this by secretly switching work clothes and transferring his work quota to fellow prisoners. When the authorities discovered that, they again locked him up in the *shizo*.

After returning to the camp, Ogorodnikov discovered, to his amazement, that he no longer had to do any hard labor; instead, he was assigned to work on the production of shopping bags. He continued to pass on part of his production quota to fellow prisoners in order to have enough time to provide advice and support, but the prison authorities turned a blind eye on this for the time being. Soon he was even exempted from work altogether and was allowed to read the newspaper in the camp library. After being transferred to the barracks for invalids and the sick, his living conditions and food improved considerably. A few days later, during roll, the commander of the camp suddenly shook Alexander's hand, to the great consternation of his fellow prisoners.

Ogorodnikov realized all too well that this unexpected charm offensive had everything to do with the fact that his sentence would soon be up. On August 11, 1979, he received the following proposal from the prison director: "You will be freed if you promise never to return to Moscow."

Ogorodnikov refused this emphatically. "It is my duty to go to the capital and to continue my work there," he said. "You can do only one thing to stop me: kill me."

The KGB response came from its headquarters in Moscow: Ogorodnikov was to be locked up in the isolation cell immediately. When he returned to the camp thirty-five days later, on September 15, 1979, a KGB official was waiting for him with a declaration to sign: it said that from then on he would no longer participate in the activities of the Christian Seminar.

"We'd rather not make a new martyr of you," the man said with a smile. "Or would you prefer to stay a while longer in prison? All you have to do is sign this form."

Ogorodnikov refused once again, even when they offered him a comfortable apartment and a good job in exchange for denouncing his past on television. Once again, the KGB referred to his approaching release date, November 20. Wasn't that the day he was longing for with such urgency? The day when he would finally see his family and friends again? The secret service turned up the psychological pressure even further by solemnly promising that Ogorodnikov would be allowed to publish his new book, "The Culture of the Catacombs," the manuscript of which had been confiscated during his arrest. He fully realized that this was just a trick and an indirect way of discrediting him with unsuspecting outsiders.

The last move of the secret service was to read to him the interrogation proceedings of Vladimir Poresh, who at that moment was in pretrial detention in Leningrad. Poresh was supposed to have recently testified that "Ogorodnikov did not play any role of significance in the Seminar."

I myself wrote all the articles signed by him. I signed them with his name because he was well-known and I was not. I was constantly using his name improperly. You are wrong. Ogorodnikov has been wrongfully imprisoned. I am the head of the Seminar and Ogorodnikov is the victim. I appeal to you to release Ogorodnikov immediately.

The KGB wanted to play the two men against each other in the hope of obtaining more information on what went on behind the scenes at the Seminar. But Ogorodnikov refused to fall for such a transparent ploy. "I take full responsibility for the articles signed by me," he said. "Morally it is impossible for me to answer your questions. Our activities conform fully to the Universal Declaration of Human Rights, which was signed by the Soviet Union. You have absolutely nothing to do with the rest."

On that same day, September 15, 1979, Ogorodnikov learned that a new case was being prepared against him based on the "anti-Soviet agitation and propaganda" prohibition in Article 70 of the Penal Code. One day later, September 16, he was flown to Leningrad in connection with the legal investigation in the case against Vladimir Poresh.

The two agents who accompanied Ogorodnikov on the plane — he was the only other passenger — released his handcuffs once they were in flight, drank vodka, and took naps. The path to freedom was open to him, with the guards' pistols there for the taking and the plane with enough fuel to fly on to the West. Yet he passed up this unique opportunity. Such flight from his situation would solve only *his* problems, not the problems of all things dear to him: his family and friends, his faith, the Christian Seminar, and his homeland. He saw it as his moral duty to keep on fighting within the Soviet Union — in spite of everything — to change the system from within, no matter how utopian that idea may have seemed at the time.

Upon his arrival in Leningrad, Ogorodnikov was transported by *voronok* to the "Big House," as KGB headquarters was called. As a cynical Russian saying has it, you can see Siberia from the roof. Right next door was the prison, the "House of Detention IZ 45/1," better known as "the Crosses." The cell that Ogorodnikov was locked up in was only two cells away from the famous No. 193, where Lenin had spent some time in custody in 1895, and which had been turned into a small memorial museum.

During the interrogation, Ogorodnikov remained uncompromising: he refused any form of cooperation out of principle. After sixteen interrogators had questioned him in turn, all unsuccessfully, he was delivered into the hands of Viktor Cherkesov, who was notorious for his cynicism, his sadistic tricks, and his unorthodox interrogation methods. Ogorodnikov later learned that Cherkesov was the best friend of Vladimir Putin, who, as head of the dreaded Fifth Directorate of the Leningrad KGB, was part of "the struggle against ideological aberrations" and was deeply involved in maintaining dissident dossiers until the end of 1977. Putin then left for Moscow and made a career for himself; but he did not forget his good friend Viktor Cherkesov, who became head of the Russian antidrug brigade until 2008. An old Russian says, "If you want to know someone's true worth, look at who his best friends are."

In October 1979, Cherkesov tried to make Ogorodnikov confess during hours of interrogation, in which he made threats that grew increasingly severe. But Ogorodnikov was not like other Christian Seminar members, and Cherkesov was not able to extract a statement from him. So, for punishment, he once again had Ogorodnikov locked up in the *kartser*. All that time, the cunning KGB interrogators led him to believe that he was going to be released on November 20, 1979, the day his sentence was up. Indeed, when that day arrived, he was surprised to hear, "Ogorodnikov, pack your stuff!" There was every indication that he was actually going to be released. But right at the prison gate he was suddenly taken aside by Cherkesov, who told him that new facts had come to light;

unfortunately, it meant that a new charge was being prepared — this one also under Article 70.

The preliminary investigation started immediately. "On November 22, 1979, Ogorodnikov's mother refused to sign his report after being interrogated by Cherkesov," said the *Chronicle of Current Events*. "His father was questioned regarding the source of the money for the purchase of the house in Redkino."

Religious Persecution Intensified

In the meantime, the Christian Committee in Moscow was suffering great hardships. Gleb Yakunin's house was searched on September 28, 1979, and Yakunin himself was arrested on November 1. That day, a number of believers, including Tatiana Velikanova, also a member of the Moscow Helsinki Group, published an appeal protesting the new religious persecutions; and the group again denounced the arrests of Alexander Ogorodnikov and Vladimir Poresh.

Father Dmitri Dudko was harshly reprimanded by the church authorities, and his sixteen-year-old son was sent for further psychological testing following an army medical exam, which had been done because he was found wearing his baptismal cross. The same thing happened to a number of frequent visitors to the Pochayiv Monastery in western Ukraine. In the city of Krasnodar, Father Nikolai Goretoy, who had helped a group of Pentecostals to emigrate, was sentenced to seven years of hard labor and five years of internal exile, though he was virtually blind as a result of an earlier ten-year internment in the Gulag.

The political climate soured even further after Soviet troops invaded Afghanistan on December 24, 1979. After the murder of Hafizoellah Amin, the Afghan head of state, on December 27, the Soviet Union threw its support behind the regime of Babrak Karmal and his struggle against the partisans. The Soviets wanted to build a strategic bridgehead in order to control the surrounding region. The anticipated quick victory did not happen, however, and it was impossible to subdue the Afghan resistance because of the massive support of the population.

The longer the war lasted, the more brutal it became. Four million Afghanis — one quarter of the population — fled to Pakistan and Iran. Internationally, the invasion resulted in the isolation of the Soviet Union, rapprochement between the United States and China, a review of the

Western armaments programs, and the refusal of the American Congress to ratify the Salt II treaty, which had been signed between the United States and the Soviet Union on June 18, 1979.

As the Soviet Union sank deeper and deeper into the quagmire of the civil war in Afghanistan, the KGB was given greater authority to preventatively silence opponents in the run-up to the Summer Olympic Games that were to be held in Moscow in 1980. On December 24, 1979, Lev Regelson, who had taken over the leadership of the Christian Seminar since Ogorodnikov's arrest and imprisonment, was picked up in the Estonian capital of Tallinn and taken to the Lefortovo Prison in Moscow. On January 8, 1980, Tatiana Shchipkova and Viktor Popkov were put in jail. Shchipkova was charged with "malicious hooliganism" for striking a police officer in February 1979 during a secret police raid on her house; she was sentenced to three years in a prison camp in the Far East, where she would come down with dysentery.

On that same date, Andrei Sakharov, the best-known Soviet dissident, was exiled to Gorky (called Nizhny Novgorod since 1991), a "closed city," to prevent him from having contact with foreign journalists and observers during the Olympics. On January 15, 1980, Father Dmitri Dudko was arrested. And when Eduard Fedotov, a Seminar member, made this known to Western correspondents in Moscow, he was imprisoned once again (the first time had been in 1976). Viktor Savin of Moscow, also a Seminar member, and Vladimir Burtsev shared his fate. On March 12, 1980, Viktor Kapitanchuk was picked up. He had been head of the Christian Committee since the arrest of Gleb Yakunin in November 1979.

Force-feeding

In the meantime, what had become of Ogorodnikov? On December 5, 1979, he went on another hunger strike in the *kartser* of the Leningrad prison to protest his internment. According to the prison regulations at that time, a hunger striker was to be artificially fed starting on the seventeenth day. But in practice that did not happen until his body began to smell of acetone. And in order to be admitted to a hospital — which took place after thirty days, according to the book — you had to be half-dead.

In late December 1979, Ogorodnikov was force-fed for the first time. With his hands manacled behind his back, a tube was brutally shoved down his nose and into his stomach, after which a sprayer was used to inject liquid food: a nutritious gruel consisting of milk, butter, sugar, eggs, meat, and groats. That is, it was nutritious on paper. Here, too, the best ingredients were stolen by the prison personnel. And the porridge was also deliberately overheated so that it burned his stomach. This is one of the worst forms of physical torture because for weeks afterward the smallest sip of water can produce unbearable stomach pain. Ogorodnikov was force-fed every two days until he decided to end his hunger strike on January 10, 1980, after thirty-six days.

At the time of Joseph Stalin, opponents were mercilessly done away with. Under the regime of Leonid Brezhnev they died a slow death by means of constant physical and mainly psychological torture. Many prisoners made a compromise with the guards by simply drinking the gruel. Then the prison management would report to the higher authorities that the hunger strike was over, even if the prisoner continued his activity the following day. But Ogorodnikov refused any form of compromise.

....

CHAPTER SIX

"Rapes," "Confessions," "Trials," and Prayer

The "Rape" of Tatiana Polyakova

Shortly thereafter, Ogorodnikov was moved from Leningrad back to the Kalinin prison to await his new trial. There, on February 16, 1980, he was locked up in the *kartser* for ten days for using "coarse obscene language" toward a *vertuchai* (the guard who brought the prisoners to work). This was a lie: Alexander never used obscene language due to his fundamental respect for every human being, even his enemies. That incident was just the umpteenth battle in the psychological war being fought against him.

The preparations for his trial were endless. In its attempt to turn Ogorodnikov into a *zek* (an ordinary convict, not a political prisoner), the KGB had to charge him with a civil offense. The team that studied his dossier was increased to sixteen members. The reason this case was considered so important was that Ogorodnikov was the first major religious dissident who was at risk of being given a severe sentence. In Chistopol and Moscow, the KGB interrogated hundreds of family members, friends, and acquaintances of Ogorodnikov, but no one was willing to institute legal proceedings against him.

But on March 19, 1980, Ogorodnikov learned from investigator Yegerev that "the rape of Tatiana Polyakova" had been added to his dossier. While digging into the details of Ogorodnikov's private life, the KGB agents had discovered that in 1969 he had been engaged to a certain Tatiana Polyakova. Her parents, who were leading citizens in the provinces, had opposed the marriage, and the engagement was broken off. The secret service persuaded Polyakova to institute legal proceedings against Ogorodnikov on the charge of rape. In accordance with the legal procedure, a face-to-face meeting between the two was arranged. Accompanied by her mother, who was also prepared to testify against Alexander, Polyakova flew to Kalinin. In the presence of law enforcement officials and official witnesses, Tatiana Polyakova repeated her charge of rape, which was supposed to have taken place in the apartment of Alexander's parents.

Ogorodnikov then began questioning her in greater and greater detail. The more deeply he probed into the allegation, the fewer details Tatiana was able to remember and the more she began contradicting herself. Finally she broke down in tears and confessed that it was all a fabrication and that she had lied. When Ogorodnikov asked why she had slandered him, she answered him in all honesty: "The KGB promised me a house." If Polyakova had stuck with her accusation, she would have been given something that everyone in the Soviet Union was dying to have.

If Ogorodnikov had been convicted of rape, not only would he have been given a heavy prison sentence — one Ukrainian dissident was given twelve years during the same period for the same unfounded charge — but in fact it would have been a sentence of death. In Soviet prisons, pedophiles and rapists were the most hated group, and they were constantly victimized by both fellow prisoners and staff. Most died before their release date. In the Tatiana Polyakova case, though Ogorodnikov had every right to initiate proceedings against her for perjury, he decided not to.

On March 19, 1980, during his stay in the *kartser*, Ogorodnikov began another hunger strike and made a number of demands on behalf of himself and all the other believers in the prison: the right to own a Bible, a prayer book, and religious literature; the right to have access to a priest for confession; the right of access to other prisoners' literature; the right to study at a religious school from within the confines of the prison. During his hunger strike Ogorodnikov was repeatedly force-fed. Finally, he was given a Bible, a prayer book, and a number of religious magazines that dated to before the Revolution of 1917.

Shortly thereafter, another prisoner called Ogorodnikov a *koz'jol* (goat), the worst term of abuse in prison — an insult that every prisoner would immediately challenge, usually with physical violence. But Ogorodnikov remained silent. He believed that to be his only proper response as a Christian. But the person who had insulted him was given a beating by an influential fellow prisoner. The latter was locked up in the *kartser* for a few days, and Ogorodnikov's time in the *kartser* was, in turn, lengthened.

The Trial of Vladimir Poresh in Leningrad

At the trial of Vladimir Poresh in Leningrad, which was held April 23-25, 1980, the court refused to look into the extent to which the texts for which he was being charged were anti-Soviet and libelous. The judge and the public prosecution service took particular exception to a letter in which Poresh asked Alexander Solzhenitsyn to put him into contact with young Christians in the West. They wanted to know more about Poresh's foreign relationships. Poresh answered as follows:

> I am on trial here because of my belief. I broke the law by defending my belief — which I have never hid and about which I have always spoken with honesty and candor. What I have done is the natural result of my conviction. In accordance with the law of our land, I now have to sit here peacefully and listen without responding. But for a Christian, the rite of the Divine Liturgy is not enough. We cannot limit ourselves to that alone.

By talking mostly about the church and not about himself, Poresh made it clear that he and his friends were involved in a purely spiritual movement. As the verdict was being read — he was sentenced to five years in the Perm-35 prison camp and three years of internal exile — a few friends cried out, "Christ is risen," "We love you, Volodya" (Vladimir's nickname), and "We're proud of you, Volodya." As he was being roughly removed from the courtroom, they loudly sang the familiar Easter hymn "Christ Is Risen from the Dead."

On May 27, 1980, Ogorodnikov was officially charged with "anti-Soviet agitation and propaganda." Out of protest, he went on a hunger strike once again, but this time he was determined to continue to the end. He wrote a letter to U.S. President Jimmy Carter with a fervent appeal not to participate in the Olympic Games, which were to begin in Moscow in July 1980, but it was intercepted. On June 6, 1980, when KGB agents entered his cell to conduct a search, Ogorodnikov threatened to slit his wrists if they didn't leave immediately. This protest action resulted in three days in the isolation cell.

On June 20, 1980, a few weeks before the start of the Olympic Games, the KGB celebrated one of its greatest triumphs. Father Dmitri Dudko, who had weathered many ordeals during his earlier nine-year confinement in the Gulag, finally capitulated after six months of pretrial detention and confessed on television: "I distance myself from everything I have done so far. I now realize that my so-called struggle against atheism was actually a struggle against the government of the Soviet Union." The text of his self-renunciation was published in full in the *Journal of the Moscow Patriarchate.* Dudko looked dazed and broken during the broadcast as a result of intensive interrogation, and it is still unclear whether he was also drugged at the time. In the dissident community, this "confession" exploded like a bomb. What a decline for the man who had baptized more than five thousand adults and whose sermons and enthusiasm had inspired so many people in the past! He had been persecuted — and had withstood persecution — almost his entire life. His faithful followers despaired, and some even considered suicide.

Ogorodnikov, who had already broken with Dudko in 1978, was shocked by the latter's confession, though he had expected it. Because the guards were aware that Dudko's "confession" had had little impact on him, he was not shown the TV images. "If Dudko is going to stand on the side of my persecutors," Alexander said, "then I will carry his cross as well. His capitulation only makes me stronger."

After his release, Dmitri Dudko was moved to a parish outside Moscow, where he was no longer allowed to have contact with anyone. A few weeks later he circulated a bitter message via samizdat: "It is not only your spiritual father who is being put to the test by the KGB but the entire Russian Orthodox Church."

In early July 1980, Ogorodnikov was so weakened after forty-one days of hunger strike that his legs would no longer support him. He could barely turn over in bed. But no one was interested. The whole country was caught up in the Twenty-second Olympic Summer Games, whose mascot was the bear cub Misha. The boycott by fifty countries, including the United States, which was a protest against the Russian invasion of Afghanistan in December 1979, overshadowed the first Olympics ever held in a Communist country. But Moscow shone as never before, and no dissident noises could be heard anywhere. Those who had not been put behind bars or exiled were sent out of the country. That was the fate of the leaders of the Religious and Philosophical Seminar, founded in Leningrad in 1979 on the initiative of Tatiana Goricheva, which was particularly popular among young female intellectuals. This women's group, which called itself Maria, a reference to the mother of God, distributed the samizdat magazine *Women in Russia.* Goricheva also regularly attended meetings of the Leningrad Christian Seminar.

The Olympics themselves became an athletic success: six new world records were established, and the big winner was the Soviet Union, with a total of 195 medals, 80 of them gold. The gymnast Alexander Dityatin, who won eight medals, three of them gold, was one of the stars. Other "gold stars" of the Soviet team went to the swimmer Vladimir Salnikov and the canoeist Vladimir Parfenovich. With so many sporting triumphs and such flawless organization, nationalism in the Soviet Union was reigning supreme once again. Just a day after the closing ceremonies on August 3, 1980, the trial began of the dissidents who had been arrested in the run-up to the Olympics. The first victim was Father Gleb Yakunin. On August 28, 1980, he was sentenced under the notorious Article 70, "anti-Soviet agitation and propaganda," to five years of prison camp with hard regime, plus five years of internal exile.

Lev Regelson, who followed Ogorodnikov as head of the Christian Seminar, publicly confessed on television that he was guilty of "anti-Soviet activities" only four weeks after defending the activities of Father Gleb Yakunin at his trial.

Ogorodnikov and Poresh Moral Victors

In mid-August 1980, Ogorodnikov was finally given access to his dossier. He learned that he had been charged with involvement in the publication of the Seminar magazine *Obshchina*, with verbal anti-Soviet agitation, with distributing books that had been published abroad, and with distributing samizdat writings. Because this charge fell officially under the category "exceptionally dangerous crime against the state," his dossier was moved from the people's court in Konakovo to the supreme court of the Kalinin Oblast. In addition, the preliminary investigation was no longer in the hands of the Ministry of the Interior but the KGB, and from now on Ogorodnikov could only appeal to a lawyer with a *dopesk*, or special KGB permission, who was listed on the KGB lawyers' list. None of the lawyers on this list had ever carried out a vigorous defense in a political criminal case. The lawyer Dina Kaminskaya, for example, not only immediately lost her job after her convincing defense of dissident Anatoly Sharansky, but she herself also had to emigrate after being threatened with a lawsuit under Article 70.

Because Ogorodnikov could find no one to defend him, he was appointed a lawyer by the court: Maria Duksova. She had to study all thirty-five files of the dossier, which contained thousands of documents, though she was only willing to provide him partial defense out of fear for her future career — despite her respect for Ogorodnikov. In reality, she functioned mainly as a mediator between Ogorodnikov and his family.

In the run-up to the trial, which was to begin on September 3, 1980, the KGB did its best to get Ogorodnikov back in shape. After almost a hundred days of hunger striking he could hardly stand upright, despite the daily force-feeding. On the first day of the trial only his mother was allowed to sit in the courtroom. Alexander's father, Iol Ogorodnikov, and his wife, Yelena Levashova, were the last witnesses called, so they could not attend most of the hearing. (Raphael Ogorodnikov, Alexander's brother, who had entered the Pskov-Pechory monastery, was not given permission to visit him in prison and was even told to leave the diocese of Pskov by order of Metropolitan Ioann.)

On this occasion, too, the room was filled with a "special audience," which meant that there was no room for Ogorodnikov's family members and friends. At the beginning of the trial Ogorodnikov asked that all the "human trash" be removed from the courtroom, but the judge silenced him. Then he contested the composition of the court — also to no avail — and after that he dismissed his lawyer, Maria Duksova, to her great joy.

Vladimir Poresh and Viktor Popkov, two Seminar members who were also behind bars, were called as witnesses. Poresh entered the courtroom with the words *Christus resurrexit* (Christ is risen). Ogorodnikov beamed upon seeing his friend again after almost two years. While the KGB had hoped to play them against each other, the glances they exchanged radiated such power that it further strengthened their inner resolve. Most dissidents experienced a second conviction as a psychological blow, but on this occasion Ogorodnikov and Poresh felt themselves moral victors. Poresh denied the charges that were made against Ogorodnikov, taking all the blame on himself. Other Seminar members also testified in Alexander's favor, with the exception of Viktor Popkov. Popkov gave the court important information on the policy and the activities of the Christian Seminar. But Ogorodnikov felt mentally alert and ready to carry on with the fight. Remarkably, all the other witnesses — from a distant neighbor to detainees from the prisons in Kalinin and Komsomolsk-na-Amur with whom Ogorodnikov had been locked up over the past two years — had, without exception, only good things to say about him, though they did confirm his anti-Soviet statements. "This is the first time in my career that we've had so much trouble finding people to testify against someone," snarled a KGB agent when Ogorodnikov was brought back to his cell in the evening.

On the second day of the trial, the report of the forensic psychological assessment was presented. It found that Ogorodnikov was responsible for his actions, but that he was also suffering from "pathological hysteria." The doctor who had examined him had advised him confidentially to have himself declared mentally ill: "The living conditions here are quite a bit better than in the camps, and after a while we'll release you." But Ogorodnikov did not go along with this idea.

During the subsequent examination of witnesses, the judge ordered Alexander's mother to be expelled from the courtroom, which was an effort by the KGB to further isolate him. As he shouted, "Don't go away, Mother, or I'll slit my wrists," she was roughly removed by police officers. In protest, Ogorodnikov did indeed slit his wrists that night. The guard who was checking on him at regular intervals saw what he had done and immediately raised the alarm. The KGB refused to allow him to be taken to a hospital for fear that the trial would have to be postponed, but they did send for a doctor right away.

The next day, the third day of the trial, Ogorodnikov appeared in the courtroom with bandaged wrists, and an ambulance was stationed in the courtyard of the courthouse as a precaution. His mother was allowed to attend the hearing while her husband, Iol Ogorodnikov, testified that he could not understand why his son was being convicted again. In an emotional plea he talked about his own life in service to his country — how during the Second Great Patriotic War he had risen from soldier to the rank of commander — and about Alexander's true character, how he had given all his money to a student whose belongings had been stolen. When Yelena Levashova took the witness stand, the judge snarled that she, too, ran the risk of being prosecuted because she had cosigned a few letters.

On the last day of the trial, September 8, 1980 — which was the 102nd day of his hunger strike — Ogorodnikov defended himself. In a five-hour argument he refuted all the charges that had been brought against him, one by one. In a cutting indictment, he exposed the failures of the Communist system, defended the values that he stood for — his faith and the aims of the Christian Seminar — and announced that he would continue his protest. He ended his passionate defense with the cry "Long live Russia!" In the meantime the judge had removed from the courtroom a large number of people who had starting ranting against him during his speech.

"A Day of Grief Has Dawned"

But none of his testimony was of any use. The court sentenced Ogorodnikov to six years in a hard labor camp with strict regime — one year under the maximum — and five years internal exile. As he had already announced in his argument, he did not appeal the sentence because of an unfair trial and administration of justice. Two Seminar members who had demonstrated in Moscow for his release during the trial were also imprisoned, and on September 28, 1980, the Moscow Helsinki Group published the following protest: "The cruelty of the judgment against Ogorodnikov is convincing proof of the determination of the authorities to annihilate the movement for freedom of religion."

The Orthodox archbishop of Geneva, Dmitri, addressed a worldwide appeal to all Christians at the end of 1980:

> A day of grief has dawned for the young Alexander Ogorodnikov. He and a number of young friends founded an Orthodox seminar to study the basic principles of the Christian faith. There was absolutely nothing illegal about this — not under any law, even that of the Soviet Union. But the Soviet authorities apparently thought otherwise. In an attempt to impose Marxist materialist ideology on the Russian youth, at any cost, they started to persecute Ogorodnikov remorselessly by means of threats, accusations and insults, and in the end he was even beaten. Finally Ogorodnikov was arrested in November 1978. The Soviet authorities urged him to renounce his faith, counting on the silence of the Western public and even on the approval of those believers who like to call themselves Christians but whose indifference is an endorsement of the actions of the godless Soviet. But that will not happen. Let all true Christians devote themselves to the defense of Alexander Ogorodnikov, who is suffering for Christ. May God come to his aid! Pray for him!

At the end of 1980, the organization Orthodox America, which took the lead in the fight against religious persecution in the Soviet Union from the United States, appealed to all Christians to write letters to the procurator-general of the Soviet Union condemning "the cruel judgment against Alexander Ogorodnikov" and demanding his immediate release. In Great Britain his case was followed closely by the Keston Institute, which studied all forms of religious oppression in the Soviet Union and the Eastern Bloc.

The World Council of Churches sent a letter to Metropolitan Yuvenali of the Moscow Patriarchate on October 1, 1980, in which the Council expressed its great concern over "the trials and convictions of a number of Christian clergymen and believers in the Soviet Union," with explicit reference to Ogorodnikov, Yakunin, Dudko, and Regelson. Yet that same month, Viktor Kapitanchuk, who succeeded Gleb Yakunin as head of the Christian Committee, was also sentenced. Kapitanchuk confessed while he was in custody, however, and was released shortly afterward.

Ogorodnikov was ordered to spend the first six years of his sentence at the Perm-36 concentration camp. But because he was carrying on with his hunger strike — now he wanted to continue to the bitter end — he was first taken to the Perm city prison, where the regime was less strict. During this stay Ogorodnikov was able to carry on a conversation with his neighbor in the next cell via the toilet drainpipe. This was the human rights activist Sergei Kovalyov, who had been sentenced to twelve years in prison on December 9, 1975, the day before the Nobel Peace Prize was presented to his friend Andrei Sakharov. Although Alexander and he had never met before, they knew each other by name.

Kovalyov was able to convince Ogorodnikov that it would be better to terminate the hunger strike and continue the struggle from Perm-36. "The prisoners there are desperately in need of a powerful figure like you," he argued. Ogorodnikov gave in, but he later regretted that decision because he was convinced that he would have caused the regime more harm if he had starved to death.

Perm-36, the "Camp of Death"

In November 1980, Ogorodnikov was taken by *voronok* to camp VS 389/36, better known as Perm-36. In this region, at the foot of the Urals, there were three camps for "especially dangerous crimes": Perm-35, Perm-36, and Perm-37. During the Soviet period no one could enter this area without a special pass because of the presence of the aerospace industry, in particular the Soyuz rockets, which were used to launch space capsules. The country's heavy war industry was also located in this region and was responsible for the production of artillery rockets, tank parts, and engines for the MiG fighter jets.

When the Gulag was in its prime under Stalin, there were more than 170 camps in the eastern part of European Russia. Perm-36 lay in the hamlet of Kuchino, about 100 miles north of the city of Perm and about 700 miles from Moscow. This camp, which dated from 1946, was involved in lumber production: they chopped down trees and sent the felled tree trunks to Volgograd (which was called Stalingrad, 1925-61) for further processing by binding them together and floating them downstream on the Kama and Volga rivers.

In 1953, the staff of Lavrenti Beria, the disgraced KGB chief who had tried unsuccessfully to seize power after the death of Joseph Stalin, were transported to this dreary place by order of General Secretary Nikita Khrushchev. Next to the camp was a psychiatric hospital. Because of the desolate swamp that surrounded the place, the residents were tormented by great clouds of botflies and mosquitoes every summer. (When the camps were shut down in 1992, the KGB ordered that all traces of them be eradicated. At Perm-36 this order was only partially carried out. Local historians, supported by the United States, set up the "Perm-36" Museum for the History of Political Repression — the only authentic Gulag museum in Russia.)

On July 14, 1972, the first crop of political dissidents had arrived in Perm-36. What made this re-education camp different from the other penal colonies and hard-labor camps in the Soviet Union was its extremely strict regime. Not only was it the camp for the most dangerous dissidents, but death sentences were carried out there as well. Due to the spartan living conditions, the incidence of death was extremely high. In the period 1972-79, at least thirteen prisoners died due to a lack of medical care. Consequently, Perm-36 was also known as the "camp of death."

Escape was almost impossible. The enormous area was surrounded by a wooden fence, five rows of barbed wire (one of which was kept permanently under electrical current), a patrol corridor for soldiers and dogs, a "forbidden zone" (a section of unplowed land enclosed by barbed wire), guard towers with machine guns, a lookout post with searchlights, a minefield and special sensors that set off an alarm as soon as anyone tried to dig a tunnel. One person did claim to have escaped from Perm-36. He was scornfully referred to as "the Baron von Münchhausen," referring to the tall tales told by the eighteenth-century German nobleman who had served for a time in the Russian army.

When Ogorodnikov arrived in Perm-36, there were between fifty and sixty prisoners of conscience in two common barracks. Earlier there must have been many more, in view of the size of the camp. Their backgrounds were varied. Some had been locked up for nationalistic or human rights activities, others for their political or religious involvement, and still others for setting up clandestine societies. Among them were various artists, historians, and scientists, such as the Estonian who had secretly translated George Orwell's book *1984*, the Lithuanian who had translated Solzhenitsyn's *The Gulag Archipelago*, and the biophysicist Sergei Kovalyov, whom Ogorodnikov had already come to know indirectly in the Perm city prison. Other detainees had unsuccessfully tried to flee to the West or had worked as spies for the CIA, the American foreign intelligence service. There was also a former officer of the "Abwehr," the Germany foreign and domestic intelligence service, who had fought with the partisans in the Baltic states and the Ukraine during the Second Great Patriotic War.

Ogorodnikov also got to know Vasily Kalinin, an active member of the underground church, who had been in the camps for thirty years. And in 1983 a prisoner arrived in the other barracks who was the only one Ogorodnikov had known before: the Catholic priest Alfonsus Svarinskas, his contact person during the preparations for the press conference in October 1978, when the matter of religious persecution in Lithuania had been raised. Svarinskas, who had been imprisoned for his contacts with the Christian Seminar, among other things, celebrated Mass clandestinely, offering sacramental wine made from dried raisins and hosts made of stale bread. He administered communion to the prisoners, heard confessions, and prayed for Russia, fulfilling the request of the Virgin Mary made to the three shepherd children in the Portuguese town of Fátima in 1917. During these apparitions, Mary had divulged three secrets. In the second secret, Mary asked that Russia be consecrated to the Immaculate Heart of Mary, in unity with the Catholic bishops of the world. Finally, in 1984, Pope John Paul II consecrated the whole world to the Immaculate Heart of Mary, but critics said this was at variance with Mary's wishes. Ogorodnikov had written an article on the Fátima apparitions in an article for *Obshchina*.

Alexander also became friends with another *zek* from the adjoining barracks, Mikhail Melah, who also spent a great deal of time in the isolation cell. The two men communicated with each other there via the toilet drainpipe. Melah even taught Ogorodnikov basic English this way, while Ogorodnikov introduced Melah to the Bible.

In Perm-36, a so-called re-education camp, the prisoners were to be "improved" and "reformed" based on a conscientious attitude toward Soviet society and work. The prisoners got up at 5:30 in the summer and 6:00 in the winter. After washing they fell into ranks for the daily roll call and then marched to the mess hall. There they were given a bowl of oatmeal — porridge mixed with water — and a piece of bread. Then they all marched in line to their work and returned at noon to the mess hall. The lunch menu never changed: borscht, oatmeal, and bread. In the afternoon everyone returned to work, and in the evening the prisoners ate oatmeal and bread once again. Very occasionally they would be served a piece of fish, but meat was unknown. During his years in Perm-36 Ogorodnikov was never given meat, though there sometimes were wisps of meat in the soup. The oatmeal was almost identical every day, but sometimes other grains were used.

Those who were sentenced to the strict regime, like Ogorodnikov, were given a reduced food ration of 1,750 calories. Each new prisoner in Perm-36 was given a special daily ration of only 1,300 calories for the first month. The food was the same, but the portions were smaller. Article 56 of the *Educational Labor Code* legalized the daily distribution of just enough food that was biologically necessary to keep a person alive. Article 20 added that prisoners "who break the rules, refuse to work or deliberately fail to meet production targets will be given less than the necessary minimum." Although there was a chronic labor shortage in the Soviet Union during the sowing and harvest seasons during those years, the prisoners were never put to work in the agricultural sector.

Those who behaved well could spend two rubles a month in the camp store to buy bread, dry biscuits, and tea. And those who had completed half their sentence were allowed to receive one annual postal package of five kilos from family members or friends. Sugar, honey, chocolate, meat products, vitamins, and food concentrates — products you could not get in the camp store either — were taboo. In addition, every prisoner was allowed to receive one one-kilo package twice a year containing nonfood and luxury food products, such as printed matter and candy; chocolate, however, was strictly forbidden. In practice, the only packages that were delivered were to those prisoners who had a good relationship with the camp administration. During the five years that Ogorodnikov spent in Perm-36 he never received a single package.

The latrines were outside, which was certainly no fun in the wintertime when temperatures regularly dropped to minus forty degrees Celsius. Inside the barracks, where the light was kept on day and night, the prisoners were not able to see outside because of the iron roll-down shutters covering the windows. Guards continuously monitored everything that went on in the barracks. Once a week the detainees did their own laundry. The black uniform, which bore the prisoner's name and barracks number, gradually became faded after all that washing. Baths were also weekly events. Everyone bathed in the primitive bathhouse, where soap was a rarity.

In the summer the barracks were broiling hot, and in the winter they were ice cold. Although the temperature inside was often barely ten degrees in the winter, the prisoners were given no extra blankets. Living together was not easy because of the total lack of privacy, the diversity of the prison population, the sounds of the inmates, and the camp's noisy public announcement system. The prisoners slept in wooden bunk beds. Each one kept his few possessions in his own nightstand: toilet articles, books, notes, and food he had bought himself.

These crushing living conditions gradually affected the spirit of the prisoners. By far the worst was the chronic hunger. Like a constantly throbbing toothache, that feeling of hunger gradually undermined the prisoners' health. After a couple of years a prisoner could no longer sit on a chair or lie on a bed without pain because his bones poked out against his skin. Other common side effects were swollen joints in the fingers and legs, red patches on the body, liver complaints, scurvy due to serious vitamin deficiency, and stomach ulcers.

Prisoners could borrow five books or magazines from the camp library, all of which were propaganda tools for "socialist realism." It's no wonder that all the prisoners were permanently consumed by a boundless longing for their wives and children, good food, and freedom.

Resisting the Exhaustive Camp System

When Ogorodnikov arrived in Perm-36, hardly anyone there put up any resistance to the arduous and debilitating camp system. His attempt to change all that meant that he was constantly being locked up in the *shizo* (isolation cell), and three times in the Pomeshcheniye Kamernogo Tipa (PKT), the camp prison, where the strictest regime was imposed. The food was identical to that in the camp, but the portions were even smaller, so the hunger pangs were even more severe. In addition, prisoners in the PKT were subjected to forced labor and had no access to medical care. The maximum length of detention there was six months.

On November 17, 1980, an exchange of words with the guard on duty
— Ogorodnikov refused to walk with his hands behind his back because,
he said, "it violated human dignity" — resulted in five days in the isolation
cell. In Perm-36 the cells were not only damp, but in the winter they were
also ice cold. The iron beds were taken down in the evening and hung
back on the wall at six o'clock in the morning. The prisoners were given
no bedding or mattresses, and slippers wrapped in handkerchiefs served
as pillows. The cell contained only a small concrete table and two or four
stools on which it was impossible to sit. The food norm here was 9B: a ration of 1,300 calories.

On the annual international Human Rights Day, proclaimed by the
United Nations on December 10, 1980, all the prisoners of conscience in
Perm-36 went on a hunger strike. On January 21, 1981, Ogorodnikov went
on another hunger strike to get his confiscated Bible back; after ten days
the authorities relented. Because the two successive hunger strikes had
weakened him badly, Ogorodnikov was taken one month later by *voronok*
to the central hospital in Vsesvyatskoye, about twenty-five miles further
on the grounds of Perm-35. The wretched road conditions made the journey a real torture.

The two-story hospital contained an operating room, a laboratory,
an X-ray unit, and a couple of rooms. Only examinations and emergency
operations could take place there. The role of the medical staff was limited to little more than alleviating pain and preventing unacceptable
deaths. The staff consisted of a therapist, three to six nurses, and Dr.
Pchelnikov, who had little competence as a physician and spent most of
his time in the administration of the hospital. His motto was: "This isn't a
health resort, it's a prison camp." The hospital was lacking even the most
elementary medical equipment, and the "best-before" dates on the limited stock of medicines had usually passed long before. Patients rarely
saw Dr. Pchelnikov, and by eight o'clock in the evening all the staff members had gone home. Doctors from outside never came to the camp except in absolute emergencies. Even in the hospital the patients had to
clean their own rooms. There was no separate toilet for the patients, so
each patient was given a *parasha* (bedpan).

Yet a stay in the hospital had a double advantage: the prisoner did
not have to work, and he was given "medical rations" according to norm
5B. In theory that was supposed to amount to between 3,100 and 3,300
calories; but in practice the sick were given a small amount of butter on
their bread and sometimes a bit of meat in their soup, and the portions

were somewhat larger. A trifling and often unconscious infringement of the camp rules was enough to send a sick prisoner straight back to the camp. When Ogorodnikov opened the ventilation window in his room without asking permission (he was the only patient in the room), he was put in the isolation cell for fifteen days. The medical team was also supposed to — again, in theory — include a dentist. But despite the many dental problems among the prisoners — Ogorodnikov lost a large number of teeth due to force-feeding — visits by a dentist were only sporadic.

During his stay in the hospital, Ogorodnikov heard through the grapevine about a recent prime-time television interview with Boris Razveyev, a former member of the Christian Seminar, who had caved in under the psychological pressure of prison interrogation and had called Ogorodnikov "the new Rasputin."

On March 15, 1981, only a few days after his return to Perm-36, Ogorodnikov began a new hunger strike because the Bible that had finally been returned to him a couple months earlier had once again been seized. During this strike he also demanded to have a talk with a priest. After one month, on April 17, he was force-fed by the guards in the medical section of the camp. Ten days later, Ogorodnikov was admitted to the hospital once again because he was totally depleted by the hunger strike, which he had been on for forty-two days. Even so, after returning to the barracks, he continued to refuse all food.

Finally, in mid-July 1981, 120 days after he had begun the hunger strike, the camp commander decided that he could have his Bible back. Ogorodnikov's condition at that point was critical, and because of his reputation in the West, the commander did not want to let him die. Alexander's hunger strike was only a few days behind him when he was put in the isolation cell, on July 14, 1981, for refusing to work and violating the uniform code. He had invoked his self-appointed status as a prisoner of conscience.

Trusting a Warden

The lives of the camp guards, all of them civil servants of the Ministry of the Interior, were by no means easy. During the winter the wardens and their families, who lived in a separate section of the camp, were totally isolated for months at a time. They were lured to this outback by the high salaries, the large number of vacation days, and the priority given to prison guards when places were allotted in the special vacation houses for government employees. Most of them were alcoholics and were driven by sadism and lust for power. They nourished a deep hatred for everyone under their command and had no qualms about using force. Others yielded under the pressure exerted on them by the prisoners and grabbed their piece of the pie at every opportunity. Since the barracks guards were constantly walking in and out, there was a great deal of contact.

In the camp prison, a relationship of trust developed between Ogorodnikov and his guard, Sergei. This man, who had himself been locked up in the prison by his fellow guards, spoke openly with Ogorodnikov through the cell door. "Sergei" was, of course, an alias; his true identity was unknown. The KGB gave aliases to the guards to prevent former prisoners from tracking them down later. Sergei was trained by the KGB to carry out clandestine operations in the West; but after a conflict he had within the agency, he was punished by being transferred to Perm-36. Ogorodnikov managed to convince him of the falseness of Communism, after which Sergei promised to smuggle out letters for him. This was a very dangerous risk to take, because the guards themselves were regularly checked. In addition, Sergei had to find a reason to go to the city (the camp was a hundred miles from the city of Perm) in order to find someone there who would be prepared to carry the letter to Moscow, where the smuggling route to the West continued. If the guard were to be caught, it could mean his death.

The three letters that Ogorodnikov entrusted to him did indeed reach their destinations. Sergei also met with Vladimir Burtsev in the city of Chusovoy, near Perm-36. Burtsev was one of the most important members of the Christian Seminar, and thanks to Sergei, Burtsev was able to gather information about the living conditions in Perm-36.

But one day Sergei, the former KGB agent, suddenly vanished. He had probably been unmasked, because camp surveillance was suddenly tightened, and the camp prison was monitored by two guards instead of one.

Besides such help from the inside, there was another way to smuggle information out: via the infrequent visitors. The strict controls that had been imposed forced the prisoners to devise extremely ingenious ways of communicating. One tested method was to write messages on cigarette papers. The papers were wrapped in plastic and then swallowed at just the right moment, since before entering the visitors' room the prisoners were frisked from head to toe. The prisoner then went to the toilet in the visitors' room and excreted the plastic bag, washed it with water, and secretly passed it to the visitor, who in turn swallowed it and walked out with the information.

"Your Husband Is a Hooligan"

On August 14, 1981, Ogorodnikov's few belongings were seized, and he was put in the *shizo* for fifteen days "for cursing." The real reason for this punishment was his refusal to work in the forbidden area, that is, the zone behind the barbed wire, which the prisoners were in principle not allowed to enter. The camp administration also punished him for the damning articles that had been published by Viktor Pronin in his column entitled "Aliens," in the popular weekly *Ogonjok* (Fire). In those articles he fiercely attacked Ogorodnikov and the Christian Seminar in response to Western radio broadcasts about their persecution. Pronin called Ogorodnikov "vain, weak, lazy, lecherous, egotistical, cowardly, and without scruples." He denied that Ogorodnikov had been dismissed from the VGIK Cinematographic Institute in Moscow for ideological reasons. And he repeated the accusation that Ogorodnikov had lived with a minor. He also accused him of "spreading unmistakably ridiculous rumors about the persecution of the Seminar."

Pronin further declared that in 1976 the mother of Eduard Fedotov and the father of Alexander Argentov had themselves requested the internment of their sons. Finally, he accused both Ogorodnikov and Vladimir Poresh of being paid foreign agents. The sharp tone of these articles suggested that the secret service was greatly annoyed by the fact that Ogorodnikov and the Seminar had by no means been forgotten in the West.

On September 5, 1981, Ogorodnikov was once again put in the isolation cell for ten days. The official reason was cited as a "careless work attitude"; in reality, it was because he had been caught writing down the text of the penitential Psalm 51 of King David for a fellow prisoner: it was the *miserere,* commonly used as a prayer by the Orthodox.

After much insistence, Yelena Levashova, Alexander's wife, was finally given permission to visit him, which the two also saw as an opportunity to have their marriage officially registered. The visit proved to be extremely complicated because Levashova's employer at first refused to give her time off — at the instigation of the KGB. She also had to stand up to the pressure from her parents, who still objected to her marriage to

Ogorodnikov. But Yelena pressed on and finally arrived at Perm-36 on October 12, 1981.

To her dismay, however, she was not allowed inside. The visit had been canceled because Ogorodnikov had been in the isolation cell for three days. "Your husband is a hooligan," a member of the camp administration told her. "He is being punished for a serious offense, which is why you cannot see him. And he's not your husband because you're not married to him." The whole matter was simply a cynical joke. Although Ogorodnikov had been put in the isolation cell on a trumped-up charge before Yelena's departure from Moscow, she had not been informed that her visit had been canceled. The same camp employee also made it clear to her that Ogorodnikov was never getting out of prison. This incident proved fatal to their relationship, which was exactly what the KGB was trying to achieve.

In November 1981, Andrei Sakharov wrote a letter from his place of exile in Gorky with a worldwide appeal to all scientists to devote themselves to defending both their persecuted colleagues and all political and religious prisoners, including Ogorodnikov. A few weeks later, Ogorodnikov succeeded in smuggling out a letter, via Sergei, the friendly guard, to his mother on December 26, 1981.

Mama,

How can I express the love for you that fills my heart to overflowing and gives my choking lungs the air I need to breathe again? I love you so very much and even more now, although that extra of love has been obtained at the cost of much pain. My intense love for you, which I was never so aware of before, has become even stronger within these bare, terrifying walls. It's as though, in spite of everything, an endless spring or a feeling of peace has been awakened in my heart, a hidden spring that once lay dormant somewhere deep in my subconscious. My mind cannot find words enough to express all that I feel and my thoughts and prayers for you. How rarely do your letters reach me!

The head of camp administration has returned the packet of medicines you sent me recently. So it's not just letters but also the essential medicines that don't get through. I know that you are living in Redkino now because I was recently told that a letter of yours was confiscated and sent back to Redkino. When I am not given your letters I am occasionally shown a notice of confiscation with the name and address of the sender on it (not always, because sometimes the KGB doesn't even let you know that a letter has arrived).

Thanks to these notices I know that you have finally moved to Redkino. I was also informed of your move by the KGB officials from Kalinin: by G. P. Petrov, head of the investigation section, and by his colleague, head of the operations unit, a man with malevolent, mocking eyes and a cruel smile. They both came to the camp on October 27, 1981, and tried, once again, to persuade me to recant. My dear ones, there is so much I have to say to you. Pray God this letter reaches you!

On October 9, 1981, I was placed in the punishment cell where the regime is harsher than in prison. Food is minimal rations, but I am refusing it. I have been conducting a hunger strike since October 28 because I am demanding the following: the return of my confiscated Bible and prayer book, contact with a priest, permission to receive religious literature, to subscribe to those religious periodicals that are published in the USSR and to enroll as a correspondence student in the Theological Academy, to receive visits from you and to register my marriage with Yelena. I am also protesting the lack of light in my cell. It is switched off from 10 a.m. until 4 p.m. Sometimes they switch it off even earlier, so you spend literally the whole day in semi-darkness.

I started the hunger strike on October 28, 1981, to coincide with the resumption of the CSCE talks [Commission on Security and Cooperation in Europe] in Madrid. Today, December 26, is the sixtieth day of my hunger strike. The conditions in this zone of the camp are appalling, even worse than those in a criminal camp. There are no medical facilities, and the inmates in the punishment cells are deprived of all forms of assistance. All you can get here are some kind of tablets that have no effect whatsoever.

Although I am on a hunger strike, instead of medical examinations I get reprimands and threatening lectures persuading me to stop fasting. They began force-feeding me liquid food on the 27th day of the hunger strike, and have repeated this treatment every seventh, eighth or ninth day ever since. I have become very weak, feel constantly dizzy and can barely sit up in bed. Pressure on me has increased; I am no longer given any new books, and the few books I have are exchanged only every ten days.

My health, unfortunately, is not very good. I have already lost nine teeth and soon I will probably lose four more. There is no dentist in the camp. My eyesight is much worse. The glasses I got in May 1981 are no longer strong enough. Deliberately darkening your cell during the daytime is in fact a kind of refined torture for me because reading in such poor light is such a strain on the eyes. When the lights are switched on in the evening, my bulb is so weak that it gives off merely a dim gleam.

The administration is also stepping up its efforts against me. I receive almost no letters, and the letters I write are either confiscated or not forwarded — which is why you have not heard from me in such a long time. My dear forsaken ones, I could write a whole book on this matter alone. If I ever see you again, when I am out of prison and God willing, I'll tell you all about it. But for now I must be brief. In the three years of my imprisonment I have spent 176 days and nights in punishment and isolation cells. In the Kalinin prison the floor was covered with water. In Konsomolsk the sewage system was deliberately blocked off so human excrement was constantly floating around in my cell. I tried to keep from making it worse by doing my business on a short concrete post. In winter the temperature in the punishment cell never rises above fourteen or fifteen degrees, while you're sitting on a concrete floor without any underwear. Daily rations are minimal. One day you get 350 grams of bread and water and the next day you get a hot meal, but according to the "reduced" norm, which means it's mostly water. In this camp I have spent most of my time in the punishment cell. For instance, between August 11 and September 15, 1979, I spent a total of 35 consecutive days and nights in the punishment cell without being taken out once. I was placed there for no apparent reason on orders from Moscow. The administration misses no opportunity to exercise repression. It's impossible to describe it all. According to prison regulations, hunger strikers must be hospitalized a month after the beginning of the strike. In my case, I have received a flat refusal. They violate their own laws, although it's already harsh enough.

Your letters are withheld from me, mother, because of the prayers in them. The censor has demanded that I forbid you to quote prayers. But how could I do such a thing? What would I want to say, or be able to say? Absolutely nothing! All I can tell you is that I'm in a labor camp and I'm not allowed to have any visitors. According to camp regulations I can only write one letter every two months, and even that letter can be confiscated. My dear ones, don't be too downhearted as you read this. It's embarrassing what I write here, but unfortunately it's the harsh truth. All my religious literature has been confiscated, so has every scrap of paper and even the textbooks I was using to learn languages.

The authorities have stripped me of the right to all visits except that one that was supposed to take place in October. But a few days before the visit I was sent to the punishment cell, so the visit fell through and I wasn't able to register my marriage to Yelena.

You can be sure that as soon as I'm released from the camp I'll be put right back in. And by the way, the amount of time you spend in the punishment cell is deliberately not included in calculating the time you've spent in the camp.

At some point I'll probably be transferred to the Chistopol political prison — the camp administration has made me a formal promise in that regard! I figure I'll be sent there either at the end of the summer or the beginning of the fall for a period of three years, until the end of my sentence. So those are the prospects for the future. In any case, this neither frightens nor saddens me.

I put my trust in God and believe with all my heart that He has blessed all my ordeals and that He will lend strength to my weakness by His merciful grace. My faith in the Lord is indestructible. So don't grieve for me. All my trials will be over one day, so that I will be cleansed of all my sins. All is subject to God's providence. All I ask of you is to pray for me. Your prayers give me strength. They are my greatest form of encouragement. The Lord gives us both trials and joys. His infinite mercy brings me much spiritual happiness. I am absolutely not depressed or despairing. My mental health is good. I keep my mind as active as possible. I look forward to the day when I will see you again. During the long, hungry and sleepless nights I often think back to your culinary skills. I dream of being reunited and try to imagine what our lives will be like when my imprisonment is behind me and my term of internal exile begins. I hope you will come to live with me then. My greatest care right now is your present solitary situation, which makes it impossible to see your grandson or to exercise a religious influence on his formative years.

I would very much like to hear from a priest. Perhaps you can arrange this for me, or ask my friends to do so? It would mean a great deal to me if I were to receive a letter from a priest. Don't worry about me too much. I love you, and every day when I recall our earlier life together it fills me with joy. Pray for me, as I will pray for you.

Your devoted son, Sasha, December 26, 1981

Despite his physical decline, Ogorodnikov's great mental stamina was still undiminished, thanks to the strength he drew from his faith. The transfer to the re-education camp in his native city of Chistopol had only been a threat. In order to arrange that, the authorities would have to change the sentence that was handed down by the court in Kalinin. In addition, the KGB discovered that Ogorodnikov knew quite a few people there, such as one of the men responsible for the Chistopol camp, who had been his fellow student.

Pandemonium in Perm-36

In 1982, Dan Wooding, a journalist for the American tabloid *The National Enquirer* and the British Sunday newspaper *Sunday Mirror*, and a commentator on the radio stations BBC Radio 1 in London and United Press International/Radio Network (UPI/RN) in Washington, D.C., launched an international letter-writing and prayer campaign for Ogorodnikov. And in early 1982, the British Keston Institute published detailed information about 350 Christians being kept in Soviet camps, which number had doubled since 1978. The Keston Institute registered 81 new arrests in 1979, 113 in 1980, and 120 in 1981. Besides Orthodox Christians, those being persecuted were mainly Seventh-day Adventists, Baptists, and Lithuanian Catholics.

In March 1982, all of Perm-36 was suddenly plunged into a state of pandemonium. To their horror, the guards discovered that a large group of prisoners had slit their wrists. The bedding in the dim barracks was stained red, and blood was dripping from the beds onto the floor. The alarm was sounded immediately. Sixteen prisoners, Ogorodnikov among them, had chosen this act of desperation because the health of their fellow inmate Viktor Nekipelov, who was suffering from acute nephritis, had visibly deteriorated, and now was mortally ill. Such a mass action was unique in the history of the camp. In no time at all, the prisoners' demands, which had come to nothing for weeks, were suddenly granted. An internist had Viktor Nekipelov immediately transferred to a hospital, where he was saved from certain death. However, in retaliation against those who had slit their wrists, the camp leaders locked up ten prisoners in the *shizo* and three in the PKT, including Ogorodnikov.

On April 15, 1982, Ogorodnikov was punished for insulting one of the guards on duty. This happened during a dispute after he had shared a spoonful of soup with Oles Shevchenko in the *shizo*. The prisoners were constantly "fighting" with the camp administration for more freedom. But those skirmishes had little effect, especially when it came to religious matters. On Sunday, April 18, 1982, for instance, an improvised Easter vigil was roughly terminated by the wardens, after which the organizers were thrown into isolation cells. Shortly thereafter, the Easter group wrote an open letter to Pope John Paul II:

> Prisoners are not allowed to have Bibles, not even following a long hunger strike — which Alexander Ogorodnikov did in 1980-1981. Confessing to a priest is absolutely impossible. Crosses in the prisons are violently removed, and conducting religious rites, even praying, is strictly forbidden, even while the prisoners are being transported.

This letter was one of those that reached its destination via Sergei, the friendly guard with whom Ogorodnikov had built up a relationship of trust.

In May 1982, ten prisoners from Perm-36 wrote an open letter to President Ronald Reagan, who had been inaugurated in January 1981, with a detailed list of the violations of human rights in the camp, including the brutality and physical and psychological torture with which they were continuously being afflicted. They asked Reagan to send an international inspection team to the labor camps in the Soviet Union. Among the signatories were the Ukrainians Mykola Rudenko, Myroslav Marynovych, and Oles Shevchenko, founder/chairman, cofounder, and member, respectively, of the Ukrainian Helsinki Group. The letter was also signed by Viktor Nekipelov, writer and member of the Moscow Helsinki Group; the Armenian Henrich Altunian, former army officer and human rights activist; the Estonian Viktor Niytsoo, architect and human rights activist; the Lithuanian historian Antanas Terliatskas; the translator Vladimir Balakhonov; Norair Grygorian, former KGB officer and American spy; and Alexander Ogorodnikov. This letter was also smuggled out by Sergei.

> Mr. President,
>
> It is often difficult for a resident of the West to imagine the atmosphere of lawlessness in which the inmates of Soviet political prison camps exist today. Recently the conditions of our imprisonment have worsened so sharply that we feel compelled to appeal to you. It is probable that this "tightening of the screws" — or, as it was said during the Stalin years, "clampdown" — is just as much the result of individual instances in which the Soviet regime has disgraced itself (Poland, Af-

ghanistan) as of the general crisis that the system is undergoing. The ever-present brothers-in-arms of a tyranny in decline — cruelty and absurdity — today permeate all spheres of our lives, all aspects of our prison existence.

On April 18, 1982, the prisoners Myroslav Marynovych, Viktor Nekipelov and Mykola Rudenko were abruptly dragged away from a small prison table at which fourteen prisoners had gathered to celebrate Easter with prayer and an Easter meal. They were thrown into a punishment cell, or *kartser*, for two weeks as "organizers of a clique." Strange as it may seem, the celebration of Christ's Resurrection was regarded as a gathering of a "clique" that had to be dispersed. It is difficult for us to imagine that there can exist another prison in the world in which the observance of a religious ritual would be punishable by incarceration in a punishment cell. Even in 1932, the authorities at Stalin's Solovky Special Regime Camp permitted not only the Easter service but even the procession with a cross that precedes the Easter Divine Liturgy.

On February 13, 1982, Rudenko, a World War II invalid with a severe spinal injury, was deprived of his invalid status for no known reason and thereby declared capable of performing heavy manual labor. We can only assume that this was done because a collection of his poems was published in the West.

In March of 1982, the prisoner Vladimir Balakhonov was suddenly deprived of a visit from his daughter on completely absurd and immoral grounds, namely, his failure to fulfill his work quota. This was to have been his first visit in ten years. The use of punishment cells as a form of harassment is becoming commonplace, a part of our everyday life. Anyone can be thrown into the punishment cell for any arbitrary reason, even the most insignificant: a button left undone, leaving the work site ten minutes before the end of the shift (even if the prisoner has met his daily output quota), or even, as happened in the case of the prisoner Alexander Ogorodnikov, who was in the punishment cell at the time, for sharing a spoonful of soup with a cellmate who was to have spent the day on bread and water under the conditions of his regime.

Just as frequently and thoughtlessly are we deprived of what is most precious to us, that is, visits with our relatives. Since visits are allowed not once a week or once a month, but once a year, this constitutes a very harsh punishment indeed. Between February and April 1982, visits from relatives were canceled for Oles Shevchenko (for celebrating Easter, among other reasons), Viktor Niytsoo and others under various ridiculous "pretexts." After traveling thousands of kilometers to the camp, the relatives of Henrich Altunian, Norair Grygorian and Ogorodnikov were simply turned away and not permitted to meet with the prisoners. Supposedly there was no room available for the meeting; Grygorian was placed in the punishment cell just before his expected visit; and Ogorodnikov's wife was bluntly told that she could not meet with her husband because their marriage had been registered only in church.

Repressions and privations stalk us at every step. Our correspondence is subjected to the harshest ideological censorship imaginable, our letters are shamelessly confiscated (for this to happen, it is enough for a letter to be deemed "suspicious in content") or they "disappear along the way." Not a single letter from abroad has reached us in the camp in the last several years. Since all those who send letters are also regarded as "suspicious in content," almost the only letters that get through the censor's fine sieve are from family members.

The confiscations conducted in the camp are senseless and absurd: poems are confiscated from poets, written prayers from believers. The authorities confiscated the Universal Declaration of Human Rights from the prisoner Nekipelov as also being "suspicious in content." It had been sent to him by his wife in a letter. The Bible and other religious literature are strictly prohibited in the camp and have been confiscated from several prisoners. The hunt for the written word is being carried to such absurd lengths that every scrap of paper and every handwritten line is wrenched from our hands.

There are even frequent instances of what might be called "ideological revenge." A prisoner's independent stance and his participation in collective protests, especially signing human-rights documents and appeals that are meant for publication in the West, leave him open to a wide range of repressions — up to and including several months of imprisonment in the camp prison or even several years in the special prison in the city of Chistopol. For example, one of the real reasons for incarcerating the prisoner Dan Arenberg in Chistopol prison in September 1981 was his attempt to send a congratulatory telegram (in a perfectly legal manner) to Menachem Begin, who had just been reelected prime minister of Israel.

As far as our foreign publications are concerned: at the very moment that you are reading this letter, Mr. President, KGB officers are quite probably conducting severe repressive measures against prisoners in connection with our appeal to you. Antanas Terliatskas was warned that he and the other authors of this appeal might receive new prison terms for their action.

Punishments were meted out to all sixteen participants in the "strike of despair," which took place because the camp authorities refused to call a specialist to examine Nekipelov, who was critically ill with acute nephritis and was failing rapidly. In the end the prisoners' demand was met and a physician arrived, but at a very high cost to all involved, as we later learned. Ten strikers were placed in the punishment cell, three of whom — Altunian, Ogorodnikov and Rudenko — were transferred to "cell-type premises" (PKT) in the camp. One month later, Nekipelov was also taken there straight from his hospital bed. The prisoner Yuri Fedorov was transferred to a special regimen camp.

The list of similar examples of lawlessness could be continued without end, Mr. President. They are so widespread that it is no longer merely a question of incidental human rights violations but of premeditated cruelty, of physical and psychological torture, of terrorizing the spirit and exhibiting open moral contempt for culture.

This forces us to raise an issue which our predecessors raised ten or fifteen years ago, namely, international inspection of Soviet political prison camps. An impartial commission of independent and politically unaffiliated Western humanitarians — writers and lawyers — after visiting the camps of any country, be they in Ulster, South Africa or the Soviet Union, could draw up an authoritative report of their findings on the number of prisoners there and, consequently, about the moral duty of the government of that country to condemn others for using imprisonment to suppress dissent.

Knowing of your determination to defend freedom and humanity in the world, Mr. President, we appeal to you to support the creation of such a commission. We would be deeply appreciative if your "Truth" project were to include the facts about Soviet political prison camps. By whatever means best suit you — be it the Madrid Conference on Security and Cooperation in Europe or in direct talks — you could help to rid the world of this cruel madness. The existence of political prisoners in our enlightened age is as anachronistic as the slave trade. The champions of worldwide morality have long known that no measures or spheres of trust have the slightest chance of success in a country that incarcerates its political, national, religious and moral opposition in prisons and camps.

This letter did not reach the West until March 1983, ten months later. On February 17, 1983, Ogorodnikov was put in the isolation cell for twelve days on charges of "organizing a gathering" and "seriously disturbing the peace" because he had refused to hand in his clothing. In his unheated cell Alexander had noticed one morning that he was paralyzed on one side, which meant that he could no longer close his left eye. After three weeks there was partial recovery, but not total.

Back to the Prison in Kalinin

Ogorodnikov's ultimate form of protest was to ascribe to himself the status of political prisoner, and he stubbornly refused to talk during the new wave of interrogations to which he was subjected. He also maintained an inflexible silence after his temporary transfer to the prison in Kalinin at the end of March 1983.

Why the return? The reason was that the camp administration wanted him out of Perm-36 for a while, hoping that his absence would reduce the defiance of the other prisoners. In addition, a new form of psychological terror was being tested to bring him to his knees. Ogorodnikov was deliberately placed in a cell in Kalinin with a few criminals who had been sentenced to death. They were promised that their sentence would be reviewed if they were able to murder their new cellmate. Ogorodnikov carried on deep discussions with them and managed to convince them that the promised review of their trial was a lie. Instead of harming or killing him, they felt drawn to him. One of them went spontaneously to Ogorodnikov for confession. The man confessed his guilt for the crime he had committed, and though he, as a nonbeliever, could scarcely grasp the deeper meaning of Ogorodnikov's words — "even you can be saved and can partake of eternal life" — he felt relieved nonetheless.

The other criminal who had been sentenced to death also confessed his sins and gave vent to his emotions: his anger, but most of all, his fear of having to die. Although both men underwent a spiritual rebirth in the last hours of their lives, the atmosphere in the cell was so tense that one could cut it with a knife. When would the executioner come get them? Ogorodnikov kept vigil with them for the whole time. Finally, they were taken away in the dead of night and executed by firing squad at daybreak. The contrast between his experiences in the death cell and the warm reception he was given the next day by the neat young man from the KGB was hard to imagine.

"We're not asking you to make a statement on television," said the young KGB man in a friendly tone. "You'll even get an apartment in Moscow and a good-paying job. There's only one condition: that you terminate all your activities."

When Ogorodnikov did not respond, the man said to him cheerfully, "By the way, I have good news for you. Your wife and son Dima are on vacation on the Black Sea right now." To Alexander's consternation, the man pulled out a photo of his son, who was now five years old, playing on the beach in the presence of his wife, Yelena Levashova.

"Just one signature and you're a free man. And that's not all. We'll take you immediately by plane to your wife and son. You can be with them tonight."

Ogorodnikov realized that this was just another attempt to intimidate and discredit him, and that on no account would he ever be released. He remained silent and was taken back to death row in the Kalinin prison, where a few prisoners who had been sentenced to death were awaiting their execution in the weeks to follow. Even though these men were in other cells, he invariably woke up in the middle of the night just when they were about to be fetched; after their execution, he prayed for them.

On Easter Sunday, April 25, 1983, Ogorodnikov went on a hunger strike once again — because he still had not been given a Bible. But after one incident, the camp commander, Major Yoravkov, had him placed in the isolation cell. Ogorodnikov warned him that he would be punished for this outrage, referring to a passage from the Bible. Hardly able to sleep, he devoted himself to prayer.

That night, one of the wardens suddenly began knocking on his cell door. Clearly overwrought, the warden asked him, "What did you do to Yoravkov?" Yoravkov, who had been in outstanding physical condition until then, suddenly had had an acute gallbladder attack. Because the doctors in Perm-36 could not help him, he was taken immediately by helicopter to Moscow. Two months later, Ogorodnikov heard the dirge and funeral music from his isolation cell. Yoravkov's coffin was being taken to the Perm-36 cemetery. As the coffin was being lowered, Ogorodnikov heard the soldiers firing in a military salute in the distance.

In the months of May and June 1983, he was questioned three times by Egorov, the head of the KGB in the Kalinin region. Ogorodnikov refused to open his mouth. Furious, Egorov screamed at him, "If you don't cooperate you'll never get out of prison!"

Whim Becomes Law under Yuri Andropov

Back in Perm-36, Ogorodnikov was punished in September 1983 for organizing an improvised volleyball game while the prisoners were being let out for fresh air. The camp regime was always strict, but it had become even stricter now that Yuri Andropov, former head of the KGB, had been appointed secretary general of the Communist Party on November 12, 1982, two days after the death of Leonid Brezhnev. Andropov had an enormous aversion to dissidents. As former ambassador in Budapest during the Hungarian Uprising in 1956, he had seen with his own eyes how quickly a peaceful movement of intellectuals could turn into a furious and uncontrollable popular insurrection. From now on, anyone who was suspected of religious or nationalistic sympathies, or who took a stand for human rights, could immediately lose his job, status, and diploma. In addition, telephone cables were cut, travel restrictions imposed, residence permits recalled, and the children of suspects were denied access to universities.

On October 1, 1983, Article 188, Paragraph 3 was added to the Russian Penal Code. From then on, anyone who violated the camp regulations would be given five additional years of internment. Whim became law because troublesome prisoners could be cunningly manipulated into the role of perpetrator, backed up by legislation. Vladimir Poresh was one of the first victims of this new article. In July 1984, just before his term of imprisonment was about to end, his punishment was extended by three years for disciplinary reasons: throwing notes over a fence between two prison lots; going on strike after a fellow inmate had been beaten by guards; and protesting the reduced bread ration.

This hard line enormously increased the distrust in the prisons and the camps, and it sowed great discord among the depleted ranks of dissidents, as well as within the foreign movements supporting them. According to the KGB, more than a hundred dissidents decided to "take the right path" between 1982 and 1986. In July 1983, the Soviet Union left the Seventh Congress of the World Psychiatric Association (WPA) prematurely

Maxim Ogorodnikov, Alexander's grandfather, collaborated with the Bolsheviks. But a recently found family photograph shows that many other family members and relatives were active in the White Army during the Civil War (1918-21), which occurred after the Communist takeover.

The Firsov family just before the second "Great Patriotic War." From left to right: Uncle Tovi Firsov and Margarita Firsova — the mother of Alexander Ogorodnikov — and their parents, Yemelian Firsov and Elisabeta Firsova.

ТУУ ТУРЫНДА
ТАНЫКЛЫК
СВИДЕТЕЛЬСТВО
О РОЖДЕНИИ

НБ № 089419

Гр. _Огородников_
(фамилиясе — фамилия)
Александр Иосифович
(исеме hәм атасының исеме — имя и отчество)
27 III 50 _тысяча девятьсот_
родился (лась) (ел, ай hәм числоны язу hәм цифрлар белән күрсәтергә—
пятьдесятого года
прописью и цифрами год, месяц и число) туды,

шул хакта гражданлык хәле актларын язу кнагәсендә
о чем в книге записей актов гражданского состояния

туу турында _Чистополь_
о рождении
гор ЗАГс
(ЗАГС бюросының исеме — наименование бюро ЗАГС)
_1950_ _IV_ _26_
года ае месяца числосында
числа
тиешенче № _языу кузелды_
произведена соответствующая запись за № _910_

34

Этисе—анисе:
Родители:

Этисе _Огородников_
Отец (фамилиясе — фамилия)
Иосиф Максимович
(исеме hәм атасының исеме — имя и отчество)
миллэте _русский_
национальность

Анисе _Огородникова_
(фамилиясе — фамилия)
Маргарита Алексеевна
(исеме hәм атасының исеме — имя и отчество)
миллэте _русская_
национальность

Баланың туган урыны:
Место рождения ребенка: город, селение
Чистополь
шәhәре, авылы,
район _____ районы
область, край, республика
ТАССР
әлкәсе, крае, республикасы.

Терҗау урыны _Чистополь_
Место регистрации (ЗАГС бюросының исеме hәм урнашкан
ЗАГс
урыны — наименование и местонахождение бюро ЗАГС)

Биру вакыты _26 IV_ _1950_г.
Дата выдачи

П. М. Гражданлык хәле актларын
М. П. язу бюросы мөдире _Шарапов_
Заведующий бюро записей актов
гражданского состояния

34

April 1950: Alexander Ogorodnikov's birth certificate, issued by the Chistopol city council.

December 1950: Alexander Ogorodnikov with his mother. He is eight months old.

1957: gathering of the Little Octobrists children's organization, in uniform. Alexander Ogorodnikov is in the second row, first on the left.

1962: Alexander Ogorodnikov with his mother Margarita Firsova.

1966: Alexander Ogorodnikov borrowing the maximum of two books from the Chistopol public library.

February 1967: members of the Komsomol Public Fighting Unit. From left to right: Balagonov, (unknown), Danilin, Ogorodnikov and Galayautdinov.

June 1969: Alexander Ogorodnikov (standing), proudly wearing a Komsomol decoration on his lapel, poses with his parents. The picture of his brother Boris was later cut out of the photograph.

September 1970: a group of philosophy students from the University of Sverdlovsk — associates of Alexander Ogorodnikov (second row, fourth from the left) — engaged in manual labor for one month at a *kolkhoz*. Next to him (third from the left) is his best friend and roommate Viktor Finkelstein, who had Jewish roots and later emigrated to Israel. When Alexander Ogorodnikov was dismissed from the university during a meeting of the Komsomol, Baris (first row, second from the left) came to his defense and was also dismissed. The student on the far left is wearing a potato sack with a skull on it as a silent form of protest against the abuse of students.

Leader of the Christian Seminar:
Vladimir Poresh.

Leaders of the Christian Seminar: Tatiana Shchipkova and Lev Regelson.

Father Ioann, the *starets,* or spiritual father, of Alexander Ogorodnikov.

Leader of the Christian Seminar: Viktor Popkov.

March 1976: Alexander Ogorodnikov in traditional Russian clothes with Yelena Levashova, his wife-to-be, at the entrance to the porter's quarters at 25 Peace Boulevard in Moscow, where he lived.

1976: members of the
Christian Seminar.

August 1976: the core members of the Christian Seminar. From left to right: Vladimir
Poresh, Alexander Ogorodnikov, Boris Razveyev, and the poet Oleg Ochapkin.

1977: consultation among members of the Christian Seminar. Alexander
Ogorodnikov is second from the right.

November 1977:
church wedding of
Alexander Ogorodnikov
and Yelena Levashova.

February 1978: group from the Christian Seminar poses after attending Divine Liturgy in Moscow. Alexander Ogorodnikov (first row, second from the right) is holding his son Dima.

Leader of the Christian Seminar: Sergei Yermolaev.

1978: Alexander Ogorodnikov shortly before his arrest.

Alexander Ogorodnikov's camp passport, signed by the head of the institute, Yury V. G. Raguzin, and the head of the section, V. Vostrikovoy.

August 1980: Alexander Shchipkov with photographs of six arrested members of the Christian Seminar in the background: Viktor Popkov (above), Lev Regelson, Sergei Yermolaev, Vladimir Burtsev, Vladimir Poresh (second row from left to right), and Alexander Ogorodnikov (below).

1980: the wives and children of the three arrested members of the Christian Seminar. The wife of Vladimir Poresh is on the right.

To Alexander's Mother
From Elsie Batchelor

Would you pray for:

Alexander Ogorodnikov

In September 1980 Alexander was sentenced to 6 years labour-camp (strict regime) and 5 years internal exile. He had organized a Christian youth seminar in Moscow. Alexander was born in 1950. His wife Jelena is left alone with 1 child.

This set of "Open Doors" - Christmas cards is a publication of "Open Doors", P.O. Box 6, Standlake, Witney, Oxon OX8 7SP, Tel. 086731 - 262.
Copyright illustrations: Rien Poortvliet/Unieboek B.V. Illustrations from: "Hij was één van ons."
Publishing firm: Van Holkema & Warendorf in Bussum, Holland. Printing: Pieters/Groede.

December 1980: worldwide Christmas card action initiated by the Protestant organization Open Doors. (From Alexander Ogorodnikov's family archive.)

Summer 1983: while he was being interrogated, Alexander Ogorodnikov was shown a photograph of his wife Yelena Levashova and his son Dima on vacation in the Crimea. "Just one signature and you're a free man. And that's not all. We'll take you immediately by plane to your wife and son. You can be with them tonight."

March 1987: Alexander Ogorodnikov shortly after his release with dissident Yuri Fedorov. Fedorov was sentenced to fifteen years in prison in 1970 for attempting to hijack an airplane to Israel. Fedorov later emigrated to the United States.

1987: meeting of Alexander Ogorodnikov (third from the left) with a delegation from the Italian Catholic Comunità di Sant'Egidio in Moscow.

12 January 1988: Alexander Ogorodnikov (right) with the released Jewish dissident
Joseph Begun, one week before Begun left for Israel.

1O DOWNING STREET

THE PRIME MINISTER   31 March 1987

Dear Mr. Ogorodnikov,

    I just wanted to write while I am in Moscow to say how
very pleased and happy I was to learn of your release. Our
joy cannot match that which your family and many friends will
feel, but is nonetheless most sincere.

    I was very sorry indeed that it has not proved possible
to meet you during my visit, but virtually every moment of my
day has been fully taken up by official engagements. But I
can assure you that you have been, and will continue to be
very much in my thoughts. I send you my warmest regards and
best wishes.

Yours sincerely

Margaret Thatcher

Mr. A. Ogorodnikov

A letter from Margaret Thatcher to Alexander Ogorodnikov.

1987: meeting of Alexander Ogorodnikov (right) and the Orthodox monk Athanasius Hart in Moscow. In December 1986, Hart organized a fasting action for Ogorodnikov's release at Saint James Church in Westminster, London.

August 1989: founding congress of the CDUR in Moscow. Next to Alexander Ogorodnikov (left) is Vitaly Savitsky of Leningrad.

1989: visit of Alexander Ogorodnikov to the Capitol in Washington, D.C., with Congressman Frank Wolf.

January 1989: Alexander Ogorodnikov with the Anglican priest Dick Rodgers (right), who collected money in the British city of Birmingham to purchase the printing press.

Winter 1990-91:
food distribution in
the open air shortly
before the opening of the
soup kitchen on Khoro-
shevskoye Shosse.

Winter 1990-91:
distributing food in
the open air to two home-
less children shortly
before the opening
of the soup kitchen on
Khoroshevskoye Shosse.

1991: visit of a British parliamentary delegation to the soup kitchen on Khoroshevskoye Shosse. The banner reads "Christian Democratic Union of Russia."

August 1991: Alexander Ogorodnikov takes a picture of demonstrators gathering around the White House during the attempt to break the reactionary coup.

Spring 1991: Alexander Ogorodnikov meets Dutch Prime Minister Ruud Lubbers at a meeting of the Christian Democrat International.

1991: a bishop of the Armenian Church visits the Armenian class at the CDUR school in Moscow.

1991: congress of the Christian Democrat International with Alexander Ogorodnikov (middle) and Anthony de Mees (right).

1992: Alexander Ogorodnikov at his desk at home.

December 1993: meeting with the volunteers who helped with the CDUR election campaign.

1996: the Island of Hope shelter in Moscow. The children and a few volunteers enjoying a meal together.

January 1998: visit of a delegation of American congressmen to the Island of Hope shelter. Next to Alexander Ogorodnikov (second from the left) are American Congressmen Christopher Smith and Tony Hall (third and fifth from the left). The banner reads "Organization for Christian Charity."

Summer 1998: Alexander Ogorodnikov in the overgrown cemetery of Perm-36 concentration camp. There are no names on the crosses marking the graves.

2003: Alexander Ogorodnikov at a congress of the Catholic organization Kairos in the Italian city of Bari, where he was given a cross of the Apostolic Nuncio of the Catholic Uniates of Belorus as a token of appreciation for his years of dedicated service.

May 2008: the shelter in Buzhorova is partly destroyed by an act of arson.

March 2008: Alexander Ogorodnikov during his second visit to the former concentration camp Perm-36.

November 2009: the shelter in Buzhorova after the completion of the reconstruction.

to prevent the country from being debarred for abuse of psychiatry for political purposes.

After Ogorodnikov's prolonged protests against the prison authorities because they refused to give him his Bible back, Ogorodnikov was once again locked up the *shizo* on November 15, 1983. At that time of year the outside temperature usually dropped to about twenty to thirty degrees below zero (Celsius); it was brutally cold in his cell because of a broken window and a breakdown in the central heating system. All he was wearing was a cotton T-shirt; the guards kept an eye on him by looking through the little window in the cell door, hoping he would get seriously ill. But Ogorodnikov was not at all bothered by the cold, thanks to his fervent prayer. After a while he felt such intense heat within him that he burst into spontaneous tears of joy and happiness. The next day the guards noticed to their amazement that his body still felt warm.

At the end of December 1983, Ogorodnikov, who was in the *shizo* again at the time, received a letter from his mother-in-law, even though that was strictly forbidden by prison regulations. "You've ruined all our lives," she wrote in a bitter tone. "Because of you I've lost my job and we were not given permission to move from our two-room apartment to a larger place. I have only one wish: that you die as soon as possible. Only then will we and Yelena and Dima finally be free." Back in the camp, Ogorodnikov went on a hunger strike once again, resulting in his being force-fed in late January 1984.

When he was not spending periods of time in the *shizo*, the PKT, and the hospital, Ogorodnikov did not escape hard labor. He worked on the production of parts for irons, sewing gloves, metal picture frames, and uniforms. But he was mainly involved in lumber processing. The heaviest work took place in the woods: chopping down trees and transporting them to the sawmill. The long working days were extremely taxing because of the constant malnutrition, the lack of experience, and the use of defective materials. Because of the paltry remuneration and frequent punishments, the prisoners were forced to work as hard as they could.

On March 1, 1984, Ogorodnikov began working in the panel section, where the production quota had just been raised. Because he was not able to make the required quota, he was assigned the lowest food ration as punishment: norm 9b. In the months of March and April 1984 he fainted three times from hunger. When he fainted the first time, Pchelnikov, the camp doctor, refused to grant him temporary time off. Ogorodnikov called him a "tyrant" and was punished for this by not being allowed to make any purchases in the camp store for the rest of the month.

On April 27, 1984, Ogorodnikov fainted again at work. He was given a sedative and taken to the *shizo*. There he had a nervous collapse, broke the window of his cell, and slit his wrists. Fellow inmates heard him screaming at night. He woke up a few times from the cold but kept falling back to sleep. As punishment for his suicide attempt, Ogorodnikov was kept ten days longer in the *shizo*. The camp administrators told Ogorodnikov's parents that he had been transferred to a camp hospital as a result of "wearing out his own body with all the hunger strikes." They did not say a word about his suicide attempt.

CHAPTER SEVEN

Hitting Bottom

Mikhail Gorbachev Comes to Power

All this time, Ogorodnikov was cut off from news of the outside world. General Secretary Yuri Andropov died on February 9, 1984, and four days later, on February 13, the baton was passed to seventy-three-year-old Konstantin Chernenko, who was already seriously ill. He died ten months later, and on March 11, 1985, Mikhail Gorbachev became the Communist Party's general secretary. During the first months of his regime, Gorbachev attempted to reduce the excessive vodka consumption in the Soviet Union by launching an anti-alcohol campaign.

But in Ogorodnikov's life in Perm-36, not much changed: he spent three days in the *shizo* again for refusing to work on Easter Sunday, April 19, 1985. Because he very much wanted to go to confession, he prayed to Seraphim of Sarov, a Russian saint and the most important of the Russian Orthodox *startsi* (spiritual leaders) of the nineteenth century. While praying, Ogorodnikov had the feeling that he was being touched by a *soutane,* which would have been normal in the Orthodox practice of confession. Immediately, his sense of desolation vanished. In the Gulag he came to realize that earlier, when he was still free, he had not prayed with enough intensity. But what he missed most of all was gripping religious literature and contacts with spiritual figures.

One day, while in the camp library, Ogorodnikov discovered the Russian translation of the novel *Franny and Zooey,* by the American writer J. D. Salinger. In this novel he unexpectedly came in contact with the wisdom of a wandering nineteenth-century Russian pilgrim who constantly and silently prayed the Jesus Prayer: "Lord Jesus Christ, Son of God, have mercy on me, a sinner." After a while, the pilgrim's prayer began to "pray itself," following the rhythm of his breathing and heartbeat. The pilgrim prayed not only during the day but at night as well. From that moment on, Ogorodnikov began to pray the Jesus Prayer silently and ceaselessly. Gradually he began to experience spiritual detachment and relief and no longer felt the gnawing hunger. Because of the constant serene smile on his face, the guards thought he was becoming demented or trying to provoke them.

Yet he could not distance himself from the horrors of Perm-36. On April 26, 1985, the Armenian dissident Ishtshan Mkrtchian committed suicide in the isolation cell. It took a few weeks before the other prisoners began to become restless because of his exceptionally long absence. When they asked the prison authorities about the fate of their colleague, they were told that Mkrtchian had been unexpectedly admitted to the hospital. At that moment everyone knew that he had taken his own life. Mkrtchian was buried like a dog in the camp cemetery, which was located over four miles away in the woods.

On May 24, 1985, Ogorodnikov was accused of "disturbing the peace" because he supposedly had influenced his fellow inmates by preaching to them during a tea break in the barracks. When he heard that another investigation was being prepared against him for violating Article 188, Paragraph 3 of the Penal Code, he went on a three-day hunger strike. On July 3, 1985, Ogorodnikov was put in the isolation cell once again for urgently asking for help for a fellow inmate who was seriously ill. When he returned to the camp, he was told the content of the charge that had brought him this punishment: "exercising an extremely negative influence on the prisoners," "an unprincipled attitude toward work" (though he was fulfilling the required production quota at the time), "actively promoting religious propaganda," and "hindering the political-pedagogical process."

On September 4, 1985, Vasil Stus died in Perm-36 following a severe beating. Stus was a Ukrainian poet and human rights activist. Four days later, Ogorodnikov began another hunger strike. He asked for a Bible, and during his stay in the PKT he protested the fact that his reading matter, work clothing, and bedding had been taken from him. On November 4, 1985, all the prisoners began a hunger strike, as they did every year to commemorate the life of Yuri Galanskov, the publisher of the literary magazine *Phoenix*, who had died that day in 1972 in a labor camp in Mordovia. A special KGB representative, who was, in fact, in charge of

Perm-36, told Alexander that his term of five years of exile would begin immediately if he would stop participating in these common actions. His fellow inmates advised him to accept this concession. But at that point Ogorodnikov was beyond compromises. He wanted to serve as an example to the younger prisoners who had recently arrived in the camp, and he knew that the Soviet regime never made compromises.

Finally, Ogorodnikov had to pay the piper. On November 15, 1985, five days before his sentence was over and his period of exile was about to begin, examining magistrate Shchukin of the KGB in Perm-36 officially charged him with "violating camp rules" under Article 188, Paragraph 3 of the Penal Code. He was immediately transferred to the city prison in Perm. To protest this action, Ogorodnikov began a hunger strike, but that was punished by four days incarceration in the *kartser* for "ungrounded refusal to consume food."

His mother, who had traveled to Perm-36 to accompany her son to his place of exile, spent days of uncertainty wondering about his fate. Only after Alexander had arrived at the prison in Chusovoy (about sixty miles away) on November 19, 1985 — in connection with the preliminary investigation of the new case being brought against him — did she learn that his exile had been temporarily postponed. During the drive to Chusovoy, a trunk containing 150 articles and books that Ogorodnikov had collected over the years was mysteriously lost. As soon as he arrived, he was locked up in the *kartser* for four days, and at the end of the preliminary investigation his personal notes and two homemade crosses were stolen from his cell in Chusovoy.

To protect himself from the biting cold in his cell — all he was wearing was thin underwear and a cotton prison outfit — he tried to move around as much as possible. He also prayed unceasingly, but, to his disappointment, it did not produce the same salutary effect that it had earlier. Finally, he became ill. On January 8, 1986, Ogorodnikov was taken by *voronok* to the Perm city prison. Because he did not keep his hands behind his back while being escorted by the prison director, he was immediately locked up in the ice-cold *kartser*. He learned from a letter sent by his mother that Vladimir Poresh had been given an early release on February 22, 1986, after his case had been reviewed — an unprecedented development in the history of the Soviet regime. But at that moment Alexander was focusing all his attention on preparing for his new trial. In reconstructing and analyzing his prison term (seven years and four months), Ogorodnikov calculated that he had spent a total of 659 days on hunger strikes, 411 days in a *kartser* or *shizo,* had been locked up three times in the PKT, and had received not a single visitor or package in all of that time. He had been denied the right to buy merchandise in the shop twenty-nine times, and his cross had been yanked off his neck thirty times.

"You're Never Getting Out of Here"

On March 11, 1986, Ogorodnikov was still in the Perm city prison, where, unlike the other prisoners, he was denied permission to go to the toilet and was refused drinking water. In addition, the wardens threw his cross out the window. Two days later he was transported to Chusovoy, where his trial would take place. When the trial began, Ogorodnikov asked that his case be postponed because there was no lawyer present to defend him — to which he had a legal right. His request was granted. This was a purely tactical maneuver on Ogorodnikov's part, since a lawyer's role was strictly symbolic in the Soviet administration of justice. When the trial finally began on April 3, 1986, Ogorodnikov immediately declined the services of the lawyer who had been assigned to him. Prisoners and guards who had been carefully selected by prison authorities testified during the trial about how he had systematically disregarded the orders of the camp personnel and broken the camp rules. (One of the guards, who fiercely lashed out at him, surprised him many years later: in March 2008, while paying a visit to the Perm-36 concentration camp, which had by then been turned into a museum, Ogorodnikov discovered that this guard had been given a job there.)

Unlike the situation at the two previous trials, the courtroom in remote Chusovoy was almost empty. Except for a few KGB agents, the only others present were Ogorodnikov's mother and his aunt Vera. The trial proceeded without any emotional displays. He was sentenced to three years of labor camp with a strict regimen, followed by the five years of internal exile from his previous conviction. After the sentencing, Shchukin, the KGB investigator in Perm, sneered at Ogorodnikov: "Have no illusions," he said. "You're never getting out of here!"

The constant threat of new convictions was, of course, one of the psychological tools the Soviet system used to break prisoners down mentally. But this time the KGB gave Alexander's parents the same message, and as a result the Christian Seminar house in Redkino had to be sold.

Furthermore, Alexander's wife, Yelena Levashova, was given the message that she had better look for another husband.

Shortly thereafter, Ogorodnikov had a few more psychological blows to absorb. Boris Razveyev of Ufa (the capital of the Bashkir Autonomous Soviet Socialist Republic, and since 1992 an autonomous republic), who had broken down, already in 1981, during an interrogation, and had been back in the Gulag since January 1984, publicly renounced his faith on April 8, 1986, via TASS, the Russian press agency. That same evening, he broadcast a personal message on prime-time television and in the trade union publication *Trud* (Work) that accused Ogorodnikov of raping and living with a minor. But the worst blow to Ogorodnikov was the loss of the forty-five notebooks in which he had carefully written down his poems, thoughts, and prayers during the preceding years.

Imprisonment Takes Its Toll

In accordance with the new sentence, Ogorodnikov was put aboard the next prisoner train — again, in the notorious Stolypin cars, often coupled to regular train cars — and taken to a camp in the region of Khabarovsk in the Far East, near the port of Vladivostok, close to the Russian-Chinese border. Compared to the prison in Khabarovsk, where Ogorodnikov had been sent for a short time in 1979, the regimen in this camp was considerably stricter. This prison camp, where between two and three thousand detainees were being held at the time, was entirely in the hands of criminal gangs. The prisoners were forced to forfeit a portion of everything they bought in the camp store to the gang leader, who then distributed the booty among the needy prisoners of his gang.

Because of his reputation and record of service in the Gulag, Ogorodnikov enjoyed a fair amount of respect among his fellow inmates; but it soon became apparent that moving to this backwater was more than he could handle. The seven and a half years of undernourishment were beginning to take their toll, not only physically (his remaining teeth rotted away one by one), but also mentally. He was increasingly tormented by hallucinations and delusions. Sometimes he would suddenly imagine that he was smelling fragrant soup, or that he had slit his wrists and drunk his own blood, or that he had put out his own eyes and was about to fry them in a pan. Ultimately, he sank into a deep depression.

In late May 1986, Ogorodnikov summoned all his courage and wrote two letters of farewell. These were smuggled out of the camp via the network that he had managed to build up in Khabarovsk. The first letter was addressed to his mother.

Mama!

Your silence — in response to my enforced silence, which stifles my voice behind the thick walls of the punishment cell — is tacit support of my persecutors. You only began to show signs of alarm when one and a half years had passed since you had had a letter from me. The relatives of other prisoners raise a hue and cry if so much as a month passes without their receiving any news of the prisoner. You realize, don't you, how important it is that every word from me be made public as quickly and as broadly as possible? My future depends in great measure on the action that you are prepared to undertake. Prisoners whose relatives are active on their behalf, who don't let the world forget about their plight, are not only the ones who are released when their sentences expire, but they also get better treatment in the camps because the KGB is forced to take some notice of international public opinion.

I am the only prisoner here who receives only one letter a year. In the past eight years I have received a total of only four or five letters from you. Other prisoners receive that much in a week. I am an Orthodox Christian and the Russian Orthodox Church is behind me. Nationalists sometimes say to me, "Where is she, then, your Holy Russia? Has she abandoned her own?" I know that some letters written to me by friends have been confiscated. I have also learned that letters have been sent to me by total strangers. At the same time, with the exception of one letter from Sasha Shchipkova, I have heard nothing from my Christian Seminar friends. Of course, maybe these letters have been confiscated, too, but the fact that nobody but you and Aunt Vera bothered to come to my trial seems to speak for itself.

Sometimes it's almost as if I have to learn to live with the idea that no one is interested in my fate or my well-being — except God. I feel so alone and so forgotten. The less publicity a person receives, the more vulnerable he becomes. You really don't have to be afraid of publicizing my case far and wide. It won't have any impact on the KGB's attitude toward you. Since my arrest I have had only fragmentary information about the Seminar, which presumably has ceased to exist. Have you had house searches? What did they take? What happened to the last photos that were taken before my arrest, especially the wedding photos? Only someone who has spent time here can understand how I value every word I get from you.

Because of your passivity, the authorities are so certain of your indifference to my fate that they go to whatever lengths they like to humiliate me. Before my trial in April they threw me into a punishment cell for no reason whatsoever and shaved off my hair and beard, and as soon as the sentence was pronounced they brought me back to the punishment cell where the temperature was zero degrees Celsius. And this despite the fact that the Western governments and certainly the Western people are becoming increasingly aware of our distressing situation, and their interest is growing! All the time I spent in the isolation cell at Perm was clearly aimed at humiliating and breaking me in every conceivable way, which would not have happened if I had been in Leningrad or Kalinin. In Perm, for instance, I was thrown into the icy cellars for up to ten days at a time for merely refusing to squat on the floor with my hands behind my back during a search of my cell. If all the details of my outrageous treatment were to become known, my persecutors would have to exercise more restraint; this is something that has been proven in the cases of other prisoners. Until this happens, they can do what they like with complete impunity. Presumably, I will soon be sent to a camp for common criminals where I can look forward to more incarceration in punishment cells, more beatings, more solitary confinement.

So I urgently repeat my request. This is a decision I reached after much thought and suffering. You must understand that death appears to be the only way to end my unendurable agony. Death is my only release. I have already committed the grave sin of attempting to commit suicide: on the 1st, 9th and 17th of May 1984. I secretly cut my veins, but every time I was discovered, unconscious but still alive, and was nursed back to health with blood transfusions. So I beg of you again — please appeal to the Presidium of the Supreme Soviet to show me a measure of mercy by ordering my execution by firing squad. This is the only way for me to end the prospect of lifelong, painfully slow torture. As a result of continuous humiliation, a total absence of human rights and frequent incarceration in punishment cells I have been robbed of the living conditions that are considered normal for all human creatures.

I am systematically deprived of books and culture and am constantly tortured by hunger and cold. They even forbid me to pray, and my cross has been brutally torn from my neck many times. I have spent a total of 659 days on hunger strikes to protest their refusal to let me have a Bible and a prayer book and to protest being locked up in the camp prison. All this is ruinous to my health, which has been deliberately wrecked step by step, so that my last flicker of hope and life is beginning to fade. This life has turned into a nightmare. It must be my fate to remain in isolation and be charged with endless crimes. I was forced into 659 days of hunger, just for the right to have a Bible. What this means in fact is a long, drawn-out murder behind thick, dark walls. I have absolutely no idea whether there was even one Christian anywhere who expressed public support for me during those days of hunger strike, and the thought that maybe there wasn't terrifies me.

Officially there are still three years of camps and five of internal exile before me, but Shchukin, the investigator in Perm, has promised me more. He showed me a file of materials they are already preparing for further charges against me, this time for "anti-Soviet agitation and propaganda" which means a further ten years of camps plus five of exile. And despite this, there is only silence. A human being is being tortured to such an extent that death seems a welcome deliverance — yet few seem to care one way or another. They shoot overworked horses when they collapse, don't they? So why am I being deprived of the chance to die? Why am I doomed to a life of torment? Suicide is a terrible sin, but if the public prosecutor orders my execution he'd be putting me out of my misery. Why shouldn't I be allowed to ask to be put to death? Mama, if you have a grain of compassion, then please convey my request to the Presidium, and make sure that all people of good will do the same.

Only the full glare of publicity can alter my fate, and that of others in the same situation. Only this can restrain the hands of those who otherwise feel free to subject me to every conceivable atrocity. Only the incorruptible light of day can force lawlessness to cease its dark dealings and to give up altogether.

If I am soon to be sent to a camp for common criminals, please realize that in fact I will be thrown into an ocean of lawlessness . . . where I will be robbed of even that moral support that the political prisoners are still able to provide each other to a certain extent. It also means that I will constantly be locked up for shorter or longer periods of time in the shizo and the PKT, and that they really will do all they can to break me, both physically and mentally — including stirring up criminals against me. Besides endless hard labor, even on days off, they make you march around like soldiers, single file, to the dining area and back again. Taking bread back to the barracks is strictly forbidden. And every day you have to attend political education sessions. You are punished for the least little thing, even for a badly made bed. You have no rights whatsoever. Of course, the Lord alone knows what will happen to us. My only hope is in the mercy of God. May this hope survive, intact and immortal, the more so because the camp regime has become even more heartless and cruel, to the extent that now it is impossible not to break the rules.

I have been told, "Get this into your thick skull: if we can't get you to confess, you'll never leave prison." So, my dear ones, this means a life sentence, provided they keep their word. The Lord alone is holding in His hand the last flicker of life within me and is granting me a faint ray of hope.

My wife Lena will finally have to come to a decision, because it's clear that they're going to keep me in prison for the rest of my life. She can still write to me once a year, even if she no longer wants to be my wife. I certainly am not rejecting her, for "what God has joined together, let no man put asunder." But she must make a decision either way. As for my nine-year-old son, Dima, I have great hopes. I pray that he will start writing to me, too. I am very much afraid that because of his home situation — where they are extremely hostile to both me and to the Church — he will be discouraged from trying to contact me. I pray that his soul will not become overgrown by weeds.

I do not even know whether Dima has been taken to church for Holy Communion. Probably not, since Lena hasn't said anything about it. Does he wear a cross around his neck — the visible symbol of our allegiance to God? Probably not, I'm afraid.

During those 659 days, in addition to the gnawing hunger you're also tormented by the illusion of the taste of food in your mouth. When you're on a hunger strike it's extremely important that you keep moving, even though it takes an enormous effort just to turn in bed or get up. In the punishment cell the weakness brought on by hunger is aggravated by extreme cold. When I spent two months on a hunger strike in a punishment cell from December 1983 until February 1984, the ceiling and walls of the cell were entirely covered with ice. My only witnesses were God and the maliciously grinning wardens. The Christian Church has created an immense civilization and a deep spiritual culture over the past two thousand years, but where is the Christian brotherhood, and the love and compassion for one's neighbor, which, in Dostoevsky's opinion, was supposed to be uppermost in the life of every Christian?

I have the distinct impression that the Christian world beyond the prison walls knows nothing about my protest fasts. I ought to point out that my hunger strikes were not meant to secure my release from prison! No! My only purpose was to obtain a Bible, a prayer book and a cross, which would enable me to address myself to the source of Divine Revelation. All of Patriarch Pimen's declarations about freedom of religion in our country are negated by the fact that all these things are systematically denied me.

I beg you all: get someone, anyone, to speak out in my defense and call on all Christians to pray for my sinful soul and the alleviation of my punishment. That is the only thing that could have any influence, and would benefit the religious renaissance in Russia. Then the Church would also feel called to intervene on behalf of the persecuted and to expose the persecutors. Who dares take on this responsibility? Isn't there a single compassionate soul left in the world? Has love become so scarce? Do I not deserve just a little attention and justice?

What's in store for me now? Only God knows. I'm locked up in a cell with violent criminals, most of them imprisoned for murder, who indirectly try to provoke me into a conflict with them. One of them, who has already murdered two people, has openly threatened to kill me. He's awaiting execution by firing squad and keeps bragging that it doesn't make any difference whether he's shot for killing three people or two. Whenever I go to bed I never know whether I'm going to wake up in the morning. I rely only on the will of God.

I've had the cross torn from my neck thirty times. Is it not possible to appeal to the members of Western churches to take it upon themselves to ensure that I receive a Bible and a prayer book? Even if it's in English, French or German? Why wouldn't the universal Christian Church send a word of support to one of her persecuted sons? Errant and sinful, but a son nonetheless.

It is terrible to realize that you are of no use to anyone, that you are doomed to lose your life without compassion, in total oblivion. That you are going to lose your life, which is still full of energy. That you must endure hunger and cold, without books, in dark cells where even the sacred gift of God — life itself — has degenerated into agony.

I embrace and kiss you. May the Lord keep you!
Sasha, May 1986

Obviously desperate, Ogorodnikov explicitly asked to be executed twice in this letter, but the real thread running through it was a cry for attention and a plea to make his case known in the West — the ultimate lifeboat. The fact that he had tried to commit suicide three times, and that in three places he talks about his fear of being transferred to a camp for common criminals, is an indication of his complete mental collapse.

In writing this letter, Ogorodnikov was fully aware that it might be intercepted by the KGB and might never reach the West. Thus he consciously mentioned the three suicide attempts. He was indirectly letting the KGB know that he had reached the end of his rope. If he had written, "I only slit my wrists as a means of protest," which was truly the case, the secret service would have increased the pressure on him even further. They did not understand that a Christian is not allowed to commit suicide.

In a second letter, written to his friends, Ogorodnikov gave a detailed description of the depressing camp regime.

For proven violation of the camp regime, with which I have often been falsely charged, I was repeatedly placed in isolation in the camp prison, or PKT. And now I've been sentenced to another three years for the same offense. By repeating and intensifying the punishment, the regime becomes the alpha and omega of correctional punitive measures for those in prison. The regime deprives people of their freedom of choice, makes moral conduct impossible and forbids, under penalty of harsh punishment, any display of such Christian stirrings of the heart as love, charity, compassion and defense of the persecuted.

The chief focus of the regime's hatred is God, the free spirit, the word, and the universal need of a form of culture. Every written thought, every summary of a book, Soviet or otherwise, every scrap of paper with writing scribbled on it, is immediately confiscated. Just as all my notebooks were. Over the past seven years I had carefully written down my thoughts in them on a number of topics: philosophy, philology, theology and history. The books also contained the prayers and Bible passages that I had written down from memory as well as my own poems and a large number of exercises for my foreign language study. About forty-five notebooks in all.

The basis for these repressive measures is exhausting, compulsory slave labor, which is rewarded by a meager ration and the ever-present camp gruel. The strict camp regime, along with the meaningless, mechanical, monotonous and sweaty forced labor with its absurdly high work quotas, reduces you to a docile automaton. If you leave your post for only three minutes, even if you've fulfilled your daily quota, it's seen as a serious violation and may result in immediate incarceration in the "shizo," or isolation cell. All this — and the feeling that you're part of an insane machine — torments you, robs you of your lust for life, and deadens you totally. The days gradually turn into a tiring, endless, overwhelming nightmare. The system is set up in such a way that after work you have neither the will nor the energy to spend the remaining brief time on something like "self-education." With the mind-numbing work, the strict camp regime, the meager rations, the continuous sleep deprivation, and the deadly uniformity, there's nothing left of your lofty calling to be a reflection of the image and likeness of God. You're reduced to the dull, apathetic status of a slave, or perhaps an animal who is only capable of stuffing his hungry belly, impulsively and instinctively, whenever he has the chance.

The camp regime is organized so ingeniously that it's impossible not to violate it. A violation can be provoked at any time, which means that the regime has everyone fully in its power. The "zek" hasn't the slightest degree of self-defense and is therefore fully subject to the arbitrary rule that prevails here. Even the most minor violation can result in being locked up in the isolation cell — a favorite means of "re-education" among the guards.

Tightly packed together in a closed, dark room, with a sense of utter hopelessness, totally cut off from the world, isolated in the dark and in a deathly silence that is broken from time to time by the rattle of keys and the cursing of the guards, shivering and frozen to the marrow by the incredible cold, measuring the long and exhausting days into tiny bits . . . you become more and more aware of just how much your flesh is affected by your spirit. At that point you feel like nothing but a small, pitiful creature being torn apart by an overpowering sense of hunger and cold.

This is how the inventors of this new anthropology deal with us. They have taken hunger and cold — the traditional tortures of the Gulag — and added to them the factor of time, so that life, the most sacred gift of God, slowly but surely becomes a curse.

Both of the above letters were successfully smuggled out of the camp. But would these urgent messages ever reach the West? In the meantime, daily life in the camp went on.

"God Will Not Be Mocked!"

Despite the fact that Major Grinko, deputy commander of the camp in Khabarovsk, had given Alexander permission to wear a cross, on August 6, 1986, a camp official, during the daily morning roll call, ordered him to remove his cross immediately. Ogorodnikov refused.

"Take that cross off! Now!" snarled the official, who wanted to make an example of him in front of the assembled prisoners.

"I will not comply with your order," Ogorodnikov answered, "because what you are asking of me is an infringement of my rights." When the official repeated his order for the third time, Ogorodnikov responded with these words: "I am a Christian. Therefore, I am expected to let the Lord prevail over men."

"Take that cross off!" barked the official again.

"I will never, ever take this cross off," was Ogorodnikov's resolute response. "This cross is a symbol of my faith. And I am determined to confess my faith openly, in front of everyone. So I'm warning you that the Lord my God must never be humiliated. I myself mean nothing, but I am a son of the Lord. When you oppose me, you oppose Him. I'm warning you!"

The camp official had Ogorodnikov dragged off to the interrogation cell. There a few prison guards attacked him in an attempt to tear the cross from his neck, but he popped it into his mouth. Then the wardens hit him in the face, but Ogorodnikov prayed as loudly as he could. Finally the official in charge of the camp screamed at him, "*I* am your Lord. Pray to me."

Unable to remove the cross, the guards decided to spray him with gas. But because the interrogation room was quite small, the gas overcame them as well. Then one of the wardens pulled out a pair of American handcuffs, the kind that get tighter and tighter the more pressure is applied to them. Ogorodnikov could not keep them from handcuffing his wrists, one by one. He was then forced to lie on the floor, and a couple of wardens held his arms on the floor while two others jumped up and down on them. The swelling against the handcuffs became so great that

Ogorodnikov's wrists almost broke. He passed out, and the guards were then able to take the cross out of his mouth.

Hours later, Ogorodnikov was awakened by the pain. His hands were swollen, and his arms were numb. Feeling gradually returned to his right hand, but his left hand would remain partially numb for the rest of his life — a constant reminder of the Gulag.

In no time, everyone in the camp knew what had happened to him. A prisoner in an adjoining cell unraveled his woolen sock and made a cross out of the wool. He then folded up a piece of paper into a tube and put the cross inside. Standing on the shoulders of two of his cell-mates, he blew the cross through an opening in the ceiling that was meant for electrical lighting cables. Like a floating arrow, the cross landed on Ogorodnikov's lap.

Alexander filed a complaint with the Public Prosecution Service, which was responsible for supervising the camps. This had never been done before, since anyone who exercised his "right" to do so was sure to be given extra punishment for using "unacceptable," "libelous," or "anti-Soviet" language, or for making "ungrounded claims."

Ogorodnikov wrote:

I know that you serve the same idols as those who are torturing me. This statement is a profession of my faith in the Lord Jesus Christ and His Most Pure Mother. It is also a warning to my persecutors: God will not be mocked, and the gates of hell will not prevail against the Church — the pillar and ground of truth. This has already been demonstrated in the past by two thousand years of persecution, trials and heresies against the Church. Persecution only purifies the Body of Christ, and our faith is tempered in its furnace. The Lord will hear our groans and the gnashing of our teeth, and He will strengthen His children with spiritual power.

The groans of Christian martyrs form the background to the American-Soviet agreement on increasing contacts and exchanging delegates and information on the situation in the two countries. But the Church is outside political structures. Liberal Western appeasement policies give state atheism a free hand but do not offer a helping hand to prisoners of conscience, who are only being incarcerated for their creed or their convictions. In isolation and in solitary confinement for our principles and our faith, we will continue to confess the saving gospel of the risen Christ and defend the image of God from every attack of the devil.

Even before the complaint was sent, however, the man responsible for this incident was arrested, probably for another offense. He was placed in a punishment cell with violent criminals, who attacked him ferociously. The man was stabbed several times and slowly bled to death.

When Ogorodnikov's two farewell letters finally reached the West in late 1986, six months after they had been sent, they immediately triggered a tidal wave of reactions. Orthodox Action, a charitable organization of the Australian ROCOR diocese, made the following appeal to its parishioners: "Every day before we sit down at the dinner table, lie down in a warm bed or when we admire our children — let us remember Alexander; enjoying our peace and freedom — let us remember Alexander; tearing off a page of the daily calendar — let us remember Alexander; and imagining, for a moment at least, that he is our son, brother or husband — let us prayerfully remember him. If our conscience is still alive, if love and Christian compassion for our neighbor has not yet left us, let us publicize Alexander Ogorodnikov's true situation, let us give him our support not once or twice, but as many times as it will take to contribute to his release."

In Britain, Jubilee Campaign, a Christian human rights organization, distributed postcards and posters throughout the country featuring Ogorodnikov's picture. This nongovernmental organization, led by David Alton, professor of history at the University of Liverpool and a member of parliament for the Liberal Democrats, also sent appeals to the Soviet ambassador and to Prime Minister Margaret Thatcher. The "Iron Lady" responded by pressing Moscow for Ogorodnikov's release.

In November 1986, the Keston Institute published a forty-four-page brochure on the case. The brochure also contained an appeal to the West from a group of Russian Orthodox Christians in Moscow:

Your Christian delegates are keen on visiting our country; your Christian preachers return home with a host of pleasant memories; you are all inspired by the simple beauty of our churches and the numbers of people filling them. This picture lingers in your memory, evoking the best and warmest emotions. But we wish you to understand that what you have seen is the sum total of what is permitted to us. In all other aspects of our lives — family, social, political and cultural — we are not allowed to be Christians. We may only "perform our cult." However, the life of a Christian is not confined within church walls; there he receives the highest fulfillment of his Christian endeavors and finds the

starting point for all other aspects of his life. But it is precisely in those other spheres of life that we are not permitted to live by simple Christian feelings — to believe, to be merciful, to entreat, to defend, to love, to bring up children, to work and to teach. All these attempts are met by harsh persecution.

But even under our atheistic and totalitarian system there are those who do not fear to profess their faith openly, and to rise up in defense of human dignity despite the threat of persecution or even death. Alexander Ogorodnikov, organizer and leader of the Christian religious-philosophical Seminar in Moscow, has already spent seven and a half years in hard labor camps under inhuman conditions. Those of Alexander Ogorodnikov's letters that have reached us ominously reflect the unending and unrestrained acts of violence directed by the heartless servants of the regime at the innocent man in his isolation and complete defenselessness.

This situation — that is, when the State intentionally delays the ultimate death of a man who is isolated from the public view in a concentration camp but who persists nevertheless in confessing his Christian faith and insists on his right to possess a Bible and wear a cross — this situation, then, tells us incomparably more about the nature of the society in question than all the declarations about religious freedom which are intended for the gullible West and are broadcast either by the faithful servants of the State or by the hierarchs of the Orthodox Church who have forgotten about their duty to protect their flock.

We appeal to you, Christians! Raise your voice in defense of Alexander Ogorodnikov and, with all the means available to you in our free and democratic way of life, to try and secure his release and the repeal of the unjust sentences passed on him.

On December 1, 1986, the Anglican priest Richard Rodgers and the New Zealand Orthodox monk Athanasius Hart conducted a public action at Saint James's Church in Westminster, London. Hart built a cage in the church, put on a prison uniform, shaved his head and went on a hunger strike. Brochures, folders, and postcards urged people to write letters to the Soviet ambassador in London and to the Soviet leader, Mikhail Gorbachev. Support came from British parliamentarians, who came to the church to read from Scripture. During the night of December 23-24, 1986, a vigil took place in the presence of Orthodox Bishop Kallistos of Diokleia and the Anglican bishop of London, followed by a silent procession to the Soviet embassy. Images were broadcast by the television networks BBC, ITV, and CBS.

In Switzerland the socialist parliamentarian Richard Bäumlin and Pierre Aubert, minister of foreign affairs, decided to apply diplomatic pressure on the Soviet Union. Orthodox Christians in America called on all believers in the United States to write a letter to their congressional representative, urging him or her to take a firm stand against the violation of human rights in the Soviet Union and against its lack of respect for the Helsinki Accords. "Be sure to call attention to the Ogorodnikov case," they were advised, "and ask him to submit a request for release to the Soviet Union."

Pastor Charles Rush of Christ Church, an ecumenical congregation in Summit, New Jersey, started a letter-writing campaign. And on June 30, 1986, Ernest Gordon, the former dean of the chapel at Princeton University, and since 1981 the chairman of CREED (Christian Rescue Effort for the Emancipation of Dissidents) in Washington, D.C., during a hearing of the Congressional Human Rights Commission, added Ogorodnikov's name to the list of twenty-five prisoners to be given preferential treatment. *La Pensée Russe — Rousskaïa Mysl,* a Russian-language weekly published in Paris, and *Cahiers du Samizdat Tetradi Samizdata,* a Russian monthly published in Brussels, came out with the full text of both of Ogorodnikov's letters.

In the Netherlands, an organization called Open Doors, founded in 1955 and supporting persecuted Christians worldwide, carried on a campaign for Ogorodnikov's release. The Catholic Order of Malta adopted Ogorodnikov "as a prisoner." The camp in Khabarovsk was flooded with thousands of letters. Ogorodnikov knew nothing about these efforts, but he did feel mentally stronger, as if he were being carried by the prayers of so many people.

Three Slogans: Economic Intensification, *Glasnost,* and *Perestroika*

In the meantime, developments in the Soviet Union were gaining momentum. After the disaster at the Chernobyl nuclear power plant on April 26, 1986, Mikhail Gorbachev gave the signal for large-scale reforms; his rallying cry consisted of three concepts: economic intensification, *glasnost* (openness), and *perestroika* (restructuring). On October 11-12,

1986, Gorbachev met with President Ronald Reagan in the Icelandic capital of Reykjavík. The talks, which failed at the last moment, dealt with the mutual reduction of nuclear weapons. But Reagan also brought up the matters of the emigration of Soviet Jews, respect for human rights, and the plight of religious dissidents. Alexander Ogorodnikov's name was on the list of twelve persons whose release Reagan was requesting.

"We will not exploit their release, should it occur," said Reagan. "We will only express our gratitude." The Americans kept up the pressure. A few days after the summit, George Shultz, the U.S. secretary of state, said: "As long as the Soviet Union continues to violate human rights there will be no progress in the arms control talks."

Mikhail Gorbachev, who was still emphasizing the need for a "war against all religious manifestations" in November 1986, nonetheless began to doubt the usefulness of the Gulag. In January 1987 he asked the journalists in Russia to fill in the blanks in Soviet history. The general secretary, whose grandfathers had both done time in the Gulag, did not see the connection at first with the many thousands who were still in the camps. In his book *Perestroika: New Thinking for Our Country and the World,* Gorbachev does not mention prisoners of conscience.

But the pressure on Gorbachev continued. In an exchange of prisoners in 1986, Anatoly Sharansky was sent out of the country; soon afterward, Yuri Orlov, human rights activist and winner of the Nobel Prize for physics, immigrated to the United States. But the point of no return was reached on December 8, 1986, when Anatoly Marchenko died in prison in Chistopol, probably after having been given a dose of drugs during a hunger strike. The wave of negative publicity that followed — the statements made by his wife, Larisa Bogoraz, became known worldwide — led Gorbachev to decide to gradually free the political prisoners. On December 23, 1986, Andrei Sakharov and his wife, Yelena Bonner, were given an official pardon by Gorbachev and allowed to return to Moscow after six years of internal exile in Gorky.

In the camp at Khabarovsk in late December 1986, Ogorodnikov was visited by his mother and his brother, Raphael, for the first time since his incarceration in November 1978. They were told not to talk about current events, that doing so would put the rest of the visit in jeopardy. Even so, Alexander did detect that a great deal was going to be happening within a very short time. After the three-hour talk, they were all permitted to shake hands.

In late 1986, KGB boss Viktor Chebrikov concluded that the dissident movement had grown so weak that it could no longer do any harm. Therefore, early in February 1987, the Presidium of the Supreme Soviet decided to release a number of political and religious prisoners. In mid-January 1987, Ogorodnikov, much to his astonishment, was suddenly admitted to the camp hospital, where he was treated extremely well and given good food to eat. This obvious sudden change of attitude on the part of the camp administration, of course, made him suspicious that something was up. Then, on February 14, 1987, a military general appeared before him in full regalia and read aloud a letter in which General Secretary Mikhail Gorbachev personally ordered Ogorodnikov's release.

Ogorodnikov was so thunderstruck that he could no longer move his legs. Because he had failed to absorb the actual contents of the letter, the general read it again in the same solemn tone. Only then did it dawn on Ogorodnikov that he was going to be released.

Because he was being pardoned and thus was not being given amnesty, he had to sign a declaration promising that from then on he would no longer commit anti-Soviet acts. This Ogorodnikov refused to do. The camp directors, however, had no other choice than to let him go. His fellow prisoners refused to show up for the second work shift that day until the staff officially confirmed that Ogorodnikov was indeed being released.

"O Death, Where Is Thy Victory?"

On February 14, 1987, when Ogorodnikov, dressed in his prison rags, finally walked out the door after ninety-nine months in the Gulag, he cried out, "O death, where is thy victory? O grave, where is thy sting?" (1 Corinthians 15). His years in the Gulag had undermined him physically and psychologically, but he was not broken. His half-sister Ludmila and her husband, who lived in Khabarovsk, were waiting for him outside the camp. They told him that his release had been brought about by the personal interventions of British Prime Minister Margaret Thatcher and U.S. President Ronald Reagan.

Ogorodnikov spent his first days of freedom with Ludmila — to catch his breath. Overcome by emotions, he was constantly in tears. The nightmare was finally over. He could scarcely believe it. On the day of his release he learned from radio and television that the international Forum for a Nuclear-Free World, for the Survival of Humanity, was at that moment being held in Moscow, February 14-16, 1987, a meeting where

Andrei Sakharov was openly arguing for free emigration, freedom of expression, greater internal freedom of movement, and the release of political prisoners. During the forum, General Secretary Mikhail Gorbachev declared: "The broad democratization of our society is irreversible. May there be no more forgotten names or black pages in our history and literature. No names may be forgotten — and it is even more immoral to forget entire periods or to suppress the memories of those who lived, believed and worked under the leadership of the Party and in the name of socialism."

Did that mean that Ogorodnikov's years of suffering had not been in vain?

III

ISLANDS OF HOPE

CHAPTER EIGHT

Policies of Religious Tolerance

U pon arriving in Moscow on February 19, 1987, Ogorodnikov wrote a letter of thanks to everyone who had supported him:

> I bow my head with a deep sense of gratitude for your prayers and your patient struggle in defense of your Russian disciple of Christ. When you are in a concentration camp and you feel that your heart is beginning to fail, the hunger is gnawing at your stomach, the cold is numbing your body, and the despair is coursing through your blood, it's as if you have already been carried to your grave by an indifferent world and you're being flooded by waves of despair. But it was precisely in those devastating moments in that ice-cold cell that I physically felt the salutary warmth of your prayers and compassion, a power that connects us through a stream of spiritual energy as a result of our common experience of faith and the mysterious solidarity of brotherly unity.

Ogorodnikov also telephoned Bishop Hilarion of the Russian Orthodox Church Outside Russia (ROCOR) in New York City and Father Viktor Potapov, director of religious programming for the radio station Voice of America in Washington, D.C. And he went to Moscow to personally thank Andrei Sakharov.

Yet the initial euphoria quickly turned into disillusionment. In its efforts to poison his life, the KGB had brought his family to the brink of the abyss as well. Five days before his release, his wife, Yelena Levashova, had married another man. The surname of his son, Dima, had been changed to that of his mother, Levashov. At first Ogorodnikov was kept from seeing both Yelena and his son; the latter was now almost ten years old and was living with Yelena's parents, who refused to allow any form of contact with Alexander.

Shortly after his release, Ogorodnikov traveled to the Pskov-Pechory monastery to meet with his spiritual director, Father Ioann. The abbot, Gabriel Stebluchenko, who was a secret KGB agent, refused to let him in; but, thanks to an obliging monk, Ogorodnikov was able to clamber over the medieval walls at one o'clock in the morning by means of a thick rope.

Ogorodnikov was especially moved by the loving and sympathetic words that Father Ioann spoke to him: "Many people look up to you. You must serve as an example. A great deal depends on you now. You must not make any mistakes. A unique opportunity to gain more freedom is now presenting itself. We must use *perestroika* to our advantage."

Concerning his former wife, Father Ioann advised him: "You must forgive her. Give her the chance to come back to you." A few days later, Ogorodnikov had a meeting with Yelena Levashova, accompanied by her brand-new husband and a priest, Father Vladimir.

"I will always love you, Sasha," said Yelena. "But I can never go back to you. I know you through and through, and I know for sure that before long you'll resume your former activities. The KGB will arrest you again, and you'll end up back in prison. In the meantime, my life goes on. I can't wait any longer."

Because Yelena refused to go back to Alexander, their church-sanctioned wedding was immediately annulled by the attending priest. This meant that Alexander would be able to remarry in the church, should the opportunity ever arise, but not without the personal permission of the patriarch of the Russian Orthodox Church.

Every Release a Victory

Little seemed to have changed in Soviet society during Ogorodnikov's eight-and-a-half-year absence — at least not on the outside. The opening in the society that Mikhail Gorbachev had recently accomplished was still very narrow. Everyone lived with the firm conviction that the Communist regime would carry on for at least another hundred years. And fearing an implosion, the KGB kept an unrelentingly tight grip on the reins. For example, they used strong-arm tactics to suppress Jews demonstrating for the right to emigrate and for the release of their chairman, Joseph Begun. Those demonstrations had begun on February 9, 1987, on Arbat Street — in a shopping district in Moscow — and were held every day. On February 13, 1987, fifteen Jewish demonstrators were badly beaten by eighty plainclothes policemen.

The political dissidents were released in a mere trickle. Anatoly Koryagin, a psychiatrist and crusader against the abuse of psychiatry for political ends, left the Gulag on February 17, 1987. Joseph Begun followed two days later. In each of those cases the government resisted to the last moment; indeed, every release was a laborious struggle.

At the end of January 1987, Tatiana, the wife of Sergei Khodorovich — who from 1979 to 1983 had managed Alexander Solzhenitsyn's foundation to support Soviet prisoners and their families — received the message that her husband would be freed on February 14 under the condition that both of them would agree to emigrate. Tatiana reluctantly agreed to this compromise — out of sheer necessity because of her husband's critical state of health — and decided to quit her job. But when the promised date finally arrived, Sergei was still not released. Only after a campaign was carried on in the United States by several members of Congress, the International Society for Human Rights (ISHR), the Committee for the Defense of Persecuted Orthodox Christians (CDPOC), the Christian Rescue Effort for the Emancipation of Dissidents (CREED), and the Russian Orthodox Church Outside Russia (ROCOR), was Sergei Khodorovich finally allowed to leave the Gulag on March 17, 1987.

On that day, Andrei Sakharov and Yelena Bonner announced that eighty-six dissidents had returned to Moscow in the previous three months. On March 27, 1987, dozens of dissidents, Christian Seminar members, friends, and acquaintances got together in the apartment of Viktor Popkov to congratulate Alexander Ogorodnikov on his thirty-seventh birthday.

Ogorodnikov worked for the release of as many religious prisoners as possible, regardless of their creed. He gathered information on unknown prisoners of conscience and sent this material to the government, to foreign correspondents, and to Western politicians who were visiting the Soviet Union. Thus did George Schultz, the American secretary of state, receive a list of 180 names of Christians, Muslims, Jews, and Hare Krishna adherents who were still in the Gulag. Those who were being freed would be struck from his list.

Emigration No Option for Ogorodnikov

Ekaterina Vasil'eva, one of the most popular movie stars in the Soviet Union, happened to recognize Ogorodnikov on the street in Moscow a few days after his return, much to his surprise. Although they had never met, Vasil'eva admired him greatly. She took Ogorodnikov back to her apartment and let him spend the night there, in view of the fact that he had no place of his own since returning to Moscow and had been forced to find temporary housing with friends.

Vasil'eva managed to convince Ogorodnikov to wait for his son, Dima, at the school he attended. Having such a famous movie diva pay a visit to this gray suburb was an event in itself. But when Dima first saw Alexander, he shouted, "You're not my father! You're a criminal!"

Vasil'eva tried to change Dima's mind: "You mustn't believe what others say. Your father is an exceedingly good man."

But Dima said, "I want to be a Communist."

For Ogorodnikov, this first meeting with his son after eight and a half years was a genuine horror. It was very difficult for him to realize that his son had not been raised to be proud of his father or to respect him. Obviously, it was the result of Dima's spending most of his young life with his grandparents: they were the ones who were chiefly responsible for turning their grandson against his father. After this painful incident, Ogorodnikov began to give serious thought to the idea of emigrating — which many released prisoners of conscience were doing at that time. Anatoly Koryagin, for example, moved to Switzerland with his family. Anatoly Sharansky left for Israel, followed shortly by Viktor Brailovsky, a standard-bearer for the refusenik movement. And on January 18, 1988, Joseph Begun took the same step. In 1987 alone, 8,011 Jews left the Soviet Union, the highest number since 1979; indeed, one year later, in 1988, the Soviet Union issued 108,000 emigration permits.

Although the BBC announced that Ogorodnikov had received permission to emigrate, he did not, in the end, see it as an option. Despite his deteriorating family situation, he could not reconcile such an idea with his own conscience. The challenges in "his" Russia were just too great. An opportunity — small though it was — had presented itself to change the system from within, and he wanted to seize it with both hands.

The movie star Vasil'eva did what she could to get Ogorodnikov a passport. When he had left the Gulag, all he had been given was a document confirming his release. But all doors swung open for the star of cin-

ema; some officials even asked for her autograph. After a month and a half
— exceptionally fast by Soviet standards — Ogorodnikov once again pos-
sessed a passport. But he still did not have a residence permit to live in
Moscow. He applied for one, but the procedure was deliberately prolonged, partly due to KGB interference. This meant that Ogorodnikov was
permanently at risk of imprisonment for breaking the law covering internal passports. In mid-July 1987, he left Moscow for a while after receiving
actual threats. "Freed, but Fugitive" read the headline of an article in the
British *Buzz Magazine* in August 1987. In the interview under that head-
ing, Ogorodnikov described his new life as a free man: "I'm a stranger and
an outsider in my own country. As a non-official and illegal inhabitant in
my own city of Moscow, I can be arrested anytime and anywhere."

When he returned to the capital a few weeks later, Ogorodnikov kept
in constant touch with Western journalists, because such contacts — as
he had discovered in the 1970s — were his best life insurance. The more
press conferences he gave, the stronger his position was. He was repeatedly picked up by the police or the KGB, after which his friends would
immediately alert the foreign correspondents. Each time that happened,
Ogorodnikov would hammer away at the proper enforcement of the law.
According to the law, a suspect could be held in custody for only three
hours before a time-consuming administrative procedure had to be
started, something that the government was not keen on doing because
of Ogorodnikov's reputation. Feeling strengthened by the new wind that
was blowing through society during Gorbachev's time, he managed to
play this card — a "weak point" in the law that had been blatantly ignored
in the past — with great skill. "You can arrest me, but then you've got to
follow the rules down to the letter," he told the police laconically. Thanks
to this argument, he was always released after just a couple of hours.

Tension with Gleb Yakunin Mounts

No role of significance, however, was reserved in Soviet society for former dissidents. Their names had circulated only in the underground
press and in the West. In the tidal wave of changes inundating the country at the time, most of the dissidents stood at the back of the line, as if
there was no room for them. Foreign journalists and Western press agen-
cies approached Ogorodnikov repeatedly, but in his own country he was
barely known. Furthermore, within the new social context, the dissidents

had become each other's rivals. The smoldering internal tension, which for a long time had been stifled by the repression, now suddenly came to the surface.

Gleb Yakunin had been released from Perm-37 in 1985, and since then had lived in internal exile in the Yakut Soviet Socialist Republic (since 1992 it has been known as Yakutia, or Sakha). In mid-March 1987, Yakunin was granted amnesty by General Secretary Gorbachev, at which time he returned directly to Moscow, where he immediately appointed himself spokesman for the religious dissidents. Yakunin, who as a priest enjoyed a certain amount of social prestige, looked with envy at the activities being conducted by his coreligionist Ogorodnikov, sixteen years his junior, and at the good relationships the latter enjoyed with foreign journalists. When the Christian Committee for the Defense of the Rights of Believers in the Soviet Union was founded in 1976, the relationship between the two men had quickly cooled, and now — in 1987 — it cooled even further.

In his letters Yakunin called Ogorodnikov an extremist who was impossible to talk to. It was also hard for him to swallow the fact that Ogorodnikov had been given the Prize for Religious Freedom and Human Rights Activities in 1987, awarded in the United States. Ogorodnikov had not accepted that award in person, fearing that he would be denied reentry to the USSR upon his return. Instead, he picked it up later at the American embassy in Moscow.

Yakunin and his confidant, Markus Sergei, tried to discredit Ogorodnikov via a direct samizdat attack, an action that had been planned by the KGB, as it turned out later. The tension between Ogorodnikov and Yakunin escalated with the distribution of an article by Ogorodnikov on the persecution of the church in the Soviet Union. The idea for the article had been Ogorodnikov's, and he actively participated in writing the text. But Yakunin advised him not to sign the article — "You're far too radical, after all," he said — and when Ogorodnikov said he would anyway, Yakunin had the final version signed by twelve others, not including Ogorodnikov. Yakunin's aim was to isolate him internationally and put himself forward as the leader of the Christian dissidents. After Ogorodnikov informed Western journalists of what had really happened, *The New York Times* ran a front-page article with the headline "Schism in the Russian Christian Movement."

Shortly after his release from the Gulag, Ogorodnikov was given temporary shelter in the home of Viktor Popkov, a former member of the

Christian Seminar. The two had been reconciled since Popkov's negative testimony at Ogorodnikov's trial in 1980. But after a couple of months, Popkov gently hinted that Alexander should seek lodgings elsewhere. This hint followed a conversation between Yakunin and Popkov, Ogorodnikov later discovered. After leaving Popkov's apartment, Ogorodnikov spent each night at the home of a different friend or acquaintance, and this went on for quite some time.

As a result of this incident, the relationship between Ogorodnikov and Popkov cooled again. In the meantime, Popkov tried to ingratiate himself to the foreign guests who were always coming in search of Ogorodnikov, but did not know that he had left or where he was staying. Popkov also pocketed money that had been entrusted to him in good faith by foreign guests in Ogorodnikov's absence.

Due to the openness engendered by Gorbachev, more and more foreign politicians and religious leaders were coming to visit the Soviet Union; but numerous invitations to Ogorodnikov from the American, Dutch, German, and British embassies went missing during that chaotic time. For example, when Prime Minister Margaret Thatcher, during her visit to the Soviet Union, held a breakfast for a number of dissidents, including Joseph Begun, at the British embassy in Moscow on April 1, 1987, Ogorodnikov was not among them — even though Thatcher had sent him a personal letter. The fact that the British prime minister did not meet with the dissident whose release had been the object of such a struggle in the United Kingdom caused something of a stir in Britain. However, Ogorodnikov did meet with Prime Minister Jacques Chirac of France during the latter's visit to Moscow in May 1987. And when the monk Athanasius Hart visited Moscow, he gave Ogorodnikov the icon he had painted during his fast in December 1986 at Saint James's Church in London. In gratitude, Ogorodnikov gave Hart the "floating" cross that a prisoner in Khabarovsk had once made for him.

The strained relationship with Alexander's son, Dima, thawed somewhat after Ekaterina Vasil'eva invited a number of clowns and actors she knew to a party for Dima's tenth birthday. Dima could hardly believe that the move star had organized this especially for him. Once again she attempted to convince him of his father's good heart, after which Dima Ogorodnikov called him "father" for the first time. Years later, Vasil'eva was to enter a women's monastery. The British singer and songwriter Graham Ord wrote the song "Am I Forgotten?" which was inspired by Ogorodnikov's lengthy stay in the Gulag.

Policy of Religious Tolerance

Basically dissatisfied with the pious and introverted approach to faith in the Russian Orthodox Church, where the emphasis was mainly on the liturgy, fasting, and the use of icons and candles, Ogorodnikov attempted to breathe new life into the Christian Seminar. With a climate of openness to the Christian religion finally seeming to emerge in the Soviet Union, he pressed for an engaged and extroverted faith. In point of fact, after seventy years of dogmatic atheism, the systematic persecution of the Russian Orthodox Church was coming to an end. The activities of the Seminar were still closely monitored by the KGB, but agents no longer harassed its members. After two years of *glasnost, perestroika,* and tumult, the Orthodox Church in Moscow was rising like a phoenix from its ashes. The concept of *bogoiskatelstvo* (searching for God) was quickly becoming trendy among Russian intellectuals and young people. As the most important spiritual leader and most popular theologian in the Soviet Union, Father Alexander Men gave lectures and religious courses at the Moscow State Institute for History and Archives. Young people recorded his lectures and distributed the tapes.

One by one, churches, monasteries, synagogues, and mosques were returned to their rightful owners. They became beloved meeting places where *babushkas* could get together and reminisce about the time before the Revolution of 1917. These places also became centers for religious education. Yet, hanging over that spontaneous revival of religious life was still the black shadow of the past. The *nomenklatura* of the Russian Orthodox Church, many of whom had openly collaborated with the Communists, remained at their posts — just as before. The church synod did not respond to the request of six Orthodox dissidents, among them Gleb Yakunin, who called for the resignation of Patriarch Pimen I of Moscow, head of the Russian Orthodox Church. In an open letter, Ogorodnikov asked the patriarch and the synod to publicly apologize for their collaboration with the regime: "Only when the legacy of the past is shaken off can the Church resume its activities with a clean slate." In response to this, only one bishop offered his apologies for what had happened in the past.

In the meantime, Konstantin Kharchev, chairman of the Council for Religious Affairs and architect of the policy of religious tolerance, was sending mixed signals. Sometimes he encouraged Christians to disregard the ban on religious education and the practice of charity, and sometimes he cautioned them.

The Christian Seminar Organizes Relief Actions

When the Christian Seminar in Moscow started up again, only a handful of former staff members were involved. Because of faulty communication, Ogorodnikov had no idea where most of them had gone; for example, it was not until later that he learned that Tatiana Shchipkova had moved to Leningrad. Most of the new participants were socially engaged young people with a great spiritual hunger. The discussion of the role of the church in the future of society resulted in a number of articles. Ogorodnikov sent these articles to the Synod of Bishops of the Russian Orthodox Church, and they were also read aloud on Radio Liberty, the BBC, and Voice of America.

The Seminar strove for the full separation of church and state and remained loyal to the ecumenical approach that had been observed during the seventies:

"What we have in mind," said the Seminar, "is an authentic experience of faith, and our goal is a free Church and a free State. That does not mean a return to the state religion from before the 1917 Revolution, however. Our idea is a broad ecumenical movement of Orthodox as well as Catholics and Protestants."

Due to a lack of available meeting facilities, the meetings of the Christian Seminar always took place in the homes of members. As before, those who attended came from all over the Soviet Union. "There were three hundred at the most recent meeting," wrote the American professor James A. Scherer of the Lutheran School of Theology in Chicago in October 1988.

> You get the impression of a clandestine home party abuzz with subversive theological ideas, reminiscent of the underground solidarity that once characterized the party of Marx and Engels before it turned into the party of the official, established order and the entrenched bureaucracy.

With all the social developments that were taking place at the time, the Seminar began to focus more attention on the public dimension, some of what it had already been doing back in the 1970s. During the slow implosion of the Soviet empire, Moscow had begun to exert a strong attraction on the poor and needy from every corner of the country. Despite the compulsory residence permit policy, which enabled only a small number of outsiders to move into the capital, the population of Moscow increased from eight to ten million. In 1988, there was a migration of tens of thousands of Armenians, who had initially come to escape the violence of war-torn Nagorno-Karabakh, or Artsakh, a region in Azerbaijan where ethnic Armenians made up the majority. In late 1988 there was a new stream of refugees resulting from the severe earthquake of December 7, 1988, which had destroyed 40 percent of their homeland.

Yet, despite the massive need, charity played only a marginal role in Soviet society. It simply had never been an inherent element in the Orthodox soul. In addition, the initiatives and activities of the private charitable associations were strictly curbed by scores of government regulations and controls. Because some of these organizations had a suspicious aura about them — there were rumors that "black" money was being laundered there by the Russian mafia — they first had to convince the distrustful population of their bona fide character. In Leningrad, free food was distributed to single elderly persons and disabled Afghan veterans by a group of volunteers who formed around the writer Daniil Granin. In Moscow, the Center of the Holy Family, an initiative of the Catholic nun Teresa Kim (better known as "Sister Tank"), extended help to the homeless sick in the worst of the city slums. A couple of other Orthodox voluntary organizations did exist, such as an initiative of Archimandrite Dionisi in the former Saint Nicholas Church and the private project "Right to a Future."

Ogorodnikov began to develop relief activities with the help of foreign gifts. There was no infrastructure for these activities, so goods were temporarily stored in the homes of Seminar members. Ogorodnikov also gave financial help to prisoners of conscience who had spent time in the Gulag, as well as to the poor, orphans, former psychiatric patients, and lonely old people — population groups who had fallen between the cracks. The fissures in the previously monolithic Soviet system were growing both in number and size. Intellectuals gathered in the big cities in so-called "glasnost clubs" and "perestroika clubs" to hold uncensored debates concerning social problems.

General Secretary Mikhail Gorbachev refused to turn a blind eye to corruption and the abuse of power. Procurator-General Alexander Rekunkov reported that 200,000 government officials had been subjected to disciplinary action in 1986 for "irresponsible deeds." KGB chief Viktor Chebrikov confessed to the beating of a Ukrainian journalist, and in Karelia two police officers on the Finnish border were given prison sentences for the maltreatment of detainees. Dinmukhamed Konayev, a confidant of former General Secretary Brezhnev, was deposed as the Communist Party leader of Kazakhstan for "gross violations of Party norms and establishing a personality cult."

The government newspaper *Izvestia* (Messages) reported that three hundred leading public officials in the republic of Turkmenistan, on the Iranian border, had had country homes built for themselves that were paid for by the state.

Perhaps the greatest achievement of the new political wind was the disappearance of censorship. Driven by the thirst for sensationalism, loyal pen-pushers broke one taboo after another in writing about prostitution, vagrancy, drug addiction, homosexuality, juvenile delinquency, environmental pollution, slums, privileges for party bosses, unemployment, health-care abuses, and abuse of psychiatry for political purposes. The trade journal *Meditsinskaja Gazeta* reported the death of the journalist Viktor Bertshin, author of a report on abuse of power and corruption in the secret service. After Bertshin had lost consciousness during an interrogation, he was given an injection that proved fatal.

People had to stand in line at that time — not only for their daily groceries but also to purchase a newspaper. Most newspapers sold out in no time every day because the paper shortage meant that circulation had to be kept to a minimum. Thirty kilograms of paper and cardboard were produced per person each year, compared to 212 kilograms in the United States. The sole reason for the paper shortage, a familiar problem in the Soviet Union, was the use of obsolete production techniques and the failure to recycle old paper.

The progressive weekly *Moscow News* was popular, and so were *Ogonjok,* a weekly, and *Komsomolskaya Pravda,* the daily publication of the Communist youth movement Komsomol, which was issued in a print run of twenty million. The somewhat more conservative periodicals *Moskovski Komsomolets,* the Moscow city newspaper, and the magazine *Sotsialisticheskaya Industriya* were no less driven by sensationalism. The government newspaper *Izvestiya,* however, wanted to follow an independent course, and it evolved into a quality newspaper.

On May 28, 1987, a nineteen-year-old German named Mathias Rust succeeded in landing a Cessna 172, a single-engine sports plane, on Red Square in Moscow without being spotted by the radar of the Russian military air defense, which was apparently leaking like a sieve. This stunt was an enormous psychological blow to Communist Russia and ultimately led to the dismissal of a number of highly placed military officials and fervent opponents of Gorbachev's "liberal" regime. Gradually, the Soviet Union began to lose its grip on the Eastern Bloc. Beset by economic problems, those countries also began to experiment with reforms. The collaboration within the Comecon — the economic alliance composed of Cuba, Mongolia, and the Eastern European Communist countries, and led by the Soviet Union — came under extreme pressure, all the more so because the various currencies were not convertible.

In September 1987, the Soviet domestic press reported for the first time that strikes were taking place in the USSR. Bus drivers stopped working in the city of Chekhov in the Moscow Oblast, followed by workers in the bus factory in the city of Likino, also in the Moscow Oblast.

Starting in December 1987, the police held weekly press conferences on criminality in Moscow. The venue was 36 Petrovka Street, for decades one of the most feared addresses for dissidents. These press conferences were an aspect of the new political climate under Gorbachev, which had resulted in open discussions of domestic problems. Television also began to play a more critical role in discussing societal changes and problems. The programs *Vzgliad* ("Outlook") and *Do i posle polunochi* ("Before and After Midnight") made mincemeat of Communist propaganda. The first issue of the magazine *Semya* ("Family") reported that, in 1987, 14,000 young people had been arrested for drug-related offenses, that an equal number had been treated for venereal diseases, and that the number of children growing up in single-parent households had risen to 700,000.

Winds of Change in the Cultural Sector

New winds also began to blow in the realms of literature, theater, and film. In early March 1987, the Soviet news agency *Novosti* reported the appointment of a new chairman of the Writers' Union and also announced that sweeping changes had been made in the management of publishing houses and on the editorial boards of literary magazines.

After the journal *Sovietskaya Kultura* announced that a special government commission had finally decided to publish Boris Pasternak's novel *Doctor Zhivago*, the secretariat of the Writers' Union reversed Pasternak's expulsion, which had occurred in 1958, almost thirty years before. But the publication was held up due to strong resistance from the opposition. A few excerpts from *Doctor Zhivago* were published in December 1987 in the progressive weekly *Ogonyok,* the standard-bearer of the *glasnost* ideology, and the appearance of the first chapters in the magazine *Novi Mir* in January 1987 was a great moral victory for the policies of General Secretary Gorbachev and for the rehabilitation campaign being conducted by Yevgeni Pasternak, the author's son.

In January 1988, Sergei Zaligin, the editor-in-chief of *Novi Mir,* announced his intention to publish two banned novels by Alexander Solzhenitsyn, *Cancer Ward* and *The Gulag Archipelago.* But it would be another year and a half — August 1989 — before the first chapters of *The Gulag Archipelago* would appear in that journal.

Several exiled Soviet artists returned home, such as the dancer Mikhail Baryshnikov of the Bolshoi Theater in Moscow, Yuri Lyubimov, the former director of the Taganka Theater, and prima ballerina Natalia Makarova, who had worked with the Kirov Ballet in Leningrad. The cellist, composer, and conductor Mstislav Rostropovich, who had chosen voluntary exile after a ban on leaving the country had been imposed in 1971 and had immigrated to the United States in 1974, was readmitted to the Soviet Composers' Union in 1990. Each weekend, tens of thousands of Muscovites visited a nonofficial art market to become acquainted with the latest currents in the world of art.

At the International Film Festival in Moscow in 1987, all the films of director Andrei Tarkovsky were shown posthumously, including the first Soviet screening of *The Mirror,* the film Ogorodnikov had worked on as a student. Another high point of the festival was the film *Commissar,* filmed in 1967 by director Alexander Askoldov, all copies of which had been destroyed by the KGB — except for one. The banned film *Repentance* (1984) by the Georgian director Tengiz Abuladze, a cold-eyed depiction of the horrors of the Stalin regime, was finally premiered in 1987 at the Cannes Film Festival and afterward shown to packed theaters in the Soviet Union. The fact that Russians were finally able to see this film was the result of the intervention of Eduard Shevardnadze, the minister of foreign affairs at the time.

Historians were given access to the Gulag archives for the first time. In January 1989 a number of them set up an organization called simply Memorial in memory of the victims of the Stalinist repression. The first chairman was Andrei Sakharov.

In the economy, however, innovation was slow in coming. The self-employed were permitted to practice their professions, and for the first time since Stalin's rise to power, there was room for small private enterprise as well as joint ventures with foreign companies. Yet success remained limited. Gosplan, the state planning committee, continued to control the entire economy. It was a thoroughly ossified system in which money was actually irrelevant, and there was no room at all for creativity. Quantity prevailed over quality, and the express train of technological progress passed the Soviet Union by for the most part.

On January 1, 1988, 60 percent of the country's industrial and agrarian production switched over to a system with an even economic balance. Companies were now required to keep their expenses in line with their income. They were given more responsibility and were permitted to spend their profits as they saw fit. Companies that lost money had no choice but to dismiss superfluous personnel or shut their doors. In practice, economic developments were seriously hampered by the notorious scarcity of machinery, trained personnel, and raw materials — and by the requirement that at least two-thirds of the production had to be contracted out to government institutions. Eighty percent of the businesses were still dependent on the government, and in the end the ministries responsible for industrial planning pocketed the profits.

The fears of radical reformer Nikolai Shmelev and of Gavriil Popov, economic adviser to Gorbachev, were confirmed. Because the political omnipotence of the planning committee and the ministries remained unshaken, independent enterprise was really no more than window dressing. On February 6, 1988, Gorbachev fired Nikolai Talizin, head of Gosplan, whom he himself had appointed in 1985. Instead of putting any reforms into effect, Talizin had emerged as one of the most fervent defenders of the centralized economy.

In the meantime, cracks began to form throughout the Russian monetary system. There were four currencies in circulation in the Soviet Union at that time: *rubles,* which were intended for most of the Soviet public and which one could use to buy exclusively inferior products after waiting in line for hours; *check coupons,* for Soviet citizens who earned hard currency abroad; *D-coupons,* for foreign diplomats; and hard currencies such as American dollars and West German marks — especially for tourists. Foreigners and the wealthy class could shop in luxury specialty stores, where the most trendy Western consumer goods were for sale. For "ordinary" Russians, however, these luxury items were unaffordable. In July 1987 the official rate of exchange was 1.58 American dollars to the ruble, but on the black market a dollar was worth about five or six rubles.

Gorbachev Caught between Conservatives and Radical Reformers

In pushing through his policies of reform, Mikhail Gorbachev was constantly being impeded by resistance from the establishment and lower party officials, who were determined to retain their positions at all costs. The policies of *glasnost* led to great discord within the Communist Party: on the one side, there were reformers, who wanted to link more private initiatives with the dismantling of the Communist Party's power monopoly; on the other side, there were conservatives, who did not want to do harm to the system. Yegor Ligachev, the number-two man at the Kremlin, argued in favor of an educational system that would "only form people who are capable of implementing Party policies."

Gorbachev was involved in a constant give-and-take between these two power blocs. In the Ukrainian city of Dnepropetrovsk, the power base of the late General Secretary Brezhnev, Gorbachev dismissed party leader Viktor Boyko after Boyko's open resistance to the new liberalization policies; but he also threw radical reformer Boris Yeltsin out of the Politburo. The population was stupefied and lethargic; ordinary people viewed the party changes and struggles with indifference and apathy, as they had always done before.

In addition, it was unavoidable that the old nationality problem would rear its head, with the Crimean Tatars playing a central role. On July 29, 1987, after President Andrei Gromyko had received a small Tatar delegation, hundreds of Crimean Tatars demonstrated in the center of Moscow for a return to their homeland. But two days later, on August 1, the twenty-one most important leaders were put on a plane and flown to Central Asia, leading to a diplomatic incident with the United States.

The government was gradually losing its grip on events. In 1987, thirty thousand independent organizations were set up to develop activities for recreation and environmental care. A number of these organizations also acquired political aspirations and developed into political movements, varying from the ultra-right-wing Russian nationalist and anti-Semitic movement Pamyat (which means both "memory" and "remembrance") to the ultra-left-wing Socialist Initiative.

Pressure grew on the all-powerful Communist Party as the *glasnost* being preached by Gorbachev made it increasingly clear how much the party had been deceiving everyone for years. The ideological basis of the party had melted away during the 1970s, so *glasnost* did not trigger a social discussion that would stimulate the emergence of ideas concerning the renewal of the party. The only taboo that remained untouched was criticism of Marxist ideology.

Samizdat Lives

Although censorship had ended, there was absolutely no freedom of the press in the Soviet Union. The printing offices were still in the hands of the government, and every new publication had to be authorized by the Glavlit censorship service. This assured the continued existence of samizdat — at least for the time being. In early July 1987, the magazine *Glasnost* was launched by a few former dissidents: the historians Sergei Grigoryants and Henrich Altunian, the journalist Lev Timofeyev, Father Gleb Yakunin, and Mustafa Djemilev, head of the Crimean Tatars. Fifty copies of the first issue — forty-nine pages long and typed on a typewriter — were circulated via the underground press. Ogorodnikov contributed an article on *glasnost* and the relationship between church and state.

But the KGB didn't wait long to step in. On October 5, 1987, a few members of *Glasnost*'s editorial board were arrested as part of an investigation of "criminal activities" because a government photocopy machine had been used in the distribution of the magazine. And on March 19, 1988, a house search was carried out in the home of Sergei Grigoryants, the magazine's editor-in-chief. The government had already curbed the activities of the independent publishing houses and print shops. These businesses marketed limited editions of books that the state publishing companies had refused to print. The shortage of paper and machinery was the official explanation for what was ultimately an attempt to maintain the state monopoly on publishing books and magazines.

In the meantime, Ogorodnikov was busy starting his own religious magazine, convinced that it would be a powerful weapon in the church reform that he envisioned. On July 13, 1987, he announced the forthcoming publication of the *Bulletin of the Christian Community*. He applied for official permission to publish but received no answer. The aim of the magazine was "to stimulate the discussion of religious questions and to distribute as much information as possible on the state of the Orthodox Church and other religious organizations." On behalf of the project's thirty initiators, and in his capacity as editor-in-chief, Ogorodnikov presented the first issue of the *Bulletin* at a press conference in Moscow on August 3, 1987.

His name and temporary address were prominently and confidently featured on the title page. On the same day, he had a presentation copy delivered to the Central Committee of the Communist Party, but the gesture was politely declined. The twenty hand-typed mother copies of the first issue, 150 pages in length, found their way to believers throughout the Soviet Union. The magazine also contained a number of articles in English and French because of its distribution in the West, where interest in the developments taking place in the Soviet Union was considerable. After the press conference, the KGB took Ogorodnikov in for questioning. The agents threatened to arrest him again because he still did not have a residence permit for Moscow, but a few hours later he was back on the street. The secret service took subtle revenge by distributing a samizdat letter that slandered Ogorodnikov.

By publishing current information from around the country, the *Bulletin of the Christian Community* quickly grew into a leading voice of the Christian community in the Soviet Union, each issue numbering a few hundred pages. Ogorodnikov built up an information network that was partly based on informants who had lent their support back in the 1970s. Soon after the publication of the *Bulletin* began, it was no longer possible to publish the overabundance of information.

The third and fourth issues of September/October 1987 (published as a double issue) contained chronicles of religious life in the Ukrainian and Lithuanian Catholic churches, in the Lutheran Church in Latvia, and in the Russian Orthodox Church. This was followed by various documents, letters, and appeals from several Christian communities, an article on the position of the clergy, an overview of recently opened churches, a discussion of a few theological questions, and an up-to-date report on religious prisoners. Also included were reviews of the domestic and foreign press and various articles on the role of Christianity and the meaning of the Christian identity in a secular Marxist state.

Dissidents Released . . . and Rounded Up

But what about the human-rights situation? The government veiled itself in silence, and the foreign reports all published different statistics. For instance, the 1987 annual report of the U.S. State Department noted an increase in travel and emigration possibilities for dissidents and a drop in the actual number of prisoners of conscience, while it also noted that living conditions in the camps and prisons had still not improved, and that Jews and other minorities were still being discriminated against. Another American report pointed to the release of 274 prisoners in 1987; it observed that at least 430 persons were still being held in labor camps, prisons, psychiatric hospitals, or internal exile, charged with "anti-Soviet agitation and propaganda." More than half of the prisoners of conscience were *religious* activists. In 1987, Amnesty International reported the release of 250 political prisoners — the largest number in many decades — and published data on 300 people who had been imprisoned because they "exercised their fundamental human rights in a nonviolent manner."

Conversely, in 1987, at least twenty Russian believers were convicted because of their religious activities. In Kiev, during an open-air worship service, a minister of the Protestant Pentecostal movement was arrested and charged with "public indecency." Several Jehovah's Witnesses who refused to serve in the Soviet army on religious grounds suffered the same fate, as did many Lithuanians. On January 15, 1988, Andrei Sakharov had a talk with General Secretary Gorbachev at the Kremlin and handed him a list of two hundred Russian political prisoners whose release he was requesting. Afterwards, Sakharov declared that he came away with "a higher opinion of the general secretary as a man and as a government leader."

On October 6, 1987, the former dissidents Alexander Podrabinek, Valery Sendorov, and Alexander Ogorodnikov held a press conference in Moscow to announce the formation of the Moscow branch of the International Human Rights Organization (IHRO), which was based in Munich. The aim of this branch was to serve as a stimulus in the struggle toward the respecting of human rights. By connecting with an international organization, the Moscow branch could call on the expertise, financial resources, and logistical support of the mother organization. However, setting up the secretariat was anything but easy. The KGB was systematic in pressuring property owners not to offer leases to human-rights organizations. It took months before they could find someone who was not intimidated by the threats from the secret service.

The former dissident Anatoly Koryagin, who had moved to Switzerland, testified to this problem: "The repressive abuse of psychiatry has still not been uprooted. I know of 20 to 30 cases at the moment. The only way to improve the situation for good is to apply continuous pressure. The government and the KGB will never voluntarily renounce this extremely useful means of repression."

For his part, Ogorodnikov kept calling for the release of prisoners of conscience. He also devoted himself to bringing an end to religious persecution and to the recognition of all religions. With the support of Vladimir Chernik of the Greek Catholic Church — the Eastern rite Uniates in the western Ukraine — he launched a campaign in the fall of 1987 for the legalization of the Uniates and the return of the property that had been seized from them after the 1917 Revolution. Ogorodnikov intensified this demand at a press conference held in his Moscow apartment, at which several underground bishops from the Greek Catholic Church were present.

In November 1987, Ogorodnikov married Paulina Bogdanova, a theater and art reviewer. With the help of a priest, they were able to have their marriage registered by the Christian mayor of a village six hundred miles from Moscow. (Registering in Moscow was not possible because Ogorodnikov still did not have a residence permit.) Their son, Vladimir, was born in May 1988.

Celebrating the Seventieth Anniversary of the Revolution

In the run-up to the celebration of the seventieth anniversary of the October Revolution, November 7, 1987, a hundred prisoners of conscience, most of them lesser known, were given amnesty. On the basis of archival research, historians were able to demonstrate that Stalin's forced collectivization and Great Purge had cost the country more than a million lives, including scores of people who had played leading roles in the 1917 Revolution. The best known among them were Nikolai Bukharin, Karl Radek, and Grigory Zinoviev. The review of the most high-profile convictions from the years 1937-38 led to the rehabilitation of nineteen historical leaders and of Leon Trotsky, for whom a statue was erected in the Lenin Museum in Leningrad.

On the anniversary of the revolution, Mikhail Gorbachev gave a speech in the Congressional Palace in the Kremlin that was broadcast live on television. In it he denounced Stalin's personality cult, illegal actions, and arbitrary behavior: "Continuing to cover this up would mean ignoring the historical truth and would indicate a lack of respect for those who were the innocent victims of lawlessness and arbitrary decisions." The general secretary also announced his intention to see that "history is truthfully and fully rewritten." At a meeting of the Communist leadership a short time later, Gorbachev refused to grant permission for a new international conference of Communist parties.

Yuri Samodurov, of the Moscow "Perestroika Club," collected signatures for the erection of a monument in memory of the victims of Stalinism. And on October 22, 1987, the day Joseph Brodsky was awarded the Nobel Prize for literature, the magazine *Kommunist,* the theoretical organ of the Communist Party, apologized to the writers, artists, and intellectuals of the Soviet Union for the cultural policies of the preceding seventy years. While Gorbachev was signing a disarmament agreement with President Ronald Reagan in early December 1987 in Washington, D.C., Jewish refuseniks in Moscow were being brutally beaten during three days of demonstrations. The American Jewish community held a protest demonstration in Washington, D.C., to show their solidarity with the refuseniks.

Gorbachev made sure that the hard-liners were never given the chance to recover. On January 28, 1988, the magazine *Literaturnaja Gazeta* came down hard on Andrei Vyshinsky, the prosecutor-general under Stalin. This architect of the Great Purge of the thirties was notorious for his brutal behavior. He reversed the right of defense and made defendants write and then sign their own confessions. The article signaled a review of the judicial apparatus, with the reformers pushing for the application of the principle of innocence until sentenced. In March 1988, the Joseph Stalin Museum in the Georgian town of Gori closed its doors. The critical magazine *Ogonyok,* which enthusiastically set about "filling in the blanks" of history, wrote about how Stalin had had the wives of two of his close associates — President Mikhail Kalinin and Vyacheslav Molotov, commissar for foreign affairs — sent to the Gulag.

Commemorating a Thousand Years of Christianity

In the meantime, Ogorodnikov was working hard on preparations for an alternative celebration: the commemoration of one thousand years of Christianity in Russia, which had been planned for June 1988. This commemoration and its expected thousands of visitors, who were part of scores of international delegations, was a unique opportunity to unmask the official Soviet government's version of the Orthodox Church's life in Russia by showing how things really were. Ogorodnikov hoped that this approach would force the government to allow more religious freedom and to return all the property that had belonged to the churches before the Revolution. He invited the representatives of all the church denominations to participate in an alternative celebration committee. Many, including Father Gleb Yakunin, responded to his appeal.

The committee drew up a program and delegated the various tasks. At Ogorodnikov's request, Dima Sakharov, son of Andrei Sakharov, and Sergei Savchenko, a physicist as well as a photographer for the *Bulletin of the Christian Community*, spent months traveling around the Soviet Union with a camera — without the KGB knowing about it. Those two succeeded in capturing on film a whole laundry list of distressing situations involving religious persecution. In its first press communiqué, the alternative celebration committee demanded the release of 238 prisoners of conscience, the repeal of the antireligious legislation of 1929, and the return of the Monastery of the Caves (the Pechersk Lavra) in Kiev.

By the end of the 1980s, the disintegration process of the Soviet Union was proceeding at a rapid pace. In January 1988 the government prohibited the abuse of psychiatry for political purposes. From then on, family members could lodge an appeal against such internment, and the control of psychiatric institutes was transferred from the Ministry of the Interior to the Ministry of Health.

Mikhail Gorbachev announced the withdrawal of Russian troops from Afghanistan beginning on May 15, 1988. Since 1979, the Soviet Union had been involved in a hopeless struggle with the mujahideen, the Islamic resistance movement. But one conflict was scarcely over when the next one reared its head: the Caucasus. In the age-old powder keg of the Caucasus, unrest was growing by the day. On February 23, 1988, in Yerevan, the capital of Armenia, 120,000 Armenians turned out in a protest demonstration to demand that the Soviet Union hand over the disputed region of Nagorno-Karabakh to Armenia. The smoldering conflict between the Christian Armenians and the Islamic Azerbaijanis was concentrated in the mountainous region in which about 80 percent of the population were ethnic Armenians, but which had been added to Azerbaijan by Stalin in 1923.

In addition to the former dissident Dmitri Volchek, Ogorodnikov was the best-informed independent observer in Moscow. He was visited almost daily by Western journalists because, given his local contacts, he had a clear picture of the latest developments. Ogorodnikov was the first to report killings in Armenia and Azerbaijan. On the day that he decided to go to Armenia himself, the plane turned back to Moscow just before it was to arrive in Yerevan because of his presence on board.

During Mikhail Gorbachev's official visit to Yugoslavia on March 13, 1988, the old Communist guard — headed by Yegor Ligachev, the number-two man at the Kremlin — published a startling letter in the daily *Sovetskaya Rossiya*, the organ of the authorities of the Russian Soviet Federative Socialist Republic (RSFSR), in which he mercilessly shot Gorbachev's ambitious reform policy to pieces. In a reaction to what was informally called the "conservative manifesto," the major artists' unions declared their unconditional support of Gorbachev, and *Sovetskaya Rossiya* was forced to apologize. Ligachev remained at his post for the time being, but he had lost all of his authority over the press and television.

Soon afterward, a veteran of the Communist Party viciously attacked Gorbachev's *perestroika* policy in an article submitted to the newspaper *Molodaya Gvardia* (Young Guard), but by then the clock could no longer be turned back.

The Democratic Union in the Opposition

On May 7, 1988, sixty representatives from several cities met in an apartment in Moscow and set up the Democratic Union, a new political movement dedicated to establishing a multiparty system based on the Western model. This was not an initiative of well-known Soviet dissidents, but a recently formed discussion group made up of Perestroika 88, the pacifist Trust Group, the Democracy and Humanism Seminar, and the Committee for a Memorial for the Victims of Stalin. The spokesperson for this new liberal party was the former Soviet dissident Valeria Novgorodskaya of the Trust Group. The police, who were waiting outside in massive numbers, arrested all the participants after the meeting was over.

Two days later, when several members of the Democratic Union approved the statutes and program of the new party at a meeting held in the dacha of *Glasnost* editor Sergei Grigoryants, the police stepped in again. They conducted a house search and seized all the newspaper's documents and cash. Grigoryants, who resisted his arrest, was sentenced to seven days in jail, and five members of the editorial board were thrown in jail for three to five days. At a demonstration on Pushkin Square in Moscow, where supporters of the Democratic Union were protesting the sentencing of Grigoryants, twelve participants were arrested. A short time later, a second demonstration was held with five hundred participants. The

Democratic Union, which used a pre-Revolution Russian flag as its symbol, developed into a nationalistic opposition movement.

The Democratic Union was not the only organization with political aspirations. Elena Zelinskaja, publisher of *Merkurii*, the most successful
samizdat magazine at the time — with a circulation of a thousand hand-
typed mother copies — was busy preparing for the congress of the Union of
Democratic Forces. Tatiana Zaslavskaya, a confidante of General Secretary
Gorbachev, then launched an idea that was already circulating in intellectual circles: the establishment of a political alternative that would not function as an opposition party but as a combination of all non-Communist unofficial groups and of all persons interested in social change. In March 1988,
Konstantin Kharchev, of the Council for Religious Affairs, gave a speech
that was circulated in samizdat, in which he acknowledged that the attempts to eliminate religion from society had failed:

> The government never had control over the Protestants and Catholics
> as they did over the Russian Orthodox Church. Not only has religion
> survived the persecution but it is also undergoing a revival. What is
> best for society: someone who believes in God or someone who be-
> lieves in nothing? Or someone who believes in God and Communism?
> We have to choose the lesser evil. Since religion is never going to dis-
> appear, the government is well advised to make the best use of it.

On Easter Sunday, April 10, 1988, Russian state television broadcast a report about the divine liturgy being held at Epiphany Cathedral in
Elokhovo, a village near Moscow, which was being led by Patriarch Pimen.
Because the police had sealed off the streets around the cathedral, believers were forced to walk past a row of hostile Communist youths, who insulted them.

On the eve of the 1st of May parade on Red Square, Gorbachev received Patriarch Pimen and five metropolitans of the Synod of the Russian Orthodox Church at the Kremlin. "Believers have the right to express their convictions with dignity," the general secretary told them. He
also said that a new law on religious freedom was in the making. That
same day, the TASS news agency published an interview with Metropolitan Filaret of Minsk. During a press conference later that day, Ogorodnikov declared that "the meeting with Gorbachev was mainly meant to
pull the wool over the eyes of Western public opinion. The Communist
regime, which has always been officially atheist, hopes to rob the

thousand-year anniversary of Christianity in Russia of its religious significance and turn it into a big show."

Ogorodnikov continued to support believers who wanted to emigrate. In the spring of 1988 he asked Richard Schifter, the American
ambassador to the United Nations Commission on Human Rights
(UNCHR), to help members of the Russian Pentecostal church immigrate to the United States. Ogorodnikov convinced Schifter, an experienced diplomat, of the merit of this operation: "The members of the Pentecostal church are dedicated Christians and hard workers. Most of them
have large families with many children. Their future in the Soviet Union
remains uncertain, but they can make an important contribution to
American society." In the end the American government decided to admit to the United States 25,000 members of the Pentecostal church.
Ogorodnikov helped with the selection, making sure that only genuine
members of this church were given exit visas, which was no easy task
considering the size of the operation.

In May 1988, he succeeded in obtaining the release of an Orthodox
believer who had spent a total of thirty-seven years in a psychiatric hospital. Due to all the injections the man had received over the years, he had
difficulty functioning normally. Because he no longer had any family, he
was entrusted to Ogorodnikov's care. The man lived for a time in Alexander's apartment until he was admitted to the Orthodox Holy Trinity
Stavropegial Monastery of the ROCOR (the Russian Orthodox Church
Outside of Russia) in Jordanville, New York, thanks to the intervention of
Dick Rodgers, an Anglican priest. He died there in 2007.

It was during this period that perhaps the last taboo was breached
when the magazine *Novi Mir* dared to publish an article that criticized
Lenin, who until then was regarded as the unassailable founder of the Soviet state. In his article, economist Vasily Salyunin said that Lenin's policy
of "wartime Communism" (1918-21), or the systematic and deliberate rationing of consumer goods, was actually the cause of the great famine
that raged between 1921 and 1924 in the Ukraine and parts of Russia.

Official Celebration of a Thousand Years of Christianity

By the end of May 1988, the Soviet Union had become the focus of international interest. First came the visit by President Ronald Reagan, accompanied by five thousand staff members and journalists. During his

visit Reagan kept hammering on the importance of freedom, especially religious freedom, much to the displeasure of the Soviet authorities. Ogorodnikov and his son, Dima, along with twenty former dissidents and Jewish refuseniks, had a meeting with President Reagan at Spaso House, the residence of the American ambassador in Moscow. During his inspiring speech at the close of this memorable meeting, Reagan said:

> I came here in the hope of giving you some strength. But as it turns out, you have given me strength — you have given me a memorable message. Indeed, while we press for the improvement of human rights through diplomatic channels, you are doing the same thing by giving your own lives, day in and day out, year in and year out, and in doing so you constantly put your jobs, your homes, and all your property at risk.

One of those present, the biologist Sergei Kovalyov (who had been in Perm-36 with Ogorodnikov), was dismissed from his position at the research institute where he worked on June 2, right after Reagan's departure.

A few days later, the celebration of a thousand years of Christianity in Russia began. In the days prior to the celebration, hundreds of prisoners of conscience were freed, and a new series of churches and sanctuaries were given back to the Russian Orthodox Church, making a total of 325 since 1986. One of them was the eleventh-century Monastery of the Caves (the Pechersk Lavra) in Kiev, the oldest monastery in the country. The registration of baptisms and church congregations became less rigid, and the government temporarily agreed to the importation of hundreds of thousands of Bibles, Bible commentaries, and prayer books.

On June 4, 1988, the TASS news agency argued that Orthodoxy "gives expression to love and compassion; condemns laziness and the greedy accumulation of money; and impresses upon the population high moral standards, of which our socialist society is in such dire need." This wave of good will had a significant propaganda content. The regime wanted the church to side with the politics of Mikhail Gorbachev as it conjured up a vision of religious freedom for the outside world.

Patriarch Pimen conducted a solemn service at the Epiphany Cathedral in Moscow the next day. Sitting in the first row was an imposing throng of prelates: Pope Shanouda III of the Coptic Church; Robert Runcie, the archbishop of Canterbury; and a Roman Catholic delegation led by the Dutch Cardinal Johannes Willebrands and the Italian Cardinal Agostino Casaroli, the Vatican secretary of state. Pope John Paul II was not invited, and the Patriarch Dmitrios of Constantinople, the ecumenical patriarch, failed to appear. Describing this service, Ogorodnikov told the Belgian journalist Bert Claerhout:

> For the people the celebration was a great feast, for the Church all that counted was the prestige, and for the government it was the show. The church leaders may drink cognac and eat caviar, but they are still slavishly dependent on the atheistic state. Because they were so fearful of irritating the Party leaders, they never even worked for the freeing of imprisoned priests, nor did the freed dissidents receive any support.

General Secretary Gorbachev had a personal meeting with Cardinal Casaroli, and on June 11, 1988, President Andrei Gromyko received the guests in the Kremlin. He repeated — this time officially — that soon a new law on religious activities would be enacted, and also confirmed that from then on religious groups would be able to carry on charitable activities. The Baptists struck while the iron was hot: they held open-air services in a number of cities — without any government interference.

What about Ogorodnikov's alternative program? After a few members of the organizational committee, including Gleb Yakunin, pulled out under pressure from the KGB at the last minute, a number of planned activities were dropped. But the real crowd magnet was an exhibition on the actual situation of the church in the Soviet Union based on the photographs taken by Dima Sakharov and Sergei Savchenko and other recent documents. The pictures showed, for example, churches that had been destroyed or turned into cowsheds and prisons, a crucifix that had been shot by a firing squad. The exhibition took place in a Moscow apartment whose owner had deliberately "disappeared" from Moscow for a few weeks, to keep him from shutting down the exhibition under pressure from the KGB.

The secret service did everything they could to divert the thousands of delegates to their approved routes. But a large number of them succeeded in attending Ogorodnikov's five-day conference in the Moscow apartment anyway. During this conference, representatives of Orthodoxy, of the Uniates — one of whose bishops literally lived underground — and of various Protestant denominations from almost every corner of the Soviet Union testified to the reality of religious persecution. For many Western journalists and visitors, this introduction to the underground church was a total revelation.

Ogorodnikov used all kinds of tricks to bring important religious leaders into contact with religious dissidents. Through the intervention of an Italian journalist, a secret meeting between representatives of the Vatican and the Uniates took place in the sacristy of the Roman Catholic Church of Saint Louis before and after a celebration of the Mass. On June 18, 1988, the focus of the Christian Millennium celebration moved from Moscow to Kiev, where thousands of invited guests attended a service at the Saint Sophia Cathedral, built on the site where Grand Prince Vladimir I had been baptized one thousand years earlier. In an interview that was published in the American magazine *Time* on June 20, 1988, Ogorodnikov talked about how disillusioned he was that the antireligious legislation of 1929 was still in force: "A positive sound during a celebration can always be interpreted negatively," he warned. "What counts is what is in the law."

The KGB Breaks Up Ogorodnikov's Second Marriage

The secret service was furious that Ogorodnikov had succeeded in throwing a monkey wrench into the works of their well-oiled propaganda machine. If he had not been so famous, he certainly would have been murdered. On July 18, 1988, Ogorodnikov temporarily left Moscow. He traveled to Lithuania, where on July 24, 1988, he set up a defense committee for Petras Gražulis, who had been sentenced to ten months in prison after refusing to serve in the Soviet army. Gražulis was a member of the Christian Seminar in Lithuania.

When Ogorodnikov returned to Moscow after four weeks, a painful surprise awaited him. His wife, Paulina Bogdanova, refused to let him into their apartment. During his absence, the KGB had repeatedly threatened to take away their son, Vladimir, unless she terminated her marriage to Alexander. Paulina refused to speak to Alexander, sent away all Western correspondents who came to visit him, and had their marriage legally dissolved. Divorce in the Soviet Union was just an administrative formality, because the Communists attached no importance to family values.

The newspapers *Krokodil, Pravda,* and *Izvestiya* simultaneously published fourteen letters to the editor in which intellectuals and former dissidents, under pressure from the KGB, referred to Ogorodnikov's family problems. They claimed that his wife had pleaded with him to emigrate because she was sick and tired of living the life of a dissident, but he had refused. The report was also broadcast in English and French by Radio Moscow.

CHAPTER NINE

Christians and Political Reform

In an ultimate attempt to curb the rise of organizations, which were now popping out of the earth like toadstools, an *ukaze*, or ordinance, was issued by the government on July 28, 1988, stating that all public demonstrations had to have the permission of the local authorities. Such permission had to be requested at least ten days in advance, and if permission was refused, there was no possibility of appeal. In the meantime, dissidents were slowly being released. On August 26, 1988, trade union leader Vladimir Klebanov finally left the Gulag after ten years of detention, and he immediately resumed his former trade union activities.

The fact that the process of reform started by Mikhail Gorbachev had still not been achieved was reflected in an article in *Pravda* in which Stalin's politics were defended as follows: "The Soviet Union had no choice at the time but to take the path that Stalin chose. Despite the enormous losses, the serious mistakes and the massive repression, our country was guarded from mortal danger, and socialism was saved for the future."

On August 6, 1988, Yegor Ligachev, the number-two man in the Kremlin, repeated his criticism of the reform policy. And the ministry of culture boycotted the plan of the Memorial society — which was now represented in 110 cities — to build a center in the capital as a memorial to the terror of the Stalin period, though Gorbachev had announced that he supported the plan. Memorial, in collaboration with the magazine *Ogonyok*, responded in November 1988 by organizing "Conscience Week," with an exhibition on Stalin's reign of terror.

Nevertheless, Gorbachev continued with his reforms. Thanks to the struggle against the privileges of the *nomenklatura*, the number of official cars was reduced by 40 percent, and the *berioshkas* — hard-currency shops where Soviet citizens who had worked abroad could make purchases with special ruble certificates — closed their doors. These shops were mainly popular among speculators, who would then sell the goods on the black market. The shops for foreigners who paid with hard currency did stay open, as did the special shops for the *nomenklatura*.

After months of turning a blind eye, the government came down hard on the anti-Semitic campaign being conducted by the nationalistic organization Pamyat. In addition, in the Lenin Library in Moscow, about eight hundred books by victims of Stalin's purges, which had been banned for decades, were put back on the shelves. The court case against Yuri Churbanov, the son-in-law of Leonid Brezhnev who stood accused of large-scale corruption, grew into an attempt to settle the score against Brezhnev's regime, which was euphemistically known as the "period of stagnation." This was the first political trial of the *glasnost* era. Churbanov was sentenced to twelve years in a labor camp.

In the meantime, the call for more autonomy in the Baltic states was being heard with greater frequency. In Estonia, the recently formed People's Front, which had added 40,000 members in only two months, emerged as the largest political organization next to the Communist Party. The People's Front was prepared to support Gorbachev's reforms in exchange for political and economic autonomy. One hundred thousand Estonians, out of a population of 1.5 million, held a demonstration in the capital city of Tallinn for the first time.

In response, Gorbachev said that opposition parties would always be prohibited "because they go against the interests of the people." He also warned, "There are limits to *glasnost*." A new law covering the maintenance of public order gave the ministry of the interior far-reaching powers, by which homes and suspicious places could be searched without a warrant. In this context, Soviet troops were deployed in the turbulent Caucasian republics of Armenia and Azerbaijan, and the government threatened to do the same in Estonia. But on September 12, 1988, during a march of 300,000 Estonians, calls for independence were heard for the first time.

A people's organization with the name *Sajūdis* (Movement) was also formed in Lithuania on June 3, 1988, by the Lithuanian professor Vytautas Landsbergis, a conservative politician. On September 29, 1988, representatives of *Sajūdis* and the Lithuanian Freedom League stood on the same podium during a demonstration of about five thousand participants protesting the violence used by the militia against peaceful demonstrators and hunger strikers. Twenty demonstrators were arrested. At the end of October 1988, in the Lithuanian capital of Vilnius, the Stanislaus and Wenceslaus Cathedral (the Arkikatedra), which had been turned into an art gallery, was returned to the Roman Catholic Church, and tens of thousands of believers attended that first mass. In the magazine *Ogonyok*, Konstantin Kharchev, chairman of the Council for Religious Affairs, called for religious freedom, an end to the registration ban for churches, and a revision of the religious legislation of 1929. Over a year later, on August 23, 1989, more than 2.5 million demonstrators formed a human chain about 400 miles long, the so-called Baltic Chain or Baltic Road, which ran right through the three Baltic states of Estonia, Latvia, and Lithuania. Their purpose was to draw attention to both the fate of the Baltic states and to the fiftieth anniversary of the Molotov-Ribbentrop Pact, or the Stalin-Hitler Pact, of 1939, which had led to the occupation of the three countries and the loss of their independence. The Baltic Chain started in Vilnius, continued to the Latvian capital of Riga, and ended at about 7:00 p.m. in the Estonian capital of Tallinn.

Economic Balances Decentralized

Over the course of 1988, dissatisfaction was becoming apparent among ordinary Soviet citizens. In just two years the price of bread, potatoes, and vegetables had shot up by 18 percent. And despite an export ban, shelves in the shops had even less merchandise than before. The value of the ruble had dropped from 100 to 42 kopeks since 1960. In September 1988, disgruntled residents of the Siberian city of Krasnoyarsk snarled at General Secretary Gorbachev: "Go to the shops and take a look. You'll see with your own eyes that they're completely empty!" and "We don't even have hot water!"

Nor did the economic reforms proceed according to plan. In 1987 the Soviet Union experienced negative economic growth. One in eight companies was operating at a loss, leaving a hole in the treasury of eleven billion rubles. In Leningrad a company shut down for the first time. On September 21, 1988, thirty-one big businesses, including the Promstroy Bank and the Zhilsots Bank, were given six months to change course. If they failed, they, too, would go bankrupt or be taken over.

On January 1, 1989, the law on financial autonomy and balanced budgets was decentralized. Yet this did not lead to the creation of a free market, because the prices were always centrally determined. But the government feared that if prices were decontrolled, they would skyrocket.

Gorbachev silenced critics by rearranging the Politburo. Yegor Ligachev, Gorbachev's conservative rival, was degraded to minister of agriculture. And after Andrei Gromyko stepped down as president on October 1, 1988, he was replaced the same day by Mikhail Gorbachev. The purging of the party executives continued unabated. On October 3, 1988, Vitaly Vorotnikov, prime minister of the Russian Soviet Federative Socialist Republic (RSFSR), who had been appointed in June 1983, made way for Alexander Vlasov, a confidant of Gorbachev.

The "closed" port of Vladivostok in the Far East, home port of the Soviet Union's Pacific fleet, was finally opened to foreigners after five decades. Andrei Sakharov was given permission to travel to the United States for the first time; because of his knowledge of "state secrets," he had never before been permitted to accept foreign invitations.

In October 1988, Gorbachev announced that all political prisoners would be released before the end of the year. According to the opposition Democratic Union Party, there were still at least 400 political prisoners in the Soviet Union, though Amnesty International's estimate was somewhat lower — between 150 and 234.

On October 20, 1988, Ogorodnikov was arrested and interrogated. The authorities seized seventy-nine books, including his Bible and a prayer book, and he had to pay a tax on the books that were not seized, after which he was released. On November 18, 1988, his brother, the thirty-seven-year-old monk Raphael Ogorodnikov, was killed in a mysterious automobile accident. Twice before, the secret service had ordered Raphael to stop his activities immediately, along with his collaboration with his brother. The "accident" happened on the way back to his parish in Porchov, 400 miles from Moscow, after a meeting with his brother, Alexander. The driver who caused the accident was immediately released, and the witnesses in the village of Kuznetsovki, in the district of Novgorod, were not questioned. Archbishop Pochovski of Pskov refused to allow Raphael to be buried in the caves of the Pskov-Pechory monastery. But believers began to visit his grave to bring flowers and burn candles. One day they discovered that the cross on his grave had been stolen.

The murder of Raphael Ogorodnikov was not an exceptional case. A similar death occurred a bit earlier in the city of Rostov. Grigory Kushin, publisher of the underground magazine *Christianin*, which was published by the Pentecostal church, was also killed in a "car crash." He had repeatedly been told by the KGB — sometimes violently — to stop publishing the magazine.

"We Have Prisoners of Conscience Once More"

At a demonstration for the release of political prisoners, held in December 1988 in Sverdlovsk, journalist Sergei Kuznetsov was arrested and jailed. The Democratic Union had mobilized three hundred supporters to commemorate the fortieth anniversary of the Universal Declaration of Human Rights on December 10, 1988, at which four persons, including Valeria Novotvoskaya, were arrested and sentenced to fifteen days in prison. Novotvoskaya went on a hunger strike in protest.

Four days later, dissidents celebrated the seventieth birthday of the exiled writer Alexander Solzhenitsyn. He was widely praised as a pioneer of *glasnost.* At that time, two American journalists were allowed to take a look at a Gulag camp in the Perm region. But it had been specially "freshened up" for the occasion, and they were shown no political prisoners. Amnesty International was finally invited to visit the Soviet Union for the first time, and in March 1989, American experts visited a few psychiatric hospitals. "The system is improved, but there is still plenty of room for abuse," they concluded. "The general diagnosis of schizophrenia is often used to keep patients interned."

After the arrest on December 11, 1988, of twelve members of the Karabakh Committee in Armenia (a group that was founded in 1988 by a group of Armenian intellectuals with the goal of reuniting Nagorno-Karabakh with Armenia), Andrei Sakharov was quoted in the American magazine *U.S. News and World Report:* "We have prisoners of conscience once more." When the seventy-five-year-old KGB chief Vladimir Kryuchkov was questioned by members of the Supreme Soviet about KGB methods, he claimed that the secret service did not tap the phones of ordinary citizens, had used informants only once, and kept current dossiers only on dissidents who were a danger to state security. A few supporters of the reforms responded with jeers.

The next step in Mikhail's Gorbachev's reform process was to change the Soviet Union's constitution. This was supposed to lead to greater power for the president and a more democratic voting procedure. From then on, all elections would be held by secret ballot, and the number of persons allowed to stand as candidates for each term of office would be unlimited. The future Congress of People's Deputies would consist of 2,250 members: 1,500 directly elected and 750 representatives of social organizations. That congress, which would elect the president, would meet only a few times a year. The real parliamentary work — passing or

rejecting legislative proposals and keeping a check on the government —
would now be carried out by the 422 members of the Supreme Soviet.

Gorbachev's aim in introducing these far-reaching reforms was to
put the parliament on a whole new footing. But on December 1, 1988, the
day the new constitution was passed, former dissidents poked fun at Gorbachev and the Communist Party in *Neva,* the Leningrad literary and political monthly; workers announced that they were going to put an end to
the privileges enjoyed by their bosses; and the popular fronts of the Baltic
states joined forces to protest the planned restriction of the republics' autonomy.

Viktor Chebrikov, a prominent member of the Politburo and former
head of the KGB, delivered a sharp attack on unofficial political organizations and called for an all-out struggle against "illegal structures and anti-
socialist elements." And Gorbachev repeated that there would be no tam-
pering with the one-party system:

> Our people have chosen socialism, and no one can replace the Com-
> munist Party. Its power monopoly is a historical achievement. A multi-
> plicity of parties cannot give society the vitality it needs. The Commu-
> nist Party is still the vanguard of society.

However, the government did decide to agree to more decentralization,
under pressure from the increasing tension in the Baltic states.

Developments in the Soviet Union at the end of the 1980s sowed
great dissension in the countries of the Eastern Bloc. The power elite in
the German Democratic Republic and in Czechoslovakia continued to
take a hard line. For example, in Czechoslovakia the playwright and dissident Václav Havel was sentenced to nine months in prison in February
1989. But Hungary was the first Eastern Bloc country to introduce a multiparty system, which it did in 1988.

The First Free Elections

Although far from democratic, the elections of March 26, 1989, produced
considerable commotion. In the first phase, 750 candidates were put forward by social organizations. These represented the Communist Party,
the Komsomol youth alliance, and the trade unions — including the Society of Filatelists, the Inventors' Union, and the Russian Academy of Sci-

ences. In this way, Mikhail Gorbachev and Andrei Sakharov each had the right to one seat in the new Congress of People's Deputies.

For the remaining 1,500 seats, an election was to be held in just that many electoral districts. Of the 2,895 accepted candidates, 85.3 percent were members of the Communist Party. In 384 national districts, where the local party bosses were still firmly in the saddle, only one person stood for office. Because of the complex selection procedure, a large number of reformist candidates could be barred from the list of candidates, for example, the liberal economist Abel Aganbegian, the space expert Roald Sagdeyev, and Vitaly Korotich, editor-in-chief of the weekly magazine *Ogonyok.* Writer Andrei Nuikin's candidacy was initially accepted, but later he was repeatedly asked to withdraw.

In the Baltic republics a showdown took place between the Communist Party and the nationalistic people's fronts. The election in Moscow was especially tense, where candidates in twenty-seven districts competed for the voters' favor. Boris Yeltsin, the former Communist Party chief in Moscow, took a stand against Yevgeni Brakov, the director of the Zil automobile factory, who was supported by the Communists. The district of Gagarin had twelve candidates, among them Dmitri Volkogonov, writer of a critical biography of Stalin; examining magistrate Telman Gdljan, who had taken the son-in-law of former General Secretary Brezhnev to court; and the former dissident Roy Medvedev, a historian who was well known for his book *Let History Judge,* concerning the history of the Stalin-era dissidents.

Yet the fight was one-sided. The Communists were the only ones with a national organization and a logistical network. And they still had the media under their control. In a television debate with Yevgeni Brakov, Boris Yeltsin was asked very tough questions by people who later turned out to be fictitious voters.

For Ogorodnikov, who still had no residence permit for Moscow, the elections were taking place much too soon. In addition, none of the candidates had his vote. Support for the Communist candidates was out of the question. But he also distrusted the "independent" candidates, including Boris Yeltsin, most of whom were ex-Communists who were only thinking of their own careers and self-enrichment.

Communists Retain Firm Control Despite Defeat

On March 26, 1989, 90 percent of the 192.5 million registered voters went to the polls. Although 87.6 percent of those elected were members of the Communist Party, the election still amounted to a painful rebuke of the party apparatus. The independent candidates, nationalists, and reform-minded Communists were triumphant. Mayors Valery Saikin of Moscow and Valentin Zgursky of Kiev even lost in districts where they had no opponents. Boris Yeltsin received 89.4 percent of the votes, and in the Baltic republics the people's fronts were victorious. The Russian-Armenian Telman Gdljan was elected in the first round.

On May 21, 1989, four days before the first meeting of the Congress of People's Deputies, 100,000 people demonstrated in the streets of Moscow under the leadership of Andrei Sakharov and Boris Yeltsin, declaring their support for democratization. During the chaotic opening session, Mikhail Gorbachev was reelected president of the Soviet Union. Andrei Sakharov caused a great deal of commotion with his questions about the war in Afghanistan and his fiery appeal for reform and parliamentary control of the Communist Party. He was interrupted by shouts and cat-calls, and Anatoly Lukyanov, the newly elected vice president, tried to silence him. In the election of the 422 members of the Supreme Soviet, the reformists suffered a defeat. Yet, Boris Yeltsin, via a clever maneuver, was able to get himself elected head of the committee charged with supervising the "architecture" of the plans.

The Supreme Soviet immediately went to work on a revision of the penal code. This led to the scrapping of two important provisions, articles 70 and 190, which had served as the basis for the convictions of many dissidents: those articles dealt with, respectively, "anti-Soviet agitation and propaganda" and "deliberate dissemination of deceitful fabrications that undermine the Soviet system."

On August 15, 1989, the ban on the importing of Bibles and works by exiled or expatriate Soviet authors was ended once and for all. After a few weeks, Russian television stopped broadcasting the parliamentary debates live because their popularity had led to a 20 percent drop in industrial production.

Due to disappointing economic figures — in 1988 growth was only 1.5 percent, contrasted to a rise in the budget deficit of 9 percent — Gorbachev slowed down the reforms, somewhat under the pressure of internal criticism. On April 29, 1989, *Pravda* published a number of speeches given by high party officials during a recent session of the party's central committee. In these speeches Gorbachev was implicitly accused of economic misman-agement, undermining the authority of the party and the armed forces, and making concessions to burgeoning nationalism.

For his part, Gorbachev conducted a major purge in the party, the cadres, and the government. Ninety of the one hundred ministers were dismissed, and the number of ministers was reduced to fifty-seven.

Communism in Chaos

In the meantime, the Communist world seemed to be coming apart at the seams. On the night of June 3, 1989, the seven-week-long peaceful occupation of Tiananmen Square (the Square of Heavenly Peace) in Beijing was ended when the government sent in the tanks. Before the eyes of television cameras, the Chinese army blatantly opened fire on the "counter-revolutionary" demonstrators, both students and sympa-thetic citizens. In Poland, the Solidarity trade union held strikes and car-ried on negotiations in 1988 and 1989 until the government finally re-lented and organized free elections. On June 4, 1989, members of the Polish Communist Party were defeated in the first free elections behind the Iron Curtain.

During his visit to West and East Germany, President Gorbachev de-clared that the Berlin Wall could probably come down, and shortly there-after, during a speech in the European Parliament in Strasbourg, he dis-tanced himself from the "Brezhnev doctrine": "The Soviet Union will no longer involve itself in the domestic affairs of its partners, but we cannot live with non-Communist governments in countries that are part of the Warsaw Pact." Yet shortly thereafter, in Poland, on August 25, 1989, Tadeusz Mazowiecki, politician and editor-in-chief of the conservative weekly *Tygodnik Solidarność*, was sworn in as the first non-Communist prime minister in the Eastern Bloc.

On May 2, 1989, Hungarian soldiers began demolishing the Iron Cur-tain by removing the blockade along the Austrian border, and on August 23, 1989, the Hungarian government opened the border entirely. In the weeks that followed, 20,000 East Germans fled to the West, and as the German Democratic Republic was celebrating its fortieth anniversary on October 7, 1989, the exodus continued unabated.

In the Soviet Union there were strikes in the Siberian coal mines that immediately spread to the Ukraine and led to the greatest social unrest since the 1920s. "This is the most important test that *perestroika* has had to undergo so far," said Mikhail Gorbachev. The government granted thirty-six of the miners' demands: more autonomy and the delivery of more soap, shoes, fresh meat, condensed milk, sugar, refrigerators, and sewing machines. The strike leaders also demanded the right to strike, as well as the right to form independent trade unions. In the Baltic republics, the call for economic independence grew louder and louder, and in the Caucasus the ethnic violence between Georgians and Abkhazians flared up again, while the conflict between Armenia and Azerbaijan over the region of Nagorno-Karabakh had still not been settled.

The World Council of Churches Meets in Moscow

On the eve of the annual meeting of the Central Committee of the World Council of Churches (WCC), which was scheduled to begin on July 17, 1989, in Moscow, Konstantin Kharchev of the Council for Religious Affairs told an Italian journalist in an interview: "It's not the government's job to meddle with religious affairs or with atheism. Atheistic propaganda must no longer be financed from the state budget." In an open letter, Ogorodnikov expressed his displeasure with regard to developments in the religious realm:

> In the eastern part of the Soviet Union it is still impossible to attend a worship service because the church buildings are hundreds of kilometers apart. That is partly the fault of the church leaders, who still adopt a docile attitude toward the regime. The Kazan Cathedral in Leningrad is still a museum of atheism, and the Tolga Monastery in Yaroslavl is currently serving as a public toilet.

Ogorodnikov calculated that, at the current rate, the return of all the church buildings would take decades.

Thanks to press credentials from the *Nederlands Dagblad*, a Dutch newspaper, Ogorodnikov was the only independent Soviet journalist to attend the Moscow meeting of the WCC. At first the credentials were taken from him at the request of Metropolitan Filaret of Minsk; but after a vociferous protest by Dutch journalists, they were given back. During the conference, hundreds of Uniates with flags gathered around the building where the Central Committee of the WCC was meeting in order to draw attention to the matter of their recognition.

Afterwards, Ogorodnikov commented on the meeting's official statements at a press conference held in a private apartment in Moscow, at which he also gave his view of the actual situation in the Russian Orthodox Church: "Between the registration of a church and the right of that church to open its doors for worship services, there is still a long bureaucratic road." He also took a deeper look at the discrimination of Eastern Rite Catholics, or Uniates, in the Ukraine. Starting in March 1989, they had been permitted to conduct their worship services in public, but they failed to receive official recognition due to the resistance of the Russian Orthodox Church and the fear of renewed outbursts of Ukrainian nationalism. A number of Uniate religious leaders went on a hunger strike, and in a church in Kiev blows were struck and a priest was arrested. On June 22, 1989, Konstantin Kharchev, under pressure from the Russian Orthodox Church, resigned as minister of religious affairs, supposedly because he had been too soft on the Uniates. The Uniates had to wait until Mikhail Gorbachev visited Pope John Paul II, in Rome at the end of 1989, to actually be recognized.

But with Muslim fundamentalism on the rise in the southern socialist republics, the president had even more religious worries. In July 1989, Mohammed-Moukhtar Babatov was elected by the Muslims of the northern Caucasus as the new mufti of Dagestan — a first in the history of the Soviet Union.

At the request of the Saint Herman of Alaska Bookstore in San Francisco, California, Ogorodnikov made an audio recording, entitled "Our Suffering Church," about his experiences in the Gulag. But at that point there was still no national museum or place of mourning to acknowledge and commemorate the suffering of the millions of victims and their families. There were no public apologies, and there was never a debate on the question of guilt. The guilty, who were easy to identify, got off scot-free.

The Soviet Union has never been able to address this black page in its history. Why not? The subject had been discussed in previous years, though never in any real depth; but since then, Russian society has undergone an unprecedented metamorphosis. The need to raise the lid on this "cesspool" became less urgent as the Soviet Union lost its international prestige, both in the Eastern Bloc and worldwide. Almost no one wanted to recall those painful memories, not least because millions of Russians had been directly or indirectly complicit in the operation of the camps. In addition, it was also in the interest of the Communists, who still were in control, to sweep this thorny question under the rug.

The nightmare of the past had to be forgotten as quickly as possible. An example of this passive attitude was the heavy-handed termination of a service commemorating the memory of Czar Nicholas II, which was held on July 16, 1989, in the house in Sverdlovsk where he had been murdered seventy-one years earlier.

While the victims of the terror had to be satisfied with a few crumbs, the bigwigs in the secret police did not have to give up their expensive apartments, luxurious dachas, and ample pensions. The fact that those who had collaborated with the old regime actually did quite well for themselves led to a great deal of social dissatisfaction that can still be felt today. In the metamorphosis that the Soviet Union underwent, political and economic upheaval went hand in hand with serious moral decay: in the first six months of 1989 the crime rate rose by 40 percent. Marx and Lenin were replaced by the free market and the mafia, whose impact became more and more perceptible. A network of an estimated three to five thousand criminal gangs, all operating at the same time in a confused tangle, left its mark on society. Three-quarters of all business owners had to hand over from 10 to 20 percent of their income in payoffs, and 150 syndicates had 40,000 private and state companies in their power and sometimes entire cities or regions. Other gangs specialized in the drug trade, the arms trade, illegal financial transactions, automobile theft, prostitution, the smuggling of raw materials and military hardware, extortion, bribery, falsification of papers, and hired killings.

Almost 30 percent of the members of the Supreme Soviet had ties to organized crime. The politicians who promised to come down hard on criminal activity were its first victims. Many teenagers were swept along by the unsavory element that was flooding society, and the average man on the street who took little notice of the economic, social, and political changes saw his buying power gradually shrink and his job disappear.

The Christian Seminar Increases Its Activities

By the end of 1988, Ogorodnikov had already published nine issues of the monthly magazine *Bulletin of the Christian Community*, the voice of the Christian Seminar, with the circulation of typed mother copies rising to 150. The *Bulletin* now had an editorial office, with Alexander Ogorodnikov as editor-in-chief, and an editorial staff that included a deputy editor, Father Valery Lapkovsky of Kerch, and Valery Nikolsky of Pskov. The American professor James Scherer remarked that Ogorodnikov "became completely absorbed in his role as underground Christian publisher." Michael Bourdeaux of the British Keston Institute called the *Bulletin* "the encyclopedia of religious dissidence in the Soviet Union."

One serious problem that inhibited the activities of the Christian Seminar was the lack of a meeting space. On August 13, 1989, for example, a literary evening that had been planned for the Krasnopresnia Culture House in Moscow was called off at the last minute because the regional committee of the Communist Party refused to make the space available. However, the lecture at the Estonian University of Tartu and the homage to Alexander Solzhenitsyn — in Moscow in December 1988 and in Vilnius in April 1989 — were given the green light.

On September 20, 1989, the Christian Seminar opened a Sunday school. The program included catechism, patrology (a branch of Catholic theology involving the study of the lives and writings of the church fathers), church history, and aspects of church life. A class in liturgical singing was later added to the lessons.

After the Christian Seminar in Moscow had been given its own storage facility, the social activities could be approached in a more professional way. The needs were immense, as indicated by the first official Russian poverty report, which had been released by the government on January 30, 1989. Forty-three million residents — one in six — could barely get by. A group of volunteers led by Katya Brodenko, later the wife of Alexander Ogorodnikov, worked on distributing clothing and food. These goods were imported in containers by the Dutch organization Dorcas Aid International (DAI), the British nongovernmental organization Jubilee Campaign, and the French Orthodox community. Only the destitute were eligible for assistance, and the names of those who received aid were carefully recorded.

The Seminar also developed charitable projects in Tatarstan and Leningrad. Forty tons of food was sent to refugees in Abkhazia, and twelve tons to Chechnya. In nine relief actions, the Seminar provided assistance to about 84,000 persons. Members of the Seminar also helped in the building of a church in a camp in the region of Ivanoskaya.

As more and more religious, journalistic, and social activities were developed, Alexander Ogorodnikov set up an umbrella organization called the Christian Democratic Union of Russia (CDUR). In 1989 this organization founded the first private school in the Soviet Union. Ogorodnikov's son Dima went to school there, as did a large number of children from Armenian refugee families. The school director appointed by Ogorodnikov was asked to prepare to have the school officially recognized, which could take a long time because of the slow-moving bureaucracy in the Soviet Union. But the director had the school registered under another name, even though it was an initiative of the CDUR. When the director refused to register a number of pupils referred by Ogorodnikov, a serious conflict arose that threatened the future existence of the school.

Because of Ogorodnikov's international contacts, ten to fifteen young people a year were able to do internships abroad: as kitchen help, journalists, or on the staff of a British parliamentarian. Others were given scholarships to an American university. But even now Ogorodnikov frequently had to face the fact that, to his regret, his trust was being abused and betrayed. The CDUR had more strings in its bow. It organized courses for Christian managers and formed the League of Christian Businessmen. But Ogorodnikov's idealistic vision was somewhat shaken when it turned out that most of the participants just wanted to get rich quick.

The Founding of the First Christian Democratic Party in the Soviet Union

After a two-year bureaucratic struggle, Ogorodnikov finally got his residence permit for the city of Moscow in the summer of 1989. This development, along with the gradually changing social and political climate in the country, pushed him to devote himself fully to political engagement in an attempt to set a Christian seal on society. In May 1989 he set up an informal Christian Democratic Initiative Group. Several organizations responded enthusiastically to the idea of political ideology along Christian lines. Then in August 1989 (Aug. 4-7), in the studio of a Moscow artist, the first Christian Democratic Party in Russia was formed in the presence of delegates from eighty social and political Christian organizations. The participants unanimously agreed to base the party ideology on the ethical principles of the gospel, personalism, and the fundamental values of Christian culture — with the spiritual revival of the Soviet Union as its goal.

In contrast to the generally accepted view — that the country would recover through the introduction of democracy and capitalism — Ogorodnikov said:

> Meaningful change can only be brought about if there is a moral and spiritual basis, and if this change is rooted in belief in God. Christianity is not something that happens in your head. It constitutes an integral part of society and of real life, and consequently of politics as well.

The CDUR planned a congress of Christian Democrats in the Soviet Union, to include representatives from all the republics.

But it did not take long for the government to react. On August 8, 1989, a day after the founding congress, the police broke into the offices of the magazine *Bulletin of the Christian Community* in Moscow, and took editorial staff member Igor Kalinichev in to be interrogated. In addition, Alexander Chuyev, the owner of the apartment that was the magazine's official address, received a summons from the police.

On the other hand, immediately after its founding, the newly founded party received the support of Christian Democrat International (CDI). This umbrella organization, composed of Christian Democratic parties from fifty-four countries in Europe, Africa, Asia, and the Americas, was founded in 1961 and was under the chairmanship of Eduardo Fernandez of Guatemala; but the driving forces behind it were the Belgians André Louis, Anthony de Meeüs, and Leo Delcroix. From 1989 to 1991, the CDI published the Russian magazine *Christianskaya Demokratiya* in French, Spanish, and English; it contained articles on political developments in Eastern Europe.

Because Ogorodnikov could not get an exit visa to travel to Paris for the August 21-26 celebration of the 200th anniversary of the *Déclaration des Droits de l'Homme et du Citoyen* (the Declaration of the Rights of Man and the Citizen, which came out of the French Revolution), Secretary-General André Louis of the CDI read aloud a message that Ogorodnikov prepared for the occasion.

The extent to which the CDUR's international contacts provoked the Russian government was something the Belgian politician Leo Delcroix experienced personally in early September during a visit to Moscow. He arranged by telephone to meet with Ogorodnikov, but shortly before his arrival, the police and the KGB broke into Ogorodnikov's apartment — his telephone had been tapped — in an attempt to prevent the meeting.

Delcroix was held for hours in a separate room, and only after his inter-preter took photographs of the heated discussion between Ogorodnikov and the KGB agents did the agents clear out.

On September 9, 1989, in the hall of the historical society Memorial in Moscow, the second congress of the political wing of the CDUR took place in the presence of the Austrian Christian Democratic politician Andreas Khol, chairman of the European Democratic Union (EDU). Amid loud ap-plause, Alexander Ogorodnikov was appointed chairman of the CDUR; Vitaly Savitsky of Leningrad, Father Valery Lapkovsky of Kerch, and Alex-ander Chuyev of Moscow were appointed vice chairmen; and they estab-lished a political coordinating board made up of ten members, three of whom were priests.

In late September 1989, Ogorodnikov took his first trip abroad. He was finally certain that the government would not take away his passport and that he would be able to return to the Soviet Union. His first stop was Brussels, where he visited the headquarters of Christian Democrat Inter-national (CDI). A few hours later he traveled with a Belgian delegation to Guatemala, where the triennial congress of the CDI was to take place (September 18-20). Ogorodnikov was given a warm welcome, and the CDUR party was accepted as a member of the congress.

Because there was so much interest in the West in Gorbachev's poli-cies of *glasnost* and *perestroika,* many people were eager to see Ogorod-nikov in person. From Guatemala he traveled to the United States for a meeting with Richard Schifter, Ronald Reagan's former ambassador on the United Nations Commission on Human Rights (UNCHR), with sev-eral members of Congress, and with a large number of American Ortho-dox Christians, most of whom had spent years working for his release. He then moved on to Great Britain, where he met with David Alton, a mem-ber of Parliament who had also spent years championing his cause. Ogorodnikov spoke at a parliamentary hearing in the presence of John Major, who was then the minister for foreign affairs, and he also ad-dressed the parliaments of the Netherlands, Malta, and France.

CDUR Secretary Sergei Savchenko Murdered in Car "Accident"

Ogorodnikov returned to the Soviet Union in mid-October 1989, where he received scores of international guests. Among those from the United States were Dr. Ernest Gordon, dean of the chapel at Princeton University, and Rev. Charles Rush of Christ Church in Summit, New Jersey. Because of his great popularity in the West, Ogorodnikov had become "inviolable" in his own country, so the KGB decided instead to come down hard on his party, the Christian Democratic movement, which had gradually come to play a leading role in the postwar politics of Western Europe and was apparently a real threat to Communism.

On October 23, 1989, Sergei Savchenko, secretary of the CDUR and Ogorodnikov's political right-hand man, was killed in a staged automobile accident. Savchenko was just about to leave for Brussels, where he had planned to study journalism, and had just come through a frustrating application procedure for an exit visa. The circumstances surrounding this "accident" were identical to those under which Raphael Ogorodnikov had lost his life the previous year. And shortly before, on October 13, 1989, Merab Kostava, a supporter of the former dissident Zviad Gamsachurdia, had also died in a suspicious car crash in Georgia. Taking leave of Savchenko was doubly bitter because his parents, as convinced atheists, were firmly opposed to a church funeral.

Because of an avalanche of invitations, Ogorodnikov soon left once again for the West, and therefore was not present when the CDUR office in Moscow was raided and plundered on November 7, 1989. Father Viktor Grigoriev, member of the political coordinating board of the CDUR, suffered a number of blows during this brutal robbery. The intruders, who were acting by order of the KGB, took computers and printers, a fax machine, a video camera, video recorders, and various other office supplies, most of which had been given to the CDUR by Christian Democrat International.

The office of the Democratic Union was also broken into and turned upside down. Sergei Kuznetsov, the journalist who had been arrested in Sverdlovsk in December 1988, was sentenced to three years in prison in November 1989 for "slandering and resisting the police." But under great international pressure, Kuznetsov — the best-known dissident of the Gorbachev era — was freed on January 9, 1990. After an article in the Paris weekly *La Pensée Russe* examined the way the KGB was controlling the Russian Orthodox Church, Viktor Popkov, who had become a close associate of Gleb Yakunin, was beaten on the street by a group of unknown assailants.

The Eastern Bloc Collapses Like a House of Cards

After the publication of a Russian opinion poll that revealed that parliamentarian Andrei Sakharov was more popular than Mikhail Gorbachev, the president called the editors-in-chief of *Ogonyok* and *Argumenti i Fakti* on the carpet. Viktor Afanasyev, the editor-in-chief of *Pravda,* was fired. While strikes were erupting among the miners of Siberia, the police crushed a demonstration of a thousand people at the Siberian KGB headquarters in Tomsk on the unofficial "Day of the Political Prisoner." And while the seventy-second anniversary of the Russian Revolution was being celebrated on November 7, 1989, a counterdemonstration was being held in Moscow — unparalleled in the history of the Soviet Union.

Two days later, on November 9, 1989, the Communist implosion reached a historic high point with the fall of the Berlin Wall. The next day, in Bulgaria, Todor Zhivkov was removed as Communist Party leader, and a few days later, on November 16, he stepped down as head of state. In Czechoslovakia, the Communist Party surrendered its monopoly position after mass protest demonstrations were held, and on December 29, 1989, the so-called Velvet Revolution reached its pinnacle when Václav Havel left prison and entered the presidential palace. Only in Romania was the fall of Communism accompanied by bloodshed. After attempting to remove László Tokés from his position as pastor in the city of Timisoara in March 1989, and to evict him from his home on December 15, 1989, Securitate, the Romanian secret security police, struggled with the local population for four days, December 16-20. A few days later the civil protests in the Romanian capital of Bucharest grew into a popular uprising, which ended with the execution of President Nicolae Ceausescu and his wife, Elena, on December 25, 1989.

On October 7, 1989, the Hungarian Socialist Labor Party — the Communist Party of Hungary — was abolished and replaced by the Hungarian Socialist Party. The Polish United Workers' Party was abolished in January 1990, and in Bulgaria, Romania, and Yugoslavia the leading role assigned to the Communist Party was removed from the constitutions. Only Albania was left, where the regime of Ramiz Alia was still holding firm.

As Communism in the Eastern Bloc collapsed like a house of cards, Mikhail Gorbachev — who had set the process in motion in the first place — held on to his precarious position for dear life. On November 27, 1989, in a two-page piece published in the Communist Party newspaper

Pravda, he declared that "Marxism will become stronger, and that will happen under the leadership of the Communist Party." But Andrei Sakharov joined in the struggle against Article Six of the constitution, which legitimated the leading role of the Communist Party. He called for a strike, and on December 12, 1989, he asked for a debate in the Congress of People's Deputies. The request was only narrowly rejected. Two days later, on December 14, 1989, Sakharov died suddenly.

Gorbachev had hoped to lead the Soviet Union in a new direction, and to do it in an orderly fashion, with the Communist Party at the helm; but the facts caught up with him. Although he continued to swear by dialogue and to guard against repression, the democratization process kept unleashing increasingly uncontrollable forces. And the Communist Party did not function as the engine in this process, but as the main obstacle to renewal.

In the meantime, Gorbachev, like a desperate fireman, scrambled from one smoldering hot spot to another, knowing that all it would take would be one serious fire to set the entire forest ablaze. When he visited Lithuania on January 11, 1990, there were 200,000 angry demonstrators waiting for him. The Lithuanian branch of the Communist Party broke away from Moscow, and in Latvia the party lost its leading role. In the Caucasus, the Armenians were involved in a dispute with the Azerbaijanis, and the Abkhazians and Ossetians wanted to break away from Georgia. But what all these peoples wanted more than anything else was to free themselves from Moscow. The key question was: Which republic would be the first to leave the Soviet Union, and how many would follow its example?

At an extraordinary session of the Communist Party on February 5, 1990, Gorbachev acknowledged for the first time that the Soviet Union had a de facto multiparty system. The president, who was still the general secretary of the Communist Party, was forced to look on in dismay as the Party — the "tower of strength" — quickly crumbled away. Parliamentarian Telman Gdljan, the former examining magistrate, was thrown out of the party after he demonstrated that Yegor Ligachev, the leader of the conservative wing and member of the Politburo, had close ties with the Uzbek mafia. In the first nine months of 1990, 600,000 members gave up their membership. "I look with contempt on all those who are now leaving the Communist Party and seeking shelter elsewhere," Gorbachev said bitterly.

The policy of free party formation, however, degenerated into total chaos. Dozens of groups came into being — independent and interchanging alliances that were based not on ideas but on personalities — only to quickly fuse with another group or to disappear entirely. On the left were the Social Democratic Party, the New Socialists, the Socialist Party of Vladimir Machanov (one of the leaders of the Siberian miners' strike of July 1989), the Anarchist-Syndicalist Confederation, and the Greens. Boris Yeltsin set up the reformist Democratic Forum. The Democratic Union — the oldest opposition movement — gave rise to the extremist right-wing Liberal-Democratic Party of Russia, headed by Vladimir Zhirinovsky. There also appeared Obshchina (the Russian People's Front); the Constitutional Democrats; the United Russian Workers' Front; the Russian Federation People's Front; and the Party of Garry Kasparov, the greatest chess player of all time. This colorful political crazy quilt, which had deteriorated into a hopelessly complex tangle, changed composition almost daily.

Christian Democracy Divided

In November and December 1989, Ogorodnikov, who had become the most popular Christian politician in the Soviet Union, traveled around the world once again. He visited the Netherlands, France, Belgium, and the United States, and David Alton invited him for a holiday in Liverpool. Visiting the Beatles Museum, where he heard the song "With a Little Help from My Friends," made him think of one night in the Gulag when he pressed his ear to the floor and heard that song far in the distance in the guards' shed. That music had been his only contact with the outside world and had been a real source of comfort.

But Ogorodnikov's lengthy absence did little to promote the further development of the CDUR in his own country, partly due to the loss of its secretary, Sergei Savchenko. The party had no social or ideological roots in the Russian Orthodox hierarchy, despite the cooperation of a number of priests, and, unlike its Western Europe counterparts, it could not turn to any Christian lay movements for help. In addition, the ecumenical position of the CDUR was still a sensitive issue for many Orthodox Christians. On December 10, 1989, during the fourth congress of the CDUR, a number of cooperative agreements were signed with the Christian Democratic parties of Belarus, Estonia, Lithuania, and Poland, and with the Free Trade Union of Vladimir Klebanov.

But the aim of the CDUR "to develop a unified bloc of Christian Democratic forces before the elections occur" was doomed to failure. The Russian electoral system and political operation were not based on parties back then, as they were in the West, but on personalities. It was not ideas but personal relationships that often hindered the development of a broad political movement.

Besides the CDUR, other Christian Democratic groups made their presence known. Viktor Akshuchits, the ambitious publisher of *Vybor* (Choice), the philosophical and cultural magazine with a Christian basis, and of a million copies of Alexander Solzhenitsyn's *The Gulag Archipelago*, also had political ambitions. And Vladimor Osipov, one of the first dissidents, founded the Patriotic Christian Union. And then there was the Church and Perestroika Movement, which grew up around Father Gleb Yakunin.

Fraudulent Elections for the RSFSR in 1990

On March 5, 1990, elections were held for both the local governments and for the parliament of the Russian Soviet Federative Socialist Republic, the largest republic of the Soviet Union. Although the electoral battle was not a fair one — the Communists censored the media and invested a great deal of money in the campaign — the reformers and nationalists were very successful once again. They captured the two biggest cities in the country: Gavriil Popov became mayor of Moscow, and Anatoly Sobshak came to power in Leningrad. In Moscow, six of those elected to the city council were from the CDUR.

There were 8,254 candidates on the various ballots for 1,068 parliamentary seats, 86 percent of whom were from the Communist Party. Boris Yeltsin, whose campaign symbols were the white-blue-and-red czarist flag and the image of Saint Andrew, patron saint of Russia, won a glorious victory. Gleb Yakunin, Viktor Akshuchits, and Father Dmitri Nesterov of Volgograd, an active member of the CDUR, each gained a seat.

Alexander Ogorodnikov had put himself forward as a candidate for the Moscow district of Dzerzhinsky, which was named after Felix Dzerzhinsky, creator of the Cheka, precursor of the KGB. This district, with half a million residents, was where the headquarters of the secret service was located. Because it was thought that Ogorodnikov probably wanted to restrict the power of the KGB, the KGB did all it could to torpedo his electoral campaign. For example, the owner of the apartment in which the CDUR was housed suddenly refused to permit entrance to Ogorodnikov and his staff members — under pressure from the KGB. They weren't even allowed to take their party materials and office supplies with them, including their computers. Not only were the computers worth a fortune, but they were also essential for running the campaign. In the weeks that followed, pamphlets slandering Ogorodnikov were circulated on CDUR letterhead. Ogorodnikov was powerless; he couldn't train a new secretary overnight. Instead he chose a "creative" solution: he and his staff members would go house to house and conduct the campaign at important Moscow intersections with the slogan "A new face for a new day."

On election day the CDUR was denied permission by the government to delegate witnesses for the counting of votes. When none of the candidates in the Dzerzhinsky electoral district won a majority, it became necessary to hold a second round of voting. Tension was also high for that round. Vadim Pergament, a member of the electoral commission who secretly had great sympathy for Ogorodnikov, told the latter about the intrigue that was taking place behind the scenes. When the votes were being counted and it appeared that Ogorodnikov would gain a majority, the results were rigged. Pergament drew up a list of the faked votes. When the winner was announced, officially the Communist candidate, Pergament raised an objection and announced that he was going to lodge a complaint with the courts. But on his way home he was attacked and wounded. Pergament survived the attack and reported the incident to the police, and the next day he went to the courthouse to make his complaint official. After that he disappeared without a trace. His relatives finally found him late that evening in a hospital in a Moscow suburb, where he soon died. Nothing ever came of Pergament's complaint, and his family immigrated to the United States a short time later.

On May 29, 1990, Boris Yeltsin was elected parliamentary chairman of the RSFSR, or Russia, defeating his rival, the conservative Alexander Vlasov. In his new parliamentary capacity, Yeltsin took the first step of challenging the authority of Mikhail Gorbachev: the parliament passed a declaration of sovereignty; decreed that the laws of the RSFSR were to take precedence over those of the Soviet Union; and removed from the constitution the leading role assigned to the Communist Party.

Yeltsin also began talks with Gorbachev concerning monetary control and control of the banks and mineral resources, and he unilaterally signed a partnership agreement with Lithuania. This put an end to the economic embargo that the Soviet Union had declared after Lithuania's unilateral declaration of independence of March 11, 1990.

CDI Promotes Fragmentation of Russian Christian Democracy

After the disappointing elections of March 1990, the idea of a great Christian Democratic party seemed consigned to the realm of utopia. On April 8 and 9, 1990, parliamentarian Father Viacheslav Polosin, Father Gleb Yakunin, and Viktor Akshuchits formed the Russian Christian Democratic Movement (RCDM). Three other parliamentarians also joined the RCDM group in the RSFSR parliament.

Although Ogorodnikov's CDUR always had many supporters and was backed by the Christian Democrat International (CDI), the CDI had bet on several organizations at the same time. On June 29, 1990, for example, Viktor Akshuchits attended the world summit of the Christian Democrats in Budapest at the invitation of CDI political adviser Anthony de Meeüs. Ogorodnikov was an official speaker at the event.

The RCDM also received the full support of the CDI. In late 1990, the magazine *Christianskaya Demokratiya* reported that the RCDM had 18,000 members and had set up branches in ninety-six cities, making it the second largest independent party in the Soviet Union.

Ogorodnikov's CDUR, which was officially registered in August 1990 as the first independent party in the Soviet Union, lost some of its supporters but continued to play a significant role, particularly in the Moscow region. In a chaotic Soviet society, where the climate was by no means ready for political parties based on the Western model, it was still difficult to translate political enthusiasm into practical realities. Father Viktor Grigoriev ended his political activities in disillusionment; but in May 1990, Alexander Chuyev formed the Christian Democratic Party of Russia. After a meeting with Anthony de Meeüs in Brussels, parliamentarian Dmitri Nesterov of the Volgograd branch left the CDUR during the congress of November 24-25, 1990, in Moscow. Following in his footsteps was Dmitri Antsiferov, who was part of a group of young Moscow Christian Democrats.

In early 1989, Ogorodnikov was given the first printing press to be legally imported into the Soviet Union. The Anglican priest Dick Rodgers had collected money in his parish in the British city of Birmingham to finance the purchase. Upon arriving in Moscow, however, the machine was immediately returned to England by customs officials. So parliamentarian David Alton went to Prime Minister Margaret Thatcher, and she wrote a letter to the Soviet authorities: "This is a special gift from the United Kingdom and we would very much like this printing press to reach the addressed party, Alexander Ogorodnikov, promptly and without problems."

The machine was sent for the second time, and David Alton later traveled from London especially to monitor the transfer of property. The authorities tried to deceive him and Ogorodnikov by telling them that the machine had never arrived. "It was loaded in London," responded Alton, "so it *has* to be here." As proof, he showed them the letter from Prime Minister Thatcher — in the original English with a Russian translation. A few minutes later the printing press was unloaded. Ogorodnikov put the machine on a truck, and that night, with Alton's help, he printed the first folder in offset.

Shortly thereafter, the *Bulletin of the Christian Community* was replaced by the new monthly called *Herald of Christian Democracy*, which was printed on the new printing press and quickly reached a circulation of 25,000. Editor-in-chief Ogorodnikov focused not only on religious reporting but also on social, political, and community problems that fell within the aims of the Christian Seminar. A few months later, in August 1990, the new press law went into effect. It guaranteed freedom of expression and put an official ban on censorship; but it also made it compulsory for newspapers and magazines to be registered.

In the meantime, the Supreme Soviet was dealing with a large-scale case of corruption in which high-level party functionaries had been acutely embarrassed by serious accusations made by two congress members, the former examining magistrates Telman Gdljan and Nikolai Ivanov.

The government revealed a new plan for switching over to a free-market economy within five years. In the first phase, which would begin on January 1, 1991, food prices would double. The operation would end with the dismantling of business monopolies, most of them state businesses, which would have to be completed by 1995.

CHAPTER TEN

New Legal Status for Religion: The Crowning Glory

The Russian Orthodox Church, which had grown into the largest organization in the Soviet Union and had more members than did the Communist Party by the late 1980s, could no longer be ignored as a power factor. What was the explanation for this success? More than anything else, the church embodied the "Russian soul," and during the gradual implosion of the Soviet empire it stepped forward as the guardian of the national interests and traditions.

Yet the church was also the object of a great deal of criticism, and it was simply not able to come to terms with its past. In May 1990, Alexei II was chosen to replace the recently deceased Patriarch Pimen by means of a secret ballot and without the interference of the government. But Alexei II had always supported the regime. In fact, in 1980 he had even declared: "Soviet citizens are never arrested on the basis of their religious or ideological convictions." A report at that time by chairman Furov of the Council for Religious Affairs contained a list of all those who had "fully submitted to state atheism," with Alexei taking second place on the list, bested on that list only by his predecessor, Pimen. But the new patriarch did not say a word about the past.

Russian Orthodoxy was also struggling with growing pains caused by limited financial resources; the laborious renovation of old churches and the building of new ones; the lack of religious reading material and religious education; a shortage of priests; and the emergence of schismatic movements. In addition, there was more and more resentment among believers with regard to the timid attitude of the church hierarchy, who hesitated to proclaim the word of God outside the church, to revive Orthodox life, and to develop lively congregations.

Orthodox Church leaders clung to their jobs and their growing social prestige. They didn't take up the torch for religious freedom, nor did they enter into discussions with believers about the difficulties with which the church was struggling, because officially the antireligious legislation of 1929 was still in effect, the last spasms of which were still perceptible. Even in 1988, the KGB refused to accept six candidates for the theological seminary. And on April 5, 1990, the Lutheran minister Harald Meri disappeared in Estonia after his house had been set on fire. One month later his tortured body was found. Shortly thereafter, the young Lithuanian priest Armands Arkentins died in the area of Riga as a result of a staged automobile "accident."

On Sunday morning, September 9, 1990, fifty-five-year-old Father Alexander Men was murdered by a man with an ax on his way to his church in Novaya Derevnya, fifty kilometers outside Moscow. The ax is a traditional Russian symbol of revolt: it was the weapon used by Raskolnikov, the main character of Fyodor Dostoyevsky's novel *Crime and Punishment.* A shock wave reverberated throughout the country. President Gorbachev immediately ordered a thorough investigation, but the murder was never solved. Alexander Men had plenty of enemies — among them the anti-Semites of the right-wing extremist group Pamyat (he was of Jewish origin), the conservative establishment of the Russian Orthodox Church, the police, and — last but not least — the KGB. His death was an unmistakable threat to everyone who might try to defy the system. Shortly thereafter, the Ukrainian priest Ivan Kupts was also murdered.

On October 25, 1990, the new law concerning freedom of conscience and religious assembly was passed by the Duma, partly inspired by a 1988 text from the Christian Seminar. The churches were given the right to acquire property and to give religious instruction, and all government interference in church affairs was henceforth forbidden. This was a great triumph for the religious dissidents in general; but for Alexander Ogorodnikov personally, it was the crowning glory of fifteen years of struggle.

All religious associations were free to register, without any restrictions. As a result, thousands of foreign missionaries overran the Soviet Union, and numerous sects descended on the country as well, including the Church of Scientology. This great diversity in religious options gave rise to a new line of division in society: a line between the Orthodox and non-Orthodox.

"500-Day Plan" as Shock Therapy

While Mikhail Gorbachev was being widely applauded in the West for making it possible to end the Cold War and bring democratization to the Eastern Bloc, his reforms were becoming less and less popular in his own country. Premier Nikolai Rizhkov, who had been appointed in 1985, preferred a cautious approach. His call for a regulated market economy with controlled price rises, slow privatization, and the gradual and staggered closing of unprofitable businesses resulted in longer and longer lines at the shops. Not only had bread become scarce, but riots broke out in 1990 over a shortage of cigarettes.

On August 1, 1990, Gorbachev, a notorious waverer, finally decided on a radical change of course by approving an alternative economic plan that had been drawn up by Stanislav Shalatin, his top economic adviser, and the economist and liberal politician Grigory Yavlinsky. The basic idea was to replace seventy years of planned economy with a market economy in five hundred days, which would unavoidably lead to price increases, except for the prices of one hundred basic products; drastic cut-backs in defense spending, foreign aid, and the KGB; the sale of state-owned companies; and the reform of the banking system. Shalatin was opting for short-term pain over long-term torture.

The Supreme Soviet — the parliament — went on to pass a law that replaced central planning with the free market without any strict timing; it gave the president a number of powers to deal with the economic crisis and to restore order in the country. Gorbachev was constantly feeling Boris Yeltsin breathing down his neck, because the latter was eager to begin implementing the "500-day plan" in "his" Russian Soviet Federative Socialist Republic.

Besides the economic shock therapy, the president was also working on a new unification agreement, since fourteen of the fifteen Soviet republics had declared some form of independence in recent months. Kyrgyzstan in Central Asia was the only republic absent from that list. But was it still possible to turn the tide? Latvia and Belarus had introduced their own customs service, and 400,000 young men of draft age refused to comply with a call-up notice from the Soviet army.

After Alexander Solzhenitsyn's citizenship had been restored in 1990, he published a 16,000-word essay in the *Komsomolskaja Pravda* of September 18, 1990, entitled "How Can We Breathe New Life into Russia?" This was his first work to appear in the Soviet Union following his banishment. The author began his article with these prophetic words: "The clock of Communism has struck its last hour, but the concrete colossus has not yet completely collapsed. Instead of finally being liberated, we may be crushed under the rubble instead." Solzhenitsyn, who refused to say the name of Gorbachev aloud, continued to play a major role behind the scenes after 1990, and his works were widely circulated.

When Mikhail Gorbachev was awarded the Nobel Peace Prize on October 15, 1990, the government newspaper *Izvestia* responded this way:

> The moment of truth has now arrived for Gorbachev and his team. Maneuvering between left and right is exhausting his possibilities. If things go on like this, the president will be in danger of missing the train for good. That is what happened to the leaders of Eastern Europe, who did introduce reforms but were too slow in abandoning the old stereotypes and old politics.

But history repeated itself. Under the pressure of the Communist Party, Gorbachev finally approved a number of economic reforms that did not go as far as the radical "500-day plan" would, and a short time later he openly distanced himself from that idea as well. He hoped to turn the tide — at least for the time being — by assigning himself a number of sweeping powers, with the support of the Supreme Soviet. Yet, despite all of that, the disintegration process of the Soviet Union continued at top speed. At the celebration of the seventy-third anniversary of the Russian Revolution on November 7, 1990, someone fired a few shots at Gorbachev from a distance of eighty meters, while elsewhere in the city, 30,000 demonstrators took to the streets at two alternative celebrations.

Gorbachev's dialogue with his main rival, Boris Yeltsin, began to flag, and hard-liner Yuri Kravchenko, whom Gorbachev had appointed head of radio and television, made drastic reductions in the selection of programs and the pool of journalists. In November 1990, Vadim Batakin, the minister of foreign affairs, was replaced by the hawk Boris Pugo. The tone of Gorbachev's speeches became more forbidding, and he openly denounced the Baltic struggles for independence, the democrats, Boris Yeltsin, and the anti-Communists.

In the meantime, the country was struggling with a food shortage. On November 20, 1990, an emergency alert was issued by Anatoly Sobshak, the reformist mayor of Leningrad: "The only way to avoid an outbreak of famine in the city this winter and to keep public opinion from turning against the democratic reforms is to send in emergency help." The food shortage led to bartering, rationing, and hoarding on a grand scale. Nine regions stopped delivering milk to Moscow in order to meet the needs of their own populations.

To a great extent, this famine was the result of the failing distribution system. Because of the dramatic socioeconomic situation — in 1989 the Soviet Union was contending once again with negative economic growth — President Gorbachev decided not to travel to Oslo to personally accept the Nobel Peace Prize that had been awarded to him. But he could do nothing about the fact that thousands of tons of imported food lay rotting in the harbors. In December 1990, Eduard Shevardnadze, the minister of foreign affairs, resigned his post in protest to Gorbachev's policies, and Premier Nikolai Rizhkov disappeared temporarily from the political arena after a heart attack.

CDUR Opens Soup Kitchen for the Poor

In Moscow, more and more poor people were seen wearing rags and scavenging in garbage containers for something to eat. Ogorodnikov's CDUR responded by opening up an outdoor soup kitchen and distributing bread to the needy. Lobbying also began for the establishment of a permanent soup kitchen. But finding a building to house such a kitchen in Moscow, where there was a lack of privately owned buildings, was extremely difficult. So a number of British parliamentarians, including David Alton, got in touch with the Moscow city council. Under pressure from CDUR city council members, the city finally made available a large building on Khoroshevskoye Shosse in the Khoroshevsky district for 7.5 million rubles a quarter in rent. Despite its social aims and nonprofit program, the CDUR still had to pay as much as any commercial organization would.

With the support of Christian organizations and businesses in the United States, Germany, France, and the Netherlands, the first private soup kitchen in the Soviet Union opened its doors in February 1991. The kitchen was run entirely by volunteers. Representatives of foreign NGOs, such as Dorcas and the Jubilee Campaign, came by regularly to lend a helping hand. Warm meals were served daily to between 450 and 550 underprivileged and homeless people and refugees. Among them were war veterans, former prisoners of conscience — the so-called "Heroes of the Soviet Union" — and even professors from Moscow State University, who had not received their salary in months. Another frequent visitor was an impoverished old man who had walked all the way from the other end of the city. His father had been a rich Russian industrialist before 1917, as well as the initiator and sponsor of a large number of charity projects, but his family had been completely ruined by the Revolution. Meals were brought to the sick in their homes. In the cellar of the building there were showers where the homeless could wash, and medical help was available in emergency cases. The food was free, but those who were not really destitute were sent away.

But the soup kitchen, which had been created out of bitter necessity, was in fact just a drop in the bucket. To alleviate the real need, a large number of such soup kitchens would have to be set up all over the city. The CDUR was eager to expand its activities, but it already had its hands full keeping this one facility running. Ogorodnikov approached the Moscow city council for substantial rental reduction or permission to buy potatoes and vegetables from the state farms, but to no effect.

Boris Yeltsin Becomes President of the RSFSR

Boris Yeltsin steadily consolidated his power position. In the elections for president of Russia — the Russian Soviet Federative Socialist Republic — held on June 12, 1991, he beat Vadim Batakin, the former minister of foreign affairs, and Nikolai Rizhkov, the former premier, in the first round. From his new position, Yeltsin was making it more and more difficult for Gorbachev, president of the Soviet Union, since without Russia (RSFSR) there was nothing left of the Soviet Union but a skeleton. At Yeltsin's inauguration as president of Russia, held in the Palace of Congresses in the Kremlin on July 10, 1991, the gigantic portrait of Lenin and the Communist symbols were covered with a Russian flag. Yeltsin did not begin his speech in the customary way, with the familiar *Tovarishchi!* (Comrades), but with "Citizens of the Russian Republic! The great Russia will rise again!" Later that day, the newly minted Russian president was blessed by Patriarch Alexei II.

It was precisely during this period in 1991 that the critically ill Iol Ogorodnikov asked his son Alexander to come to Chistopol without delay. Because of his full agenda, however, the latter could not leave Moscow immediately. This was a great pity, because Iol Ogorodnikov died soon afterward — without having seen his son before his death. Margarita Firsova, Alexander's mother, moved to Moscow after her husband's death. Ogorodnikov's civil marriage to Katya Brodenko also took place in 1991. Three children were born to them: Denil (1995), Sonya (2002), and Andrei (2007).

Through his contacts with the Jewish community, Ogorodnikov was also able to purchase (for $5,000) a small apartment in a suburb of Moscow from a Jewish family who had immigrated to Israel. He financed it with money from the sale of the Seminar house in Redkino, which his parents had given him after his return from the Gulag in 1987. He had lived in that house for years. Shortly after that, the prices of real estate would skyrocket due to the liberalization of the housing market.

Reactionary "August Coup" in Moscow Fails

Rumors of a coup d'état by the conservative Communist hard-liners in the Soviet government had been circulating for years. But on August 19, 1991, while General Secretary and Soviet President Mikhail Gorbachev was vacationing at his dacha in the Crimea, the Communist old guard actually did try to seize power. The brains behind the coup was Anatoly Lukyanov, chairman of the Supreme Soviet. He was supported by Vice President Gennadi Yanayev, Defense Minister Dmitri Yazov, and KGB chief Vladimir Kryuchkov. On that August day at seven o'clock in the morning, Yanayev declared a state of emergency for certain parts of the country in a live broadcast on state radio and television and appointed himself president of the "Committee for the State of Emergency." This caused considerable confusion in the Soviet Union — including within the army, which posted itself at a number of strategic buildings.

The incident was an important turning point in the history of the Soviet Union. Gorbachev's policies of *glasnost* and *perestroika* had brought about drastic changes, but now the reforms were once again at risk. Ogorodnikov realized that, if the coup were to succeed, he would probably be arrested again. The Communist hard-liners despised the members of the CDUR party because of their intense contact with Christian Democratic International (CDI). He prepared himself mentally for a new prison sentence. To be on the safe side, he brought his Bible with him when he left his apartment early in the morning on the day of the coup. At the

CDUR office, which was located in a building in the Dzerzhinsky district of Moscow, about a hundred party militants had gathered for a scheduled meeting with André Louis, Anthony de Meeüs, and Leo Delcroix of the CDI.

Ogorodnikov immediately sent out a call to the soldiers, asking them not to shoot. All the telephone connections with the outside world had been cut, but a message came in on the one fax line that was still open from Boris Yeltsin, president of the RSFSR, who was communicating from his dacha in the village of Usovo. He strongly condemned the putsch as a "reactionary, unconstitutional coup," and he called for a national general strike.

Ogorodnikov, who certainly was no fan of Yeltsin, had hundreds of copies made of Yeltsin's appeal. He took them with him on the afternoon that he and his associates went to the White House, the national parliamentary building on the Moskva River in Moscow. The parliamentarians had taken cover inside the building, while a crowd of citizens was gathering on the square in front of the building to offer resistance to the coup. Yeltsin's appeal heartened and motivated the demonstrators; as a result, more and more Muscovites, all of them anxious or belligerent, gathered around the White House. This motley collection of old women, young mothers, punks, workers, teachers, and former prisoners had come to defend the freedoms that had been so laboriously won in past years. A rock band played rousing music, and motorcyclists raced back and forth, informing the demonstrators of the latest troop movements.

At four in the afternoon, Gennadi Yanayev announced a state of emergency for the city of Moscow. Boris Yeltsin, who had also come to the parliamentary building, climbed up on a T-72 tank and shouted:

> Citizens of Russia! The legally elected president of the country has been deposed. What we have here is a right-wing, reactionary coup. We are responding by declaring all decisions and decrees of that Committee unlawful. We demand that the country return to a normal, constitutional course.

Improvised barricades made of scaffolding, city buses, concrete blocks, rusty bathtubs, and bricks were assembled, and as the hours passed the barricades grew larger. Ogorodnikov helped form a human chain around the White House: this served as a living shield between the soldiers and the parliament. The demonstrators screamed, *"Pozor!"* (Shame!), and

"*Rossija!*" (Russia!). Priests distributed Holy Communion, and some people spontaneously had themselves baptized. Someone even built a shrine around an icon.

Ogorodnikov was deeply moved by the enthusiasm of the people, who had thrown their very bodies into the fray. For opposite them were gigantic tanks and fanatical, elite soldiers equipped with the most advanced weapons. One young woman with two small children in her arms brought one of the tanks to a halt and shouted, "Are you going to shoot us? Aim at your officers instead!"

Ogorodnikov, too, implored the head of a military unit not to shed the blood of "our own Russian people." He realized that if the resistance was to succeed, it was vital that the demonstrators, who had come to the White House of their own free will, should stay rather than disperse. So he came up with the bright idea of engaging the services of the soup kitchen. He summoned all the volunteers to prepare thousands of sandwiches.

A few hours later, Ogorodnikov reached the parliamentary building with a delivery van full of food and drink. The people in the enormous sea of humanity, which had grown much bigger by then, were so tightly packed that no one could get in or go out.

"Who are you and what are you doing here?" one of the leaders asked.

"We're helping you mount the defenses and we're bringing you food," Ogorodnikov answered. As the delivery van approached the first ranks of the military, soldiers shot over the heads of the demonstrators. One bullet penetrated the windshield of the delivery van, but the driver was unhurt. For the entire length of the occupation — the showdown was to last three days — Ogorodnikov provided food, a total of more than four tons. At the same time, the CDUR office printed a news magazine on their printing press with an overview of all the events; that was then distributed throughout the country via the railway stations.

Three people in the crowd were killed when a tank crashed into the barricades along the Moscow ring. Having thus produced martyrs for the cause of the resisters, the coup simply caved in. On August 21, 1991, the leaders of the coup took to their heels. A triumphant Boris Yeltsin signed a decree declaring that the activities of the Communist Party were temporarily suspended. Gorbachev resigned as the Communist Party's general secretary on August 24, 1991, and became the powerless president of a country in a state of disintegration.

Silent Dissolution of a Superpower

The most important event in August 1991 was, in fact, a nonevent. In the end, the tanks and the soldiers did not shoot on the populace. When Russian Communism, in an advanced state of decay, finally breathed its last, there was hardly any bloodshed. It was like the last days of the czarist regime in 1917. Under the leadership of Boris Yeltsin, the RSFSR began to behave like an independent state — after having been frustrated by the modest role it had been allotted within the Soviet Union for three-quarters of a century. Yeltsin nationalized the mineral resources and entered into trade agreements with the other Soviet republics, just as though the Soviet Union no longer existed.

At the initiative of the Leningrad CDUR leader Vitaly Savitsky and others — and after a referendum — Leningrad was given back its pre-1917 name, Saint Petersburg, on September 6, 1991, though the surrounding oblast continued to be called Leningrad. In the months that followed, almost all the republics of the old Soviet Union declared their independence in quick succession. Unbeknownst to Gorbachev, the leaders of the former Soviet republics of Russia (RSFSR), the Ukraine, and Belarus met in Minsk on December 8, 1991, where they established the Commonwealth of Slavic States — a loose, voluntary association. A few weeks later, on December 25, when Gorbachev stepped down and the Soviet Union came to a de jure conclusion, the name was changed to the Commonwealth of Independent States (CIS).

On December 16, the Supreme Soviet of the RSFSR appointed itself rightful successor to the Soviet Union, and two days later Boris Yeltsin took over all the administrative bodies by decree. Gorbachev, who had set the entire revolution in motion in the first place, had lost control of events. There was no longer any room for him in the new constellation. The Soviet Union had broken apart. On December 25, 1991, he stepped down as president, and one day later the Congress of People's Deputies ruled that the Soviet Union would cease to exist as of midnight on December 31, 1991. The RSFSR was renamed Russia, with "Russian Federation" as its official name, and Gorbachev was succeeded by Yeltsin, who thereby became the first president of the Russian Federation.

The only visible change was the lowering of the red Soviet flag — with its familiar yellow hammer, sickle, and star — from the Kremlin. On January 1, 1992, the prerevolutionary white-blue-and-red flag of Russia began flying there once again. Cities, streets, and squares were given their former names back, and names that recalled the Communist past disappeared. Government officials went to work as they always had, but their boss was now a Russian minister, not a Soviet minister — in most cases the same person. The silent dissolution of the Soviet Union contrasted sharply with what it signified: the end of the Cold War and the virtual evaporation of one of the two superpowers that had dominated international politics since World War II.

At the end of 1991, Father Gleb Yakunin, member of the parliamentary commission charged with investigating the failed August coup, gained access to the secret archives of the KGB. There he found scores of compromising documents on the collaboration of the Moscow patriarchate with the Cheka and later with the KGB. Based on this information, Yakunin was able to prove that various highly placed church officials had once served as secret agents.

It appeared that on February 28, 1958, Patriarch Alexei II had been recruited under the code name Drozdov. Metropolitan Filaret of Kiev was called "agent Antonov," and "secret agent Adamant" was the alias of Metropolitan Juvenaly of Krutitsi and Kolomna. As the second most important church leader at the time, Metropolitan Yuvenali of the Moscow Patriarchate had dealt harshly with the dissident clergy in the Moscow region for years. Yakunin was able to demonstrate that about 20 percent of the clergy had collaborated with the KGB. According to a document issued by the Cheka in 1921, the strategy of the KGB was especially aimed at internally undermining the church hierarchy by appointing people to top positions who were easy to manipulate, so that "the Church would become the eternal slave of the secret service." But on March 6, 1992, the parliamentary fact-finding commission was again denied access to the KGB archives. One year later, Yakunin was excommunicated by the Russian Orthodox Church hierarchy, after which he joined the Ukrainian Autocephalous Orthodox Church.

Because of the open climate that prevailed in Russia during the first months of 1992, former dissidents were also given access to the KGB archives. Ogorodnikov was allowed to inspect his own dossier, and he made copies of the most important documents. "You and Vladimir Bukovsky, you are the only dissidents who never made concessions," a highly placed KGB official told him confidentially. The man asked whether Ogorodnikov would be his spiritual father, a request the latter could not grant because he was not a priest.

The documents that Ogorodnikov was allowed to see were not restricted to those about the persecution of the Christian Seminar in the 1970s. For example, he found reports from 1988 on the reprisals after the Seminar's alternative celebration of a thousand years of Christianity. He also read detailed information about the way his former wife, Paulina Bogdanova, had been put under pressure to leave him. None of the KGB reports contained the real name of the reporter or the victim, only code names. Ogorodnikov was known as "the pharmacist."

"We convinced the wife of the pharmacist to break up with him," he read in the text.

> Through the use of a special method — threatening to take away her child — we were able to persuade her to break all contact with the pharmacist immediately and to bring him into discredit with the public. This operation, which was intended to discredit the pharmacist in the eyes of the Western public, was completely successful.

Only now did Ogorodnikov understand the extent of the KGB's complicity in his wife's decision — still incomprehensible to him — to reject him so abruptly and to sully his reputation among Western parliamentarians and journalists. Later, his former wife was deeply ashamed of what had happened, but at that moment she had just wanted to save her child, whatever the cost.

Abrupt Transition to Wild Capitalism

At the end of October 1991, the Congress of People's Deputies of the Russian Federation gave Boris Yeltsin special powers to introduce a free-market economy at an accelerated rate by means of shock therapy over a period of six months, with the support of the International Monetary Fund (IMF). Under the leadership of Yegor Gaidar, the minister of economic reforms, and Anatoly Chubais, the minister of privatization, and assisted by Western advisers, the new Russian government began implementing a plan of radical economic reform, beginning on January 2, 1992. The first step was doing away with state subsidies, which meant that prices of basic products increased immediately by factors of from five to fourteen. The government encouraged free enterprise, and trade was permitted in all public places. The mafia in particular visibly expanded its activities by means of the far-flung black market, over which it had total control.

Because state businesses were no longer being supervised, many directors began to regard their company as their personal property, even though it was still owned by the state. The government did make some headway with the planned privatization; but because of a lack of money to finance this enormous operation — the Russian banking system was, in fact, nonexistent — the government devised a plan to give all citizens a "voucher" worth ten thousand rubles, with which they could purchase shares in various businesses. In the end, however, the plan did not pan out.

The most remunerative businesses ended up in the hands of the Communist *nomenklatura*, and thus the old Communists turned into the new capitalists. At the head of the financial dominions were the so-called oligarchs. Boris Berezovsky, Mikhail Chodorkovsky, and Vladimir Gusinsky made fortunes in the oil and gas sectors, and they also aspired to political roles by purchasing newspapers, magazines, and television stations. Roman Abramovich, who arranged the secret meetings between a daughter of Boris Yeltsin, Tatiana, and her lover, and who later became the private banker of the Yeltsin family, obtained Sibneft (called Gazprom since 2006), one of the largest Russian oil companies, for a symbolic sum.

The corruption, which was already running rampant during the Soviet years, increased considerably when the control mechanisms within the Communist Party disappeared. For many officials who had to wait several months before receiving their salaries, corruption became a survival strategy. At first the government continued to finance unprofitable state companies in order to combat skyrocketing unemployment, but that only served to increase the budget deficit, which led to serious devaluation. Inflation rose to 2,500 percent in 1992 and "dropped" to 840 percent in 1993, when the ruble was linked to the dollar.

The Russian market was flooded with Western products, especially in the agricultural, textile, and electronics sectors. The abrupt transition from Communism to wild capitalism — without any protection for the weaker members of society and without disciplined regulation to correct the excesses of the free market — was hardly the road to paradise. The new mottos were "every man for himself" and "earn big and earn fast."

As a result of the Gaidar government's shock therapy, a small elite was able to build up a gigantic fortune in a very short time, while the overall living standard in Russia plummeted dramatically. In no time, one-quarter of the Russian population was living under the poverty line.

The hardest hit were old-age pensioners, women, the legion unemployed, and the rural population. The government invested less and less money in health care and social services, which previously had been completely free. Diseases that had been eradicated, such as tuberculosis, malaria, and even the plague, cropped up once more, while the best doctors made fortunes working in private clinics.

The mafia imposed some order in this enormous chaos by means of extortion. All those involved in business had no choice but to hand over some of their income to the protection rackets. These criminal organizations, which had close ties with politics and the business world, were guilty of widespread kidnappings and executions of bankers, journalists, judges, and politicians. In fact, the Russian mafia was a ruthless band of thugs who by the early 1990s were operating worldwide and were able to enrich themselves with impunity through large-scale arms trafficking, drug smuggling, prostitution, and gambling houses.

President Yeltsin took every opportunity to appear in public with Patriarch Alexei II. The flourishing Russian Orthodox Church was unsurpassed in embodying the *Rodina-mat* ("Mother Russia"), the connection many Russians felt with their beloved homeland. But smoldering opposition to Yeltsin's rule began to heat up quickly. Many reformers who had been his most fanatical supporters during the August coup in 1991 emerged as his fiercest opponents. Slowly but surely, the economic shock therapy caused the country to sink into a morass, while factory directors and former Communist heavyweights hardly felt a thing and just stayed where they were.

In February 1992, Vice President Alexander Rutskoy sneeringly referred to Yeltsin's ambitious program as "economic genocide," and in April 1992, he and the parliamentary chairman, Ruslan Khasbulatov, sharply criticized Yeltsin when he asked the Supreme Soviet to extend the powers he had been granted for another six-month period. Parliament, where Yeltsin's supporters were in the minority, responded by demanding more of a say as a precondition. On December 12, 1992, after months of bickering, Yeltsin and Khasbulatov finally reached a compromise: the president got his way by and large, but the opposition managed to strengthen its position considerably.

Besides the economic derailment, Russia also had to contend with a civil war in Abkhazia, Nagorno-Karabakh, and Tajikistan in mid-1992. Large parts of Russia, from the northern Caucasus to the Sakha Republic (Yakutia), threatened to break away from Moscow. The crime rate rose as fast as inflation did, and shady businessmen managed to smuggle billions of dollars out of the country.

Christian Democracy Plays Itself Out

In 1991, Alexander Ogorodnikov placed thirtieth in a survey of the most popular politicians in Russia. He also appeared on a Russian television program, where he poked fun at the new elite, who were shamelessly enriching themselves. After that interview he was systematically banned from Russian television. Under Ogorodnikov's leadership, fifteen philosophers, theologians, and clerics, all of them members of the Russian Orthodox Church, met to discuss human rights. But the founding of a work group to deal with this important question on a permanent basis got bogged down in church bureaucracy. Nor was Christian Democracy playing a significant role in Russian politics any longer, due to its fragmentation. In addition to Ogorodnikov's CDUR and the RCDM of Viktor Akshuchits, two more Christian Democratic parties were created in Moscow: Alexander Chuyev's Christian Democratic Party of Russia in 1990, and Valery Borshchev's Russian Christian Democratic Union in 1991; the latter would later fuse with the social-liberal Yabloko party of the economist Grigory Yavlinsky, founded in 1993.

In July 1991 a number of dissident groups of the CDUR that had gathered around Vitaly Savitsky of Saint Petersburg and the Baptist Viktor Rott fused with the RCDM party of Viktor Akshuchits, but the move was not a success. The party of Akshuchits also formed the Congress of Civil and Patriotic Forces, but it came to an end in 1992. As relations between Christian Democrat International (CDI) and the Moscow branch of the CDUR cooled, the CDI openly took the side of Vitaly Savitsky.

Yet the CDI also had difficulty with this confusing tangle of Christian Democratic parties in Russia, mainly because some of the new Russian splinter groups were given the English name "Christian Democratic Union," the same name as the party of Ogorodnikov, who felt that he had been duped. In the meantime, he was still regularly accepting foreign invitations. In early February 1992 he met President George H. W. Bush at a prayer breakfast in Washington, D.C.; but in his own country he was not as popular. "You're too independent and that's why you'll never be elected," he was told by State Secretary Gennadi Burbulis, the number-two man in the Kremlin, who had first met Ogorodnikov thirty years before at Sverdlovsk University in 1970. "We don't know how you're going to vote, and that's why we don't want to work with you."

But all during the early 1990s, the CDUR was carrying on its social activities. In 1992 the first shelter was opened in Saint Petersburg for abandoned, homeless, and uprooted girls — one of the most vulnerable groups in Russian society. At first the shelter was taking in between ten and twelve girls, but later the available capacity was expanded. This shelter, called Efimiya after the former director, was of great symbolic significance because it was not in Moscow. In 1993 the CDUR opened another school, which was very successful. The attempt to create a Christian Democratic university, however, ran aground.

In the meantime, the continuous power struggle between President Boris Yeltsin and the Russian parliament brought the decision-making process to a complete standstill. Yegor Gaidar was appointed interim prime minister on June 15, 1992, as the successor to Yeltsin, who until then had been both president and prime minister. A half year later, on December 14, 1992, Gaidar was replaced by Viktor Chernomyrdin, but that did little to solve the problem. After a referendum was held on April 25, 1993, at which Yeltsin managed to rally a majority of the population behind the carrying out of his policies, he dismissed the entire parliament and called for new elections on December 12, 1993. A new draft of the constitution of the Russian Federation was also going to be presented to the voters on that occasion.

In the summer of 1993, Ogorodnikov was part of a group of five hundred delegates selected by Yeltsin, and later he was also part of the smaller commission charged with drawing up the final version of the draft text of the constitution. Meetings were held every day at the Kremlin, and at first Ogorodnikov always arrived via bicycle; but the head of the Kremlin security service begged him to take another form of transportation because the Kremlin did not have a bicycle shed.

Constitutional Crisis of 1993

On September 23, 1993, Yeltsin dissolved parliament, which was against the law — according to the constitution that was still in force at the time. But the president appealed to the results of the popular referendum held in April 1993. In response, the parliament began a procedure to have him removed from office that very day, and it appointed Vice President Alexan-

der Rutskoy as the new acting president. On October 1st, the power struggle escalated when Yeltsin ordered the army to surround the parliament
building, where a large group of anti-Yeltsin supporters had gathered.

Within a period of two years the roles had completely reversed! In
August 1991, Yeltsin had taken cover in the parliament building, the
White House, and the Communists were in the Kremlin. Now Yeltsin
was responding from the Kremlin, and the rebellious parliamentarians,
including the Communists, were barricading themselves in the White
House, where Alexander Rutskoy had his office as the new president of
Russia.

On October 2, Ogorodnikov went to the Moscow City Hall, where
the Yeltsin supporters had gathered, and then went on to the White
House, which was occupied by rebellious parliamentarians, all opponents
of Yeltsin. The atmosphere on the empty square in front of the parliament was extremely tense. From conversations that Ogorodnikov had
with the soldiers standing near the building, he gathered that the soldiers
were becoming increasingly uneasy with the orders they were receiving
from their superiors. Yet he was ordered to clear out immediately: "Get
out of here or we'll shoot!" The photographs taken by foreign correspondents that day went around the world. On October 3 a real battle took
place between demonstrators and troops, and sixty-two people were
killed. In the overall violence that took place on October 2 and 3, 1993, on
the streets of Moscow, 145 were killed and 800 were wounded.

On October 4th, at sunrise, the Russian army began shooting at the
White House on Yeltsin's orders. Encountering that show of military
force, the rebellious parliamentary leaders surrendered on the same day.

The elections announced for December 12, 1993, in which the Russian people would vote on a new constitution, were held on schedule.
Ogorodnikov's CDUR had taken all of the necessary precautionary measures to comply with the recently altered electoral law. In an effort to prevent the fragmentation of the political landscape, the new law stipulated
that every list or candidate had to submit 100,000 signatures to the Central Electoral Committee and to attain the required electoral threshold of
5 percent. As a result, resigning parliamentarian Viktor Akshuchits was
no longer able to put himself forward as a candidate.

Back in September 1992, the CDUR, which had 6,300 members at the
time, had affiliated itself with the New Russia party of Telman Gdljan, a
congressman and former examining magistrate as well as a feared champion in the fight against criminality and corruption. Working with these

kindred spirits opened up many possibilities and perspectives, but in October 1993 the CDUR was unexpectedly dealt the heaviest blow of its young existence up to that point. The political engagement of priests and bishops who had been elected in March 1990 with the Congress of People's Deputies of the Soviet Union and of the Supreme Soviet of the Russian Federation had always been controversial. The high-handed behavior of Gleb Yakunin had been particularly irritating. So the Synod of the Russian Orthodox Church decided to prohibit the clergy from taking part in elections and even from joining political parties. From now on the Orthodox Church would cooperate directly with the government.

That decision was a heavy blow to the CDUR. The core of the party, after all, was formed not by the intelligentsia but by priests and active parishes. The decision caused the CDUR to lose 70 percent of its members in one stroke.

In the elections of December 12, 1993, the first priority was to present the new constitution to the public for approval. The text, however, was not what Ogorodnikov had worked on with the constitutional commission. At the last moment, Boris Yeltsin had made a number of important changes on his own, changes that would have Russia evolve into a powerful presidential republic with only limited power for the parliament. "It's either me or chaos," was the message of Yeltsin's campaign. It was a message that could be heard and seen everywhere in the official media, since the president had silenced the newspapers and television stations of the opposition. The president hoped to capitalize on his bold action in the White House back in October, but there was one factor that he had no control over: the public's growing aversion to the way the political apparatus was being run.

The constitution could be approved only if at least half the electorate participated in the elections. At a certain point it appeared clear that this quota was not going to be met: the night of the election, the computer system stopped functioning for several hours, reducing the number of voters by a few million. Even so, according to the official results, 53.2 percent of the electorate appeared to have voted. Yeltsin had got what he wanted: 58.4 percent of the voters approved the new constitution.

In the first free parliamentary elections of the Russian Federation, which took place at the same time, twenty-one parties competed for the favors of the electorate. Yeltsin's *Vybor Rossii* Party (Russia's Choice), led by the former prime minister, Yegor Gaidar, got only 15 percent of the votes. The big winner was the Liberal Democratic Party of Russia, run by the ultranationalist Vladimir Zhirinovsky, with 23.5 percent; the Communists got 12 percent; and the new Yabloko party ended up with 7.9 percent.

Although Ogorodnikov awaited the elections with confidence, Vladimir Boxer, the new strong man behind Boris Yeltsin, warned him at the beginning of the election campaign: "There's no way you're going to be elected. You can just forget it. You're much too dangerous. We know how you're going to vote, and we know you're going to start asking tough questions in parliament. We absolutely cannot accept that."

The fear that the vote counting would be fraudulent proved to be well founded. The twelve members of the electoral commission, the ones officially charged with counting the votes, were first given an elaborate meal with lots to drink. When the commission finally got down to work, they discovered that the job had already been more or less completed. When they checked the count, it appeared that 100,000 votes had been falsified. Seven of the twelve members of the electoral commission refused to approve the "official" results, and they declared Ogorodnikov the winner. But nothing was ever heard again about the official complaint lodged with the Central Electoral Commission of Russia. All the CDUR gained were two seats on the Moscow city council. Former CDUR chairman Vitaly Savitsky of Saint Petersburg was elected from the list of candidates for Yegor Gaidar's Russia's Choice Party.

CHAPTER ELEVEN

The Island of Hope and Social Engagement

"**M**oscow: The City Where Children Are Sold for a Bottle of Whisky" was the title of an article written by British politician David Alton in 1994. According to a report issued by the United Nations Children's Fund (UNICEF), there were about 600,000 children without parental supervision in Russia at the time. In 95 percent of these cases, one or both of the parents were still living but were living the lives of vagrants. Half of these children were living in state institutions.

At the Dom Rebyonka, the Russian baby shelters for neglected children and orphans through three years of age, the rest of their lives was determined by screening conducted at age four. The "uneducable and unmanageable" children were transferred to psycho-neurological institutions. The horrors that took place there every day made the news after harrowing articles were published in international newspapers; a searing report was issued by Human Rights Watch (an international nongovernmental organization concerned with tackling human rights abuses); and a heart-rending television program was broadcast by the British television channel Independent Television News (ITN).

The intellectually gifted children were moved to a Detsky Dom, the ordinary Russian state children's home. But there, too, physical violence and sexual abuse were the order of the day. Four of ten youngsters leaving the institution at the age of eighteen became addicted to alcohol or drugs, one out of ten committed suicide, and only about one of ten began leading normal lives.

Ogorodnikov frequently saw a number of these street children hanging around in the soup kitchen. At his initiative, a roundtable discussion on this delicate and disgraceful problem was held in the office of the Russian parliamentary chairman, after which the city of Moscow decided to set up ten shelters. Because the capacity of these shelters was totally inadequate — Ogorodnikov estimated the number of street children in Moscow to be at least 60,000 — the CDUR decided to set up its own shelter. That was easier said than done, however, since it was not permitted by law. But after three years of struggle, the "Island of Hope" shelter — the only shelter in Moscow not run by the state — opened its doors in 1995. Backed by CDUR city council members, the city council of Moscow passed Decree no. 67 on January 24, 1995: under this decree, a three-story eighteenth-century villa at 2 Popov Street in Moscow was made available to the CDUR with a ten-year rental contract. It was said that the French emperor Napoleon had slept in the building during the first Great Patriotic War. A private company then donated a lump sum of 300,000 American dollars.

The Moscow Bureau of Prosecution immediately called the legal validity of the shelter into question because the building was not registered anywhere — even though there was no registration procedure at the time.

Volunteers equipped the new building with sanitary facilities and a hot-water installation, and they rewired the electrical system. In April 1995 the first guests arrived: three underage girls who had tried to survive in the neighborhood of the Kursk Station. Ogorodnikov then brought in more young girls from the other railway stations. The shelter's capacity was only thirty beds, and all of them were soon filled, thanks to word-of-mouth publicity. The guests stayed until a solution was found for their particular situation.

Girls were given priority because, almost as soon as they began living on the street, it was virtually inescapable that they would be drawn into prostitution. Those who lived on the street longer than six months could no longer adjust to normal family life. The teenage pregnancies were particularly tragic. In the state institutions the girls were given a choice: have an abortion or leave. One day, the thirteen-year-old Anya came knocking on the door of the Island of Hope, having been sent by the Salvation Army. The girl had moved from Kursk to Moscow after her parents' divorce. Her mother worked as a nurse, but in the evening she did "sideline work" as a prostitute. Anya hated her mother from the bottom of her heart. She ran away from home when her mother wanted her to become a prostitute as well. The shelter was more or less Anya's last chance to lead a normal life, since officially she was under the guardianship of her parents until the age of eighteen.

Then there was the case of a father who showed up one day at the shelter with his eleven-year-old daughter, Katya. The family had lived in a one-room apartment in Moscow until both parents traded in their home for a hut in the country to finance their alcohol addiction. When the hut burned down, the family sought temporary lodging with the grandmother. Then the mother became a vagrant. The father and Katya slept in doorways and attic rooms until the father found work and a place to live in the hall of a warehouse. Katya went to look for him there every weekend.

Removing girls from the prostitution scene was a delicate and dangerous business, since their pimps, who were often protected by the police, kept a constant eye on them. When a staff person from Island of Hope spoke to a young prostitute and told her about the help she could receive, the girl later felt so threatened that she wanted to commit suicide. The world of prostitution is ruled by fear. When the seventeen-year-old Natasha, who wanted to take the admissions exam for the University of Moscow, spent the night in a Moscow railway station because she had no money for a hotel, the police picked her up. At the police station she became the victim of a gang rape, after which the police handed her over to the mafia, who forced her to become a prostitute. A short time later, after the mafia decided she was earning too little money as a prostitute, she ended up at the Island of Hope — psychologically crushed. Ogorodnikov wanted to take the case to court, but Natasha panicked, fearing the revenge of her enemies.

There were some boys living in the shelter, too. One day, a ninety-three-year-old drifter asked whether the little boy who always accompanied him could be housed in the shelter so that he himself could die in peace.

When new residents arrived in the shelter, the first thing they got was a good washing and fresh clothes, after which each one was free to adapt to life in the shelter at her own tempo. None of the volunteers had an academic diploma or specific training in social work; but with the friendly environment and the tactful and conscientious treatment, the residents' wounds gradually healed. Slowly but surely, most of them were able to build up normal relationships again.

The living conditions were simple and the resources limited. The children helped with the tidying up, cleaning, and cooking. The girls learned to knit and sew and to do various domestic chores, and the older ones took care of administrative tasks and worked on the computer. The residents also became acquainted with Orthodox norms and values and were taught the basic principles of Christian spirituality and ethics. All this was quite the opposite of what they had seen and experienced so far.

For years, the leadership of the shelter was in the hands of Nikolai Ivanovich. A woman from Tashkent, the capital of Uzbekistan, who lived in the shelter with her young son, did all the cooking. She was assisted by a refugee from Baku, the capital of Azerbaijan, and his son. Because many of the residents were not officially registered, they could not go to school. Nikolai Ivanovich gave lessons himself, assisted by volunteers, one of whom was a retired English teacher.

A network of personal contacts with doctors, hospitals, and nurses made it possible for nonregistered children to receive the medical care they needed when they became ill. This initiative was given the blessing and sympathy of the Russian Orthodox Church in the persons of Metropolitan Kirill and Archpriest Vsevolod Chaplin, among others, but no financial or logistical support.

For Ogorodnikov, however, managing the shelter became a veritable nightmare. One day the Moscow city council ordered that a drastic renovation and restoration of the building had to be carried out as soon as possible, though Decree no. 67 said nothing about that. This was to happen in consultation with the administration for the government supervision of the use of historic and cultural monuments, and with their collaboration, because the building was a protected monument. At the same time, Ogorodnikov received a notice from the landlord that the rental contract was being terminated because the terms of the contract were not being met; but that turned out to be a false alarm.

Only a few weeks after the opening of the Island of Hope, attempts were made to drive the residents away. Rumors of irregularities in the "illegal institution" circulated in the neighborhood. Some people called it a drug den, others a brothel. Young people made a racket at the entrance, and the personnel of the shelter were repeatedly provoked. One day a girl came to the door seeking shelter. She had a dramatic life story, but soon a couple of suspicious characters showed up and demanded that she be returned to them. On another occasion, a drunken construction worker started a fight, and the police came to the house in search of a certain criminal.

Then there were the economics of the shelter: only with a great deal of difficulty was the shelter able to make ends meet. Ogorodnikov sent out a request for financial support to about a hundred banks and received just one response, a negative one. And among the generation of "new

Russians," who were earning big money on the ruins of the Soviet Union, there was a great sense of indifference. They could not care less about the old traditions. For centuries, no one in Russia could join a commercial guild without engaging in charitable works. The daily routine in the shelter was financed with the help of numerous small private gifts, which were referred to ironically as "widow's mites," and with the honoraria that Ogorodnikov occasionally managed to earn. There were also people who gave material help. One old man, who was himself poor, donated his books and clothing to the shelter. Help also came from abroad: from the Belgian Saint Egidius Community, originally an Italian Catholic lay movement called Comunità di Sant'Egidio, which was dedicated to serving the poorest of the poor in the local city, and from a Russian relief fund in Paris.

Island of Hope Staff Intimidated by Police

On October 31, 1995, at 11 p.m., four plainclothes policemen from the Criminal Investigation Unit of the Moscow police force subjected the shelter to a search; they also took volunteers Sergei Artyomov, Vladimir Kozharenyok, and Nikolai Karakozov with them to Police Station 24. Ogorodnikov was also picked up and accused of "involvement in criminal activities" and the willful creation of a "hideout for criminals" under the cover of a charitable institution. During the interrogations, the police put pressure on the volunteers to accuse Ogorodnikov of hitting residents, of being in possession of weapons and narcotics, and of being involved in the trafficking of girls for foreign prostitution networks. After denying these charges, the three were threatened with a fine of 10,000 rubles but were released at 2 a.m. without having to pay anything.

Meanwhile, the shelter was raided again at 1 a.m., again by four plainclothes policemen. They searched all the rooms. In the staff office they looked at the computer databases, seized documents, and threatened the volunteers who were still present. A few hours later, at 9 a.m. on November 1, five plainclothes detectives came to the door — also without search warrants. They appeared to be searching for certain computer data, and they also demanded the building's ownership documents and the deed of foundation of the CDUR.

Once again, Artyomov, Kozharenyok, and Karakozov were taken to Police Station 24. During the interrogation they were again pressured by the interrogator to make an incriminating statement about Ogorodnikov, this time about the illegal possession of weapons and the kidnapping and the killing of girls. Refusal, they were told, might lead to imprisonment, beating with electrical clubs, or compulsory military service in the Caucasus. The trio was freed once again, but as a result of this continuous intimidation, one of them, who could not stand up under the psychological pressure, stopped working as a volunteer — which, of course, was the whole point of the harassment.

Ogorodnikov raised this matter with several reputable international organizations. The human rights organization Amnesty International responded by urging the Russian authorities to launch an investigation "because a number of official representatives have far exceeded their authority and have broken the law in their attempt to extract confessions from several members of the CDUR on the staff of the girls' home during an illegal break-in and during intimidating interrogations at the police station."

According to Amnesty, the actions of the police were politically motivated: "This had absolutely nothing to do with apparent criminal activities. It was exclusively concerned with presumed political nominations for the upcoming parliamentary elections of December 17, 1995."

In his response of February 14, 1996, public prosecutor Andreyeshev of the Moscow region conducted an internal investigation and declared, "No investigations have been started concerning the CDUR members and ordinary citizens. Because no threats or accusations were made against Ogorodnikov, the investigation has been terminated due to lack of evidence of any illegal activity."

The First Chechen War (1994-96)

What was happening in Russian politics in the meantime? Boris Yeltsin wanted to court-martial the opposition leaders who were responsible for the occupation of the White House in October 1993 and have them executed by firing squad for conspiracy. But he could not keep the new Duma from granting them amnesty in 1994. Despite strong opposition — the Communists of Gennadi Zhuganov and the ultranationalists of Vladimir Zhirinovsky had over 40 percent of the seats — the government of moderate prime minister Viktor Chernomyrdin implemented most of its reform program. For the first time, president and parliament were able to work well together, and relations among the majority parties were good. The leaders of these parties were all from the *nomenklatura* of the former Soviet Union. Prime Minister Chernomyrdin was the main stockholder of Gazprom, the largest company in Russia and the largest natural gas company in the world. This former state-owned company, which was privatized in November 1992 and transformed into a national corporation, had a monopoly in the natural gas sector and provided half the Russian foreign currency income.

Since December 1994, the war in Chechnya, the former Soviet republic in the northern Caucasus, had been high on the political agenda. Chechnya was a traditionally Muslim republic. In the Chechen presidential elections on October 27, 1991, the strongly anti-Islamic Dzhokhar Dudayev, a veteran of the Russian Red Army and a supporter of Yeltsin, was elected president. However, the election results were declared invalid by Russia. Three days later, on November 1, 1991, Dudayev and his followers seized power in the Chechen capital of Grozny and declared independence. The name Chechnya was changed to the Chechen Republic of Ichkeria.

However, contrary to all Dudayev's expectations, the Kremlin took a negative view of these events. Because of Chechnya's rich oil fields, Moscow could never accept Chechnya's aspirations for independence. On November 8, 1991, Russia declared a state of emergency in Chechnya, and in the months that followed it tried to disrupt the greatly divided country from the inside out by delivering money and weapons to the opposition. Dudayev, however, wanted to normalize the situation in Chechnya speedily and to legitimate his assumption of power, if at all possible. When the Soviet Union was dissolved in December 1991, Dudayev hoped that the Russian Federation would disintegrate as quickly as the old Soviet Union had.

As a result of the Russian support of the opposition in Chechnya, there were three coup attempts — in 1992, 1993, and 1994 — against the Dudayev government, all of which failed. Yeltsin then closed all the borders with Chechnya, and in April 1994 he appointed his own Chechen government, headed by Umar Avtorkhanov. When the Chechen opposition parties united behind Avtorkhanov in the summer of 1994 and together joined in the fray, a civil war quickly broke out.

In November 1994, Boris Yeltsin unexpectedly broke off talks on the status of Chechnya. The Chechen pro-Russian opposition then formed an anti-Dudayev government. In early December 1994, Dudayev called for total mobilization in Chechnya. Following heavy fighting between troops of the Chechen opposition and troops of Dudayev, the Russian army invaded Chechnya on December 11, 1994. Boris Yeltsin had, with this decision, plunged the Russian army into a carelessly prepared military adventure. The Russian minister of defense, Pavel Grachev, confidently and arrogantly insisted that the fighting was expected to last for only a few hours. Russia bombed the capital of Grozny to rubble and deployed heavy artillery. But all attempts to end the rebellion failed, thereby marking the beginning of the First Chechen War.

The Russians were repeatedly forced to admit defeat at the hands of the Chechen guerrillas — in the cities as well as the mountains. In this bizarre war, the Russians were constantly stopping military operations just as they were about to triumph over the rebels. Afterwards it was discovered that the oligarch Boris Berezovsky, the deputy secretary of the Russian National Security Council, who had great influence over Boris Yeltsin and his daughter Tatiana, earned a great deal of money in the Chechen War. He sold weapons in bulk to the Chechens and made himself popular by repeatedly succeeding in freeing Chechen prisoners of war and hostages. The large number of Chechen attacks and kidnappings, each followed by bloody Russian reprisals, resulted in more than 30,000 victims in two years.

In an act of protest against these cruelties, former dissident Sergei Kovalyov, who had been in camp Perm-36 with Ogorodnikov, resigned as Yeltsin's human rights adviser on January 24, 1996. Ogorodnikov himself, who was fully opposed to the war in Chechnya, set up a new human rights organization with Sergei Arutyunov in 1996.

When Russia was focusing all its attention on the presidential elections of June 1996, the Chechen rebels saw their opportunity. On August 9, 1996, the evening of Yeltsin's inauguration after his victorious second-term election, the rebels defeated the Russian federal troops at Grozny. Yeltsin then sent the popular General Alexander Lebed to Khasavyurt, a Russian city in the autonomous republic of Dagestan, to conduct negotiations. Here a ceasefire was signed on August 31, 1996, bringing an official end to the First Chechen War. Although the accord did not mean that Russia was accepting the independence of Chechnya, independence did become a de facto reality.

The Fraudulent Parliamentary Elections of December 17, 1995

The Russian parliamentary elections of December 17, 1995, were dominated by the Chechen war and the country's socioeconomic decline. The quality of health care dropped to a third-world level, and life expectancy fell to 57.3 years. Four parliamentarians had been murdered since the elections of 1993. The last of these was the liberal Sergei Markidonov, who was shot by a bodyguard in late November 1995. And in December 1995, during the election campaign, candidate Mikhail Chelyabinsk was also gunned down. Departing parliamentarian and former CDUR leader Vitaly Savitsky was killed on December 10, in a suspicious automobile accident in Saint Petersburg.

There were 450 seats to apportion in the new parliament. Forty-three political parties vied for the voters' favor for the 225 seats that were to be filled by direct vote. In 225 electoral districts, the candidate with the most votes was chosen. A total of 2,687 candidates put themselves forward, or an average of 12 per parliament seat. The turnout was 64.5 percent, considerably higher than in 1993. The big winner was the Communist Party with 21.8 percent of the vote — almost double the results of the 1993 elections. In second place was Zhirinovsky's Liberal Democratic Party, followed by Nash Dom Rossiia (Our House Is Russia), a party formed in April 1995 by Prime Minister Viktor Chernomyrdin, with 9.7 percent of the vote; the reformist Yabloko party of economist Grigory Yavlinsky got 8.4 percent. Once again, the opposition did not gain a majority. Boris Yeltsin, who followed a somewhat more moderate course, dismissed Deputy Prime Minister Anatoly Chubais, the man responsible for the economic reforms, as soon as the election results were in.

For the Christian Democratic parties the elections were disastrous. All of the new parties inspired by Orthodoxy remained marginal: the right-wing nationalistic Russian National Council, founded in 1992 by Alexander Sterligov; the left-wing patriotic Congress of Russian Communities, founded in 1993 by Dmitri Rogozin; the ultranationalist Russian National Unity, created in 1990 by the extreme right-wing politician Alexander Barkashov; the Pan-Russian Social-Christian Union for the Liberation of the People; and Pamyat.

Ogorodnikov was eager to put himself forward as a candidate in the region of Tatarstan, where he originally came from. His objective was to break the hegemony of the Communist Party once and for all, which still held all the important posts there. The CDUR gathered the required

100,000 signatures for Ogorodnikov. But he was again breaching the tacit agreement whereby the established powers would be preserved in exchange for support to Yeltsin; thus, to keep Ogorodnikov from being elected, the KGB hauled out its heavy artillery. Dozens of KGB agents were sent out to personally intimidate anyone who had signed Ogorodnikov's nomination. Those who did not retract their signature would be put under government surveillance. As a result of this harassment, the election commission declared Ogorodnikov's nomination inadmissible. It was pointless to lodge an appeal against this decision since the pronouncement was made after December 17, 1995, making it too late to run for office elsewhere. Therefore, Ogorodnikov was not able to take part in the elections.

Attempt to Murder Ogorodnikov Fails

In 1995, Russian television devoted a special broadcast to the Christian Seminar. The producers of the program wondered: What has happened to the first participants after twenty years? With the exception of Lev Regelson, most of those early members were still religiously active. Vladimir Sokolov was a well-known spiritual writer, and Vladimir Poresh had set up a school for theology and philosophy in Saint Petersburg in 1990. Alexander Shchipkov was now chairman of the influential Club of Orthodox Journalists, and Viktor Popkov was director of the spirituality center of the conservative Catholic Italian movement Comunione e Liberazione in Moscow.

Fifteen members had become priests, including Boris Razveyev, the driving force behind the Christian Seminar in Ufa, who twice had confessed to the regime prosecutors. Working in Bashkiria (or Bashkortostan) and Moscow, Razveyev became reconciled with Ogorodnikov and later became the head of the Russian Orthodox community in the Italian city of Verona.

On January 19, 1996, the evening of the Feast of the Theophany (or the Baptism of Jesus), Ogorodnikov was on his way home after a celebration of the liturgy at the shelter when two Ukrainian gangsters waylaid him on the street. They had come to demand the return of a girl who had moved into the shelter shortly before that. According to his attackers, she was a fugitive prostitute who had been sentenced to death. Because Ogorodnikov refused to meet their demand, one of them sprayed acid gas in his face. His chin was burned but his eyes were spared thanks to his glasses. Then the other attacker tried to murder Ogorodnikov with an ax (just what had happened to Alexander Men in 1990). But as he was trying to swing the ax, the blade loosened and got stuck in a wall along the street, so Ogorodnikov was hit by only the wooden handle. Then the gangsters turned and ran. Ogorodnikov immediately reported the incident to the police, but his complaint was registered without any further investigation. Later he came to regard this failed murder attempt as his "new baptism."

On March 30, 1996, the shelter was suddenly stormed by an OMON unit, an elite unit of the Russian police, when Revolt Pimeniv, chairman of the Saint Petersburg CDUR, happened to be present. The reason for this brutal break-in was that a girl who had recently sought refuge in the shelter did not want to be returned to the special state institution. When the agents tried to take her with them, the other girls formed a circle around her and threatened to slit their wrists. Out of revenge, the agency for domestic affairs of the city of Moscow subjected the shelter to repeated inspections, supposedly owing to legal requirements. Prefect Ulyanov, of the eastern district of the city of Moscow, also repeatedly tried to put an end to the activities at the Island of Hope, though he had no authority to do so.

Police officers regularly came to interrogate the residents. A few of the residents were forced to have their heads shaved, were ill-treated, or were taken back to a state orphanage against their will. But no one ever gave incriminating evidence against Ogorodnikov. If that had happened, the shelter would have been closed immediately. While Ogorodnikov wanted nothing more than "peace and quiet," the government had but one goal: to close the shelter as soon as possible. The articles in the Russian press that reported all the problems the shelter was having had almost no effect on public opinion in Russia.

Although Boris Yeltsin had been out of circulation for months in the fall of 1995 due to a heart attack, he decided to run for a second term of office despite the disastrous conduct of the war in Chechnya and the great loss of Russian troops. In the first round of the presidential elections on June 16, 1996, the CDUR supported the candidacy of economist Grigory Yavlinsky of the Yabloko social-liberal party, which won 7.3 percent of the votes. In the second round on July 3, 1996, Yeltsin defeated his Communist rival Gennadi Zhuganov, thanks to the support he received from the oligarchs and the popular nationalist general Alexander Lebed.

In exchange for their support, Yeltsin gave the oligarchs the remaining state companies, and on June 18, 1996, two days after the first round of presidential elections, Lebed was appointed head of the national security council of the Russian Federation, which was supposed to call for an end to the crime and corruption, which had so greatly increased under Yeltsin's administration. But Yeltsin fired Lebed in November 1996. In the years that followed, Russia sank into a pool of corruption and fraud, and because of the serious financial crisis of 1997-98, the country also was saddled with a severe economic recession.

Meeting President Bill Clinton

After an interview with Ogorodnikov appeared in the *Baltimore Sun*, the American newspaper, a number of American congressmen — including Tom Lantos of California (a survivor of the Nazi concentration camps and the chairman of the Congressional Human Rights Committee) and Christopher Smith — arranged for President Bill Clinton to visit the Island of Hope shelter in Moscow while participating in the special G-7 conference on nuclear security, the Moscow Nuclear Safety and Security Summit of April 19-20, 1996, in Moscow. Because a visit to the shelter itself could not take place for security reasons, the CDUR, along with the organization Beautiful Hearts, set up an exhibition in a Moscow hotel on the activities of Island of Hope. Clinton visited that exhibition on April 21, 1996.

"How's it going, Sasha?" Clinton said, as if he had known Ogorodnikov for years. When he left, he turned around like a consummate actor, held up his thumb, and shouted, "I'll do the best I can, Alexander. I'm going to help you. You can count on me!"

The television images of that visit went around the world, and in the American Congress, Christopher Smith later declared:

> The G-7 Nuclear Security Summit was about providing nuclear safety in our uneasy world, about governments cooperating with one another to reduce danger to millions of people. Security can also be a function of mutual understanding and having genuine concern — even across borders — for other human beings, one for another. By visiting the young people of the Christian Mercy Society shelter, President Clinton exhibited that concern on behalf of all of us here in the United States, and I appreciate his kind gesture.

In February 1997, a Moscow public prosecutor brought criminal charges against the Island of Hope shelter based on Article 330 of the Russian Federation Penal Code. Ogorodnikov was accused of illegal occupation of the shelter. As part of the investigation, the prosecutor's agents confiscated many documents from the shelter without a proper inventory. During the interrogation, which took place in the shelter, the investigators also tried to get the girls of the shelter to sign a confession that Ogorodnikov had made sexual advances toward them. But even after they had been threatened with being transferred to a closed shelter, none of the girls agreed to do so. All the residents were then arrested, along with two reporters from the *Express-Chronika* magazine, and Ogorodnikov himself, and charged with "disobedience toward the authorities." In July 1997 the case ended as abruptly as it had begun: nothing could be found with which to charge the CDUR. Duma member Viktor Sheinis of the Yabloko Party took the case to the highest level, and a couple of American congressmen also became involved. Finally, the procurator-general admitted that the prosecutor in question had acted improperly.

Then the police tried a new tactic. In a raid conducted on May 15, 1997, they showed Ogorodnikov a document by two unknown men — Frolov and Zotov — stating that, during a special meeting of the Moscow Political Council, he had been expelled from his function as chairman of the CDUR. The document bore the signatures of both these men, the new chairman and the head of the political council respectively — a nonexistent function. On the basis of this forged "decree," the document said, a lower court had turned the management of the shelter over to them. The police, who were charged with carrying out this ruling, then removed some of the residents from the shelter. Frolov and Zotov took the CDUR archives, and the police seized all the financial documents for further investigation. Ogorodnikov was also picked up in an effort to isolate him. The future looked bleak because a new legal decision was necessary just to prove that the decree was a forgery.

Yet the Moscow police had completely underestimated the impact of Ogorodnikov's network. Within a few hours, the American ambassador and the representative of the European Union, both of whom lived in Moscow, became personally involved in this distressing matter, and Ogorodnikov's friends supplied Western correspondents with detailed information on the true facts in the case. A staff member of the American embassy was given permission to enter the shelter, where she befriended the few girls who were serving as hostages there.

Due to growing diplomatic and foreign pressure, the police were obliged to back off that same day. They freed Ogorodnikov, and they returned the residents who had been picked up and brought to state orphanages. They had also gone through hell. During the interrogations, the police had used violence to try to make them declare that Ogorodnikov had abused and raped them. Even then, not a single resident would make such an incriminating statement. Frolov and Zotov disappeared as quickly as they had materialized. Later it turned out that they were both part of a special department of the KGB, which called on them for these kinds of operations.

European Parliament Condemns Police Raid

The complaint lodged by Ogorodnikov was dismissed without further investigation. But on June 16, 1997, the European Parliament, at the initiative of German and Spanish parliamentarians, unanimously passed resolutions 14(e) B4-0486 and 0515/97 concerning the plight of Moscow street children. These resolutions openly and explicitly condemned the violent police raid at the Island of Hope shelter on May 15, 1997. The parliamentarians declared that they were "gravely concerned about the fact that the Moscow city council tried to close the shelter on the basis of regulations that still date from the Soviet era, and that as a result the children in question are now completely deprived of help and support." A short time later, a delegation from the European Parliament paid a visit to the Moscow shelter.

Shortly thereafter, the local police tried once again to clear the shelter by means of a raid. Their efforts failed when volunteers from the CDUR formed a living chain around the house while Ogorodnikov reported the raid to the national police. As a result of this case, a highly placed official from the ministry of foreign affairs was forced to resign.

Why was this seemingly endless campaign being waged against the shelter? First of all, Ogorodnikov had shown light on a perverse practice, and that had brought the wrath of the government down upon him. According to the law, every orphan who left a government institution at the age of eighteen was to be given an apartment or room in order to live an independent life. Because of the sharp increase in real estate prices in Russia, especially in Moscow, public housing in that city had skyrocketed in value. Corrupt officials would have eighteen-year-old orphans declared mentally ill by means of false medical diagnoses and then have them committed to state institutions, after which the officials — as "guardians" — would manage the children's homes. In practice, this usually meant renting the homes to third parties at exorbitant prices. Ogorodnikov discovered this practice quite by accident after picking up a girl who had escaped from a psychiatric hospital and had found shelter in a railway station. The girl was underfed and on the brink of starvation. Ogorodnikov publicized the case in great detail, which led to a national scandal in Russia. He also informed the United Nations of this cruel practice. After further investigation, a mass grave was discovered in which the battered and starved bodies of youngsters from state psychiatric hospitals appeared to have been dumped like animals. Ogorodnikov took photographs of the grave, but all the bodies were removed shortly thereafter.

Another reason for the raids by the Moscow police was the fact that the Chechen children in the shelter told terrible stories about the behavior of the Russian army in Chechnya.

Soup Kitchen Forced to Close

By the beginning of 1997, 1.8 million free meals had been served and 81,300 underprivileged people had been assisted in the CDUR soup kitchens since they were founded in February 1981. In all those years there had always been enough food on hand to prepare meals. Whenever the need was the highest, another generous donor from the West would step forward, as if by a miracle, with the necessary support. But this CDUR program was also constantly being harassed by the government, the police, and the mafia. During one violent raid, which took place on the very same day as the raid on the Island of Hope shelter (May 15, 1997), several people were wounded and the complete kitchen inventory was destroyed, along with a great deal of food.

Then, during the night of November 12-13, 1997, twenty unknown persons conducted a totally unexpected and violent break-in, with the consent of the local district manager. The next day they refused to allow anyone else to enter. They were there, they said, "to carry out a number of repairs by order of the person who had hired them" — whose name, however, they refused to divulge. Ogorodnikov immediately reported the break-in, but the police never showed up. All the property of the CDUR, including the printing press and all the soup kitchen's food stocks and inventory that had been purchased with the support of the European Commission, were impounded. The city council then ordered the soup kitchen to be closed, effective immediately.

On November 14, 1997, Lawrence Uzzell, the Moscow correspondent for Keston News Service in Britain, established telephone contact with Vyacheslav Ninilin, head of the Khoroshevsky district of Moscow. When Uzzell asked whether Ninilin was aware of the nighttime raid of the CDUR soup kitchen, the latter answered, "It didn't happen at night. It was during the day."

"All right, but was it your gang who conducted the raid?" Uzzell asked.

"It wasn't a gang," Ninilin responded.

"Once again," Uzzell repeated, "this is a very simple question: Were they your people?"

"There are no simple questions," Ninilin answered. "I'm not discussing this with you any further."

Then Uzzell asked for the third time: "Were they your people, yes or no?" Ninilin abruptly hung up.

The reason for this raid was a conflict over back rent that had been taken to court by the Moscow city council, though no ruling had yet been made. The city of Moscow not only demanded more rent but refused to deduct the costs for repairs and renovations that the CDUR had carried out from the rent that had been agreed to.

When Ogorodnikov visited the building on January 15, 1998, with the American congressmen Christopher Smith, Tony Hall, and Frank Wolf, it was completely empty. Not a trace of the furnishings remained. When Smith asked some workers there where the contents of the building had gone, the supervisor said that the kitchen inventory and food stocks had been stored elsewhere in the city, but he refused to say where. After signing a declaration, Ogorodnikov was able to take away two icons that had hung in the dining room and had been hidden in a back room by a CDUR staff member during the raid. Soon after that, Ogorodnikov received a message from the city of Moscow that the kitchen inventory could be picked up, but due to a lack of storage space it was impossible for him to do so. He hoped that the court would decide that everything would have to be restored to its original state; unfortunately, that did not happen.

During a meeting in the American House of Representatives on February 11, 1998, Congressman Christopher Smith criticized Moscow officials and the support that the United States government was giving Russia:

There's a man in Russia who could have gone into business for personal gain, as so many of his generation have done. But instead he is devoting his energies to helping the many poor and destitute people in his country. By way of thanks, the government is subjecting him to constant harassment: his soup kitchen has been shut down, and many underprivileged people have been deprived of the opportunity to enjoy a decent meal. All this casts human nature in a bad light, and casts a slur on the political leaders of a city with such great potential.

After the soup kitchen was closed, the homeless — led by a "Hero of the Soviet Union" — went to eat in the restaurant of the city administration. When the hero died soon afterward, the homeless were no longer welcome there. The building in which the soup kitchen had been housed was finally converted into a luxury restaurant with a fitness center and sauna.

CHAPTER TWELVE

Islands of Hope?

New Religious Law Restores Leadership Role to the Russian Orthodox Church

After the passing of Gorbachev's Law on Religion in 1990, the number of Russian Orthodox parishes rose from 7,500 to 18,000 between 1990 and 1997. The monastic congregations for male and female religious quadrupled from 117 to 478, and the number of priests and deacons doubled from 10,000 to 20,000. In 1988, 10 percent of the Russian population called themselves "religious"; seven years later, in 1995, that figure had increased to 60 percent. (Yet religious involvement and activity in Russia remained low: only 6 to 7 percent of the population regularly attended church services.)

The Russian Orthodox Church used its growing influence to bring about a change in Gorbachev's liberal Law on Religion of 1990: the Law on Freedom and Religion. The Orthodox Church wanted to recover the leading role in society that it had enjoyed for centuries, and to clamp down on the activities of sixty large and middle-sized evangelical congregations and religious sects that were not registered and were of foreign origin. The new Law on Religion, which was passed on September 26, 1997, contained a revived registration requirement for non-Russian church congregations. Under this law, such congregations now had to prove that they had been officially active in Russia for at least fifteen years before being allowed to develop any religious activities.

Although the survival of the Island of Hope shelter was no longer immediately threatened, the harassment and external attacks continued as usual. In March 1999 the shelter was raided for the twelfth time. Gangsters smashed everything to smithereens and stole important documents, and one of the volunteers, an educator, suffered a concussion. In the years that followed, it became more and more difficult for the shelter to carry out its activities, not only because of the limited financial resources but also because of the chronic lack of personnel. Because of the constant badgering on the part of the Moscow authorities, the KGB, and the police, many volunteers only stayed for a short time.

Efimiya, the home for girls in Saint Petersburg, was also saddled with major problems, and after being forced to move out of the city center, it focused all its energies on the care of lonely, elderly women.

Ogorodnikov Breaks with the West
After the NATO Bombing of Serbia

In 1999, Ogorodnikov was given a car by the Belgian Saint Egidius Community, but in March of that year he broke off all contact with official Western representatives. The reason was the intensive NATO bombing of targets in Serbia and Kosovo that began on March 24, 1999, without the approval of the United Nations Security Council. This was the means by which the Western military alliance hoped to force President Slobodan Milošević to allow the stationing of an international military force in the Serbian province of Kosovo. A humanitarian crisis had been created there by the violence that broke out between Serbian troops from Belgrade and insurgent ethnic Albanians. After eleven weeks of bombing in which hundreds of citizens were killed in Serbia and Montenegro, Milošević capitulated. On June 9, 1999, Kosovo came under the rule of the United Nations after the signing of a military technical agreement — or the Kumanovo Treaty — in the Macedonian city of Kumanovo by the International Security Force (KFOR), the Yugoslavian authorities, and the Republic of Serbia.

In March 1999, in the Belgian city of Antwerp, at the invitation of the Saint Egidius Community, Ogorodnikov took part in a protest demonstration against the bombing.

The Tide Turns under Vladimir Putin

An end also came in 1999 to the catastrophic government of Boris Yeltsin, who, when he wasn't sick, was usually intoxicated. But first came the political crisis of 1998, which occurred in the aftermath of the 1997-98 financial crisis. Yeltsin was dissatisfied with the tempo of the reforms and demanded speedier progress. The person he had in mind to bring this about was his unknown thirty-five-year-old energy minister, Sergei Kiriyenko. On March 23, 1998, Yeltsin peremptorily dismissed Prime Minister Chernomyrdin, who had served in that capacity since 1992, along with his entire administration, and replaced them with the technocrat Kiriyenko. The latter went straight to work with gusto, bringing charges against the oligarch Boris Berezovsky, the head of the state gas company Gazprom. But Kiriyenko was fired on August 23, 1998, after Berezovsky launched a television smear campaign against him. His successors were Chernomyrdin (for under three weeks), whom Yeltsin had rehabilitated; Yevgeny Primakov (September 1998 to May 1999); Sergei Stepashin (May to August 1999); and, as of August 9, 1999, Vladimir Putin, the head of the federal security service of the Russian Federation (FSB), the agency formerly known as the KGB. By that point, the country was being governed de facto by oligarchs and was in a state of total ruin.

Few believed that Putin could pull it off; but the tide turned miraculously. Putin personally went after the oligarchs, among them the formidable and influential Berezovsky, and began the normalization of authority under law. The series of bloody attacks in Moscow by Chechen rebels was like manna from heaven for Putin. On August 31, 1999, a bomb exploded in a Moscow shopping center, leaving one dead and forty wounded. During the night of September 8, 1999, an entire nine-story apartment building was destroyed by a gigantic explosion. The building was scarcely sixty meters from the apartment complex where Alexander Ogorodnikov lived, and he was one of the first on the scene. The enormous crash shattered all the windows in the nearby buildings. Cars were overturned and the street lights went out, plunging the area into total darkness. With cries of help sounding from all sides, Ogorodnikov offered any help he could provide. Twenty-three were dead, and 150 wounded were taken to the hospital that night; a total of 94 victims were eventually pulled from the rubble, including four volunteers at the Island of Hope.

The attack was in response to the atrocities committed by the Russian army in the Caucasian republics of Dagestan and Chechnya, and Chechen rebels carried out a number of other retaliatory actions in September 1999, including attacks on other apartment complexes — in Moscow and other Russian cities — in which another two hundred people were killed.

The Second Chechen War (1999-2002)

In retaliation, Putin came down extremely hard on these rebels, who formed a threat to the regime of Chechen President Aslan Maskhadov, who had become the successor to interim president Zelimkhan Yandarbiyev after winning the January 1997 presidential election. (Yandarbiyev had been temporarily appointed president in 1996, after Dzhokhar Dudayev, the president of Chechnya at that time, was killed by a missile in a Russian air attack in April 1996, after he had been detected while using his satellite phone.) President Yeltsin congratulated Maskhadov for his electoral victory at the time, though the former did not recognize the de facto independence of the Chechen Republic of Ichkeria.

On October 1, 1999, Russian troops entered Chechnya with a great display of power, marking the beginning of the Second Chechen War (1999 to 2002). After a major ground offensive, most of the area fell under Russian control. The most important Chechen leaders were killed, while a number of others were given asylum in the West, which infuriated Moscow. In April 2002, Putin declared that the war in Chechnya was officially over. President Maskhadov had been driven off by the Russian army, and he spent a number of years fighting a guerrilla war against the Russian occupiers. In March 2005 he was killed by a special unit of the FSB and was succeeded by Sheikh Abdul Halim Sadulayev, who was, in turn, killed in June 2006 by a special Russian commando.

Ogorodnikov responded with horror to the way the Chechen people were murdered, tortured, raped, beaten, and driven away, but he did not understand the Western reaction. The rebels were not just fighting for their independence; their aim was to install an Islamic regime in the region along the lines of Iran. During the Second Chechen War, Ogorodnikov was again one of the best-informed independent observers in Moscow because of his contacts with both refugees and local residents.

Vladimir Putin Becomes President on December 31, 1999

Despite the war, the Russian parliamentary elections of December 1999 proceeded as scheduled. Ogorodnikov, however, was so devastated by the loss of his close co-workers in the September apartment building explosion that he withdrew his name as independent candidate on an Orthodox-based list. The political wing of the CDUR had been dormant for years; in fact, it no longer existed. Ogorodnikov's social involvement had been absorbing all his time and energy, putting his political activities on the back burner for quite some time.

The elections were a resounding success for Vladimir Putin, who became the second president of the Russian Federation. As an independent politician, he was given the support of the Kremlin's loyalist, pro-presidential Unity Party (also known as *Medved*, or Bear), a party created in haste by Yeltsin's staff, and of the conservative, free-market Union of Right Forces (SPS, formed in 1999). These parties each brought in 30 percent of the votes. After Putin was sure of the support of the Fatherland-All Russia party, founded in 1999, he forced the Communists and the ultranationalists back into the opposition.

On December 31, 1999, Boris Yeltsin stepped down, and Putin became the acting president. This put Putin in an exceedingly comfortable position in the run-up to the presidential elections of March 2000. As Kremlin boss, he, like the czar and the general secretary of the Communist Party, was shrouded in that mysterious aura the Russians call *vlast*, or the right to power, which still inspired a certain measure of intuitive humility and respect within the population. That princely element of sovereign authority later led to Putin's introduction of the concept of "rightful succession to the throne."

Polls showed Putin with a 20 to 40 percent lead over the other candidates when the presidential elections of March 26, 2000, began. In the first round he won 53 percent of the votes, while Communist leader Gennadi Zhuganov, one of his main opponents, managed to get only 30 percent of the votes.

Brotherhood of the 21st Century

In 2000, Ogorodnikov was finally able to fulfill his old dream of publishing his own independent religious periodical, the monthly *Brotherhood of the 21st Century: A Christian Orthodox Magazine*. After years of preparation, the first number finally rolled off the presses in August 2000. This periodical, which had a maximum circulation of 125,000, was actually a continuation of his journalistic activities of the 1970s. Ogorodnikov wanted to fill a gap in the Russian media landscape caused by the poor coverage of religious events in the national newspapers, all of which were in the hands of the oligarchs. Each city or province did have an Orthodox publication with a limited circulation, but none of them was national in scope. In addition, the ecumenical approach was still an unknown phenomenon at that time.

Ogorodnikov wanted a Christian voice to be heard in society again. "We approach the Russian Orthodox tradition with an open mind," he declared in an interview.

> We are oriented towards intellectuals who are critical of the conventional clerical and Russian-nationalistic mainstream in the media, with its exaggerated patriotism and great stress on rituals and superstition. In addition, our approach is ecumenical: we also report on the Catholic Church and the Protestants in Russia, although that is not always to the liking of the hierarchy of the Russian Orthodox Church.

Resistance to this approach declined after Patriarch Alexei II, who was himself a critical reader of the magazine, gave the initiative his blessing. The articles of the new publication made every effort to avoid prevailing biases and to deal with current religious problem areas. Ogorodnikov's goal was objective, high-quality reporting from a positive perspective. He also published articles by leading Western Catholics, while translations of articles in his magazine also appeared in the West. The magazine was distributed through the churches in Russia; it was also popular in prisons. The printer's bills were paid for from the sale of single issues. The magazine had a high readership, which was indicated by the large number of letters from readers that Ogorodnikov received every day.

Island of Hope Moves to Buzhorova

In April 2001, the CDUR lost the fight with the Moscow city council over the Island of Hope shelter. After a new legal decision came down, there was no other choice but to leave the building at 2 Popov Street for good. Ogorodnikov made one last attempt to avert a calamity by submitting an appeal to the Russian Supreme Court, but that was only to buy time. Taking the case to the International Court of Justice in The Hague (the highest legal institution of the United Nations) might have offered a way out, but such a procedure would cost a great deal of money and would take a long time, and the outcome would be far from certain.

When the inhabitants left the building in June 2001, Ogorodnikov took stock of the operation for ASSIST (Aid to Special Saints in Strategic Times), the international news agency run by the British journalist Dan Wooding:

> Since 1995 we have taken in about 1,470 children and saved many others as well. In past years even the police brought children to the shelter on a regular basis. More than in the past, it functioned as a kind of halfway house where the children could stay in safety until a solution was found for them. Most of the children could be placed elsewhere. Only in exceptional cases would a child stay in the house until he or she reached the age of eighteen.

However, Ogorodnikov did not lose heart: "It is still our duty to care for these kinds of children when the parents are unable to do so. We are going to set up a unique social recovery center for children who have been abused, even if their parents are still alive." Yet for him the move came at a particularly inconvenient moment: his mother, Margarita Firsova, died in June 2001. (After the death of her husband in 1992, she had first moved into Alexander's flat in Moscow; then, in 2000, she went to live with her sister, who also lived in Moscow.)

The shelter first found accommodation in a house in a Moscow suburb. But not only was the building in poor condition, but they had to leave it after just a short time. Then, with foreign assistance, the CDUR was given the use of four new apartments on the upper floor of an apartment building in a Moscow suburb. The living conditions there were rather primitive because of the absence of decent furniture. In addition, local residents were constantly campaigning against the shelter and its activities. Ogorodnikov had already spent a couple of years looking for permanent housing for Island of Hope, and that was after years of struggle against the corruption and arbitrary rule of the Moscow bureaucracy. So he decided to continue his organization's activities on an independent footing. Far and away the best solution for avoiding future problems, he thought, was private ownership: that is, buying a building himself. Because of the unpleasant experiences the shelter had had in Moscow, he decided he would rather look for quarters outside Moscow. Finally, in 2000, Ogorodnikov was able to buy (for $3,000) almost five acres of land in Buzhorova, a village thirty-three miles from Moscow but easily accessible via public transportation. It was a private purchase. He was allowed to buy this piece of land only if he was registered as a farmer. So he took a course in farming, and by the end of 2001, he was able to complete the purchase.

In a conversation with Dan Wooding, Ogorodnikov revealed his plans to build four small houses and a farm "where at least one hundred persons would be able to live." But financial resources were limited, and Ogorodnikov was aiming too high.

In the first building phase, from 2000 to 2002, a three-story dormitory was erected. The initial step took place in the summer of 2000 — though the purchase was still not closed — when German students began working on the foundations. In the spring of 2001 the basement was built, and the main road to the house was laid. And in the summer of 2002, German and Russian students finished the rest of the building. Next came the interior. The estimate for the construction of the showers, the installation of central heating, and the purchase of doors, windows, and stairs to the second and third floors was 25,000 euros. But central heating could not yet be installed because of a lack of funds.

The construction work was already in full swing when Ogorodnikov engaged in his next battle: applying for a building permit, which, given the enormous bureaucracy and complex legislation, was a particularly time-consuming chore. In the fall of 2003, shortly after the children had been moved out of the apartment building in Moscow, local hooligans badly vandalized the new building in Buzhorova. Then, in early 2004, while work was going on to repair that damage, the building's two night watchmen were attacked: one was killed, and the other ran off.

To keep the children safe, Ogorodnikov took a number of them to stay with a woman in Diveevo, far from Moscow and near the monastery where the relics of Saint Seraphim of Sarov are kept. Other children were given shelter in the village of Pskov, near Saint Petersburg, in the region where Alexander's brother, Raphael, had lived as a monk. Slowly, the shelter in Buzhorova became occupied, first by refugees and then, beginning in the summer of 2005, by children once again.

Shelter for Refugees in Moscow

Because of the hard living conditions in Buzhorova during the winter, and especially because it was so difficult to guarantee the children's safety, Ogorodnikov's charity organization gradually turned its attention to sheltering refugees from Uzbekistan, Kyrgyzstan, and other former So-

viet republics, those who were fleeing from the regimes in their home-
lands and coming to Moscow in great numbers in the hope of building a
new future there.

Since 2005, about sixty or seventy *bomzhi* (a popular Moscow acronym for people without a permanent home or address) have been living
in a number of Moscow apartments to which the CDUR was given
usufructuary rights in 2002. Maya, an Uzbek married to a high-level ap-
paratchik, an official of the former KGB who uses his influence to protect
the building's residents, helps Ogorodnikov in the day-to-day management of the building. Once again, the relationship with the neighbors was
tense at first, but they improved after Ogorodnikov assured them that all
the residents were paying rent — which was not, in fact, true. As of this
writing, the problems have abated, but how long will that last?

More Problems in Buzhorova

In recent years, more and more homeless pregnant women and young
mothers have sought accommodations at the shelter in Buzhorova. In the
winter of 2005-6, Ogorodnikov was able to convince the management of
a local hospital to take in two women and their babies until the end of the
winter. Each winter he tries to find temporary homes for the children,
preferably with families. In the months of April and May, as soon as the
weather warms up, they return to the shelter, which still does not have
central heating. But with the passage of time, the problems in Buzhorova
have mounted. The local authorities and residents, who had been favor-
ably disposed toward the shelter in the beginning, had a sudden change of
heart. And in November 2006 the first case of arson occurred.

In the fall of 2007, fifty women and children from Chechnya were
given temporary shelter in Buzhorova, after which they were taken to a
new shelter in Chechnya. This shelter had been purchased by a friend of a
Moscow imam; Ogorodnikov provided it with furniture and food. Once
there, the Chechen women and children converted to Christianity on
their own personal initiative; they secretly left the Chechen shelter and
disappeared without a trace. Not even Ogorodnikov was able to track
them down.

Probably out of a sense of revenge — since the shelter in Chechnya
was now empty — radical Chechens made the shelter in Buzhorova their
target. In an attack in December 2007, they burned and destroyed the

staircase and furnishings on the first floor. They stole the cow and the sheep, and blocked the water supply. In May 2008 the building suffered more heavy damage in another case of arson. Mother Zoya, a demented old woman, the oldest resident of the shelter, ran away in shock and was later found dead. More recently, in 2009, the spring was sabotaged; as of this writing, the shelter has no running water. Furthermore, after almost eight years, the shelter in Buzhorova still does not have electricity, even though all the formal regulations have been met, due to Ogorodnikov's principled refusal to pay bribes. He now has no other choice but to take the matter to court and demand his rights.

Undaunted, Ogorodnikov continues to devote himself fully to the needy people at the bottom rung of Russian society. Three times a week he distributes food to the destitute in Moscow's train and metro stations. At the moment he is caring for two to three hundred people. But the weak link in his charity initiatives is his heavy dependence on foreign support. In October 2005 a subsidy from a Swiss fund was terminated after two years, so that activities had to be continued with a minimum of resources. Ogorodnikov does not receive any structural support — not from the Russian government nor from the Russian Orthodox Church. The French organization REPPER (Réseau d'Échanges de Projets et de Programmes pour les Enfants de la Rue) supported the shelter until 2005.

Ecumenical Dialogue

Beginning in the 1990s, Ogorodnikov has been repeatedly invited to attend international religious gatherings of the Dutch Christian organization Open Doors, the Catholic Saint Egidius Community (the Belgian branch of the Italian Sant'Egidio), and various other Catholic organizations in Italy, Switzerland, France, the Netherlands, and Canada. He was also a guest speaker at the World Youth Days in Rome in 2000, the World Social Forum in Porto Alegre, Brazil, in 2003, and the ecumenical event "Together for Europe" in the German city of Stuttgart in 2007. If one enters the name "Alexander Ogorodnikov" in the search field of the American website YouTube, one will find a seven-minute film about his stay in the Gulag that was produced by Open Doors.

In 2006, Ogorodnikov organized the first eight-day "Pilgrimage of the Tsar" to the Protective Veil of the Mother of God for Christians of Western Europe and the United States. During this pilgrimage, believers were able to become acquainted with the history and spiritual heritage of the Russian Orthodox Church and with life in the parishes and monasteries of the Church today. The program included visits to Moscow; to the city of Sergiev Posad, with its precious art treasure, the *Troitse-Sergieva Lavra* (Monastery of the Holy Trinity), and Saint Sergius, the most important *lavra* (monastery complex) in the Russian Orthodox Church; to Pereslavl-Zalessky, with its cathedral and various monasteries as important attractions; and to the Kostroma oblast, with the historic city of Kostroma as its big tourist attraction.

Metropolitan Kirill of Smolensk and Kaliningrad, who has been the new patriarch of the Russian Orthodox Church since January 27, 2009, extended his cooperation to this project. It was in this way that an ecumenical dialogue was started with the Orthodox Church in the places where the Orthodox Church was born.

The monthly publication *Brotherhood of the 21st Century* struggled with a dwindling circulation — first a drop down to 50,000, and later to 20,000 copies — partly because a digital version of the magazine became available in 2005. Ogorodnikov had also noticed that in recent years an unspoken opposition to his magazine had been growing in some ranks of the Russian Orthodox Church. In addition, the monthly production of each new issue was always an enormous job, mainly because the magazine was understaffed. Ogorodnikov wrote most of the articles himself, while he also edited and corrected the articles supplied by other writers, who did their work and provided their support gratis. When the magazine was hit by serious financial problems in the spring of 2007, Ogorodnikov decided to suspend its publication temporarily, despite the hole in the market and the great demand for this kind of publication in intellectual circles.

Russian Wild-West Capitalism Comes to an End

In Vladimir Putin's Russia, the second Chechen war was given the blessing of President George W. Bush after the attacks on September 11, 2001, as part of his "War on Terror." In October 2003, Putin installed a pro-Russian government in Chechnya; but in May 2004, Achmat Kadirov, whom Putin had appointed president, was killed in a bomb attack. In October 2004, Kadirov was succeeded by Alu Alkhanov, winner of the controversial presidential elections of August 2004. In February 2007, Putin removed Alkhanov and replaced him with his own puppet, Ramzan Kadirov, a thirty-year-old illiterate and son of the murdered Achmat Kadirov, as acting president. His infamous private militia, the *Kadirovtsy*, which was officially an "anti-terrorist unit" loyal to Moscow but in practice a ruthlessly corrupt gang of thugs, has the country more or less under control at the moment — with the support of the Russian federal police.

On April 16, 2004, Moscow announced that Russia was going to end its ten-year military operation in Chechnya and that the Russian troops would be withdrawn. But the future in this chaotic region remains very uncertain. In the past fifteen years, the two wars in Chechnya, which went hand in hand with crimes against humanity on a grand scale, have claimed an estimated 150,000 lives.

Putin reformed the tax system, created attractive terms for foreign investments, and limited defense spending. In crucial sectors, including energy, he upheld or restored state control. He managed to call a halt to Russia's "wild west capitalism" — the unbridled and brutal free market in the country — and restored the rule of law up to a certain point. The oligarchs were forced to respect the law and to pay taxes; those who did not cooperate fled the country or ended up behind bars. The latter was the fate of billionaire Mikhail Khodorkovsky, head of the Yukos oil company of Russia, one of the world's largest private oil concerns. Officially he was arrested for tax fraud, but in reality it was for his political aspirations.

Until 2008, the Russian economy was growing at an average annual rate of 6.7 percent, resulting in a tripling of salaries, though that increase was canceled out for the most part by inflation. Unemployment dropped, and a prosperous middle class emerged in the cities. With this economic success story, though it was lopsidedly based on the export of oil and gas, Russia found itself playing an important role in the world economy after a long absence. The first "gas conflict" with the Ukraine in late 2005 was illustrative of Russia's desire to strengthen its grip in the region.

This prosperity did not do Putin's electoral chances any harm. In the presidential elections of March 2004 he took 71 percent of the votes in the first round. In May 2008, Putin had to relinquish the presidency because he had already served the maximum of two consecutive four-year terms. The Russian constitution, which dates from 1993, did not allow for a third term. So he had his protégé Dmitri Medvedev succeed him. Medvedev, who was put forward in December 2007 as a presidential candidate for Putin's center-right United Russia party (founded in 2001), won the controversial elections of May 2008, as expected, with an over-whelming majority of votes — 70 percent.

Putin was then appointed prime minister of Russia. Since then he has been firmly in charge, and many people still regard him as the most pow-erful man in Russia. On November 21, 2008, the Russian Duma, the lower house of parliament, accepted the proposal to extend the term of office of the president of Russia from four to six years. Former president Vladimir Putin had already let it be known that he would support the proposal. Observers suspected that he wanted to return to the Kremlin. Five days later, the Federation Council (the Russian senate) agreed to a constitu-tional amendment to extend the presidential term of office (but this was not to apply to Dmitri Medvedev).

On December 3, 2009, during a live Russian television program, Putin confirmed that he was considering running for president again in 2012.

Turning a Blind Eye to Democratic Deficit

Russians have been quite willing to accept this deficit in democracy in ex-change for enhanced well-being and regained national pride. The public good will toward Putin was so great that hardly a murmur of protest was heard about his authoritarian tricks, which are manifested more and more openly. For example, Putin did not have second thoughts about placing the national television stations, newspapers, and magazines un-der full state control again, or muzzling the remaining free press.

A large number of notorious opponents of the Russian regime have been done away with by "unknown persons." One of the best known of these assassinations was that of the journalist Anna Politkovskaya, who wrote for *Novaya Gazeta* (New Gazette), an independent and democrati-cally oriented newspaper. She was working on a book about the Russian presence in Chechnya. Another case was the poisoning of Alexander Litvinenko, who had immigrated to London and was about to make some revelations about his former employer, the Russian secret service (FSB). The list of victims keeps growing. On January 19, 2009, the well-known human rights activist and journalist Stanislav Markelov was shot dead in broad daylight on a street in the center of Moscow by a masked assailant, in the presence of twenty-five-year-old Anastasia Baburova, also a jour-nalist at *Novaya Gazeta.* Baburova rushed to Markelov's aid and was shot in the head; she died of her injuries the same day.

On April 2, 2009, sixty-seven-year-old Lev Ponomarev, leader of For Human Rights, a Russian organization based in Moscow that is engaged in registering and reporting human rights abuses in the Russian Federation, was seriously wounded in an attack. The disabled journalist Sergei Protasanov, who worked for the newspaper *Grazhdanskoe Soglasie* (Civil Consensus), a small opposition newspaper in the Moscow suburb of Khimki, and was the author of a number of recent articles on electoral fraud in Khimki, was attacked on the street during the night of March 28, 2009, and died of his injuries two days later.

On July 15, 2009, a leading human rights activist, Natalia Estemirova, was kidnapped and murdered. According to Human Rights Watch, she was responsible for "extremely sensitive dossiers" on hundreds of kidnappings in Chechnya that involved Russian troops or militias with ties to Moscow. Human Rights Watch fears that the Russian secret service is also the mastermind behind that assassination.

Russia is facing great social and economic challenges at this moment in history because it has not solved the obstacles that the society has been contending with for decades: the weak economic structure, the negative population growth, the deplorable state of the Russian army, the nationality question, the enormous impact of the mafia (which has now developed into a separate class altogether), and the steady growth of corruption.

CHAPTER THIRTEEN

Fighting Corruption and Helping the Forgotten

Plans for New Political Engagement

Ogorodnikov still has political ambitions: he would like to devote himself again to promoting Christian Democracy in Russia in the near future. Indeed, for years he has been dreaming that Orthodox believers, both laypeople and priests (who are forbidden to participate in politics), would become fully politically engaged so that their interests might be defended in parliament and, if possible, in the government via elected representatives. In the 1990s, Ogorodnikov's Christian Democratic Union (CDUR) was given too little room to undertake activities in public life; nor could the party count on support from the Orthodox Church. At that time Russia had no equivalent to the social encyclical *Rerum Novarum*, issued by Pope Leo XIII in 1891. But in 2000, after eight years of preparation by the current patriarch, Kirill, the bishops' conference approved the "Basis of the Social Concept of the Russian Orthodox Church." The aim of this document is to present the Orthodox Church's religious message in terms of political theory.

In past years, Ogorodnikov has been active in the European Christian Political Movement (ECPM), a lobby group formed by the Dutch ChristenUnie party, which looks to the Bible for its guiding principles and works to make the voice of European Christians more clearly heard when it comes to family politics and ethical issues. Leo van Doesburg, of the ECPM, who supports the advancement of Christian Democracy in central and eastern Europe and is based in the Romanian city of Timişoara, would also like to see Christian Democracy get off the ground in Russia:

A gradual approach is the best. In Russia we're starting out by working on the creation of Christian social organizations, from which hopefully young leaders will emerge who at a later stage could help shape a political movement. For the younger generation, the experience of Alexander Ogorodnikov is of crucial importance.

Ogorodnikov has taken part in several ECPM conferences, including in The Hague (December 2008), Minsk (December 2008 and March 2009), and Moscow (October 2009).

In 2011, the revival of the Christian Democratic political movement began to pick up speed. At a conference entitled "The Responsibility of Christians for the Nation," held April 8-10, 2011, organizations, trade unions, and individuals established a common basis for translating the principles of Christian life, morality, and ethics in real-life situations. A commission was formed to do something about the Christian Democratic organization Moral Russia. Besides practicing love of neighbor and charity, the new political movement is hoping to create economic, social, and cultural programs. Its guiding principles are openness, transparency, the struggle against corruption, and the defense of the rights of minorities. Also high on its agenda are the improvement of health, welfare, quality of life, and morality for all Russians. It is also focusing a great deal of attention on religious education, bringing up the new generation, and supporting veterans, people with disabilities, large families, the elderly, and the poor. The basic text that was approved by the conference includes this statement:

> All our activities, as well as all interpersonal and social relationships and care for the welfare of the nation, are based on the fulfilling of God's commandments. And the social reforms we have in mind have their origin in spirituality, morality, human dignity and social justice.

The aim of the new movement is to introduce Christian moral and spiritual values into the social and political life of the country. "The Responsibility of Christians" conference was attended by representatives of the Russian Orthodox Church and other Christian churches, representatives from the academic and business communities, and foreign guests from the ECPM and the Association of Christian Democrats in eastern Europe. But it takes time to set up an actual organization to embody all these ideas and ideals — and to obtain official government approval for the party. As a result, the parliamentary elections of December 2011 and the presidential elections of March 2012 came much too soon. As a political movement, Moral Russia still wishes to play a significant role in politics; but, as Ogorodnikov observes, it "works exclusively with young people, who have no political experience."

Fighting Corruption

The unfortunate fate of the Russian lawyer Sergei Magnitsky is a harrowing illustration of the need for a new direction in Russia. Magnitsky exposed a large-scale network of corruption in Russian state enterprises; he was arrested in November 2008. On November 16, 2009, a few days before the end of the one-year period during which he could be held without being sentenced, Magnitsky died in prison under suspicious circumstances. That case has soured relations between Russia, on the one hand, and the United States and Europe, on the other, right up to the present.

Ogorodnikov, too, follows his conscience in the endless fight against decadence in Russian society today, in which a small clan of oligarchs are able to strengthen their position, thus making it impossible to end corruption, cynicism, and favoritism in the distribution of the country's resources. One of Ogorodnikov's allies in that struggle is his friend Valery Morozov. Morozov, who was also active in the Moral Russia movement, had to leave his homeland after exposing bribery in the Kremlin administration. As head of the International Anticorruption Committee (IAC), whose headquarters is in London, Morozov had spent months collecting information on the most corrupt officials in Russia. They had diverted hundreds of millions of dollars to foreign accounts. On the basis of concrete evidence, the IAC asked Western governments to put the names of the corrupt officials on a "black list," to freeze their accounts, and to deny them admission to their countries. The IAC also announced that it had proof that President Vladimir Putin was involved. Ogorodnikov says:

> We want all stolen goods to be returned to their rightful owner: the Russian people. That money should be invested in the sectors with the greatest need: health care, education, science, culture, the pension fund, housing for young families, and the fair administration of justice.

Leading Role in Anti-Putin Protest

So it is no accident that, since November 2011, Ogorodnikov has been one of the leading figures in the protest against Vladimir Putin and the way the clan surrounding him plans to consolidate its position over the coming decades after they make changes in the constitution. That protest grew spontaneously into a broad popular movement after Prime Minister Putin and President Medvedev announced that in the presidential elections of 2012 they would once again trade places — "as agreed in 2008" — and after the massive fraud perpetrated during the parliamentary elections of December 2011, which Putin's United Russia party, in truth, lost. Due to his waning popularity, Putin can only rely on the vote of people who work for the government and who have no one else to support them. In the presidential elections of March 4th, Putin won 63.9 percent of the votes — according to the official count. But the Organization for Security and Cooperation in Europe (OSCE) found that irregularities had taken place in one-third of the polling stations. Ogorodnikov, who served as an independent observer at a Moscow polling station, witnessed fraud on a grand scale. According to the law, officials are allowed to cast their vote in the district where they work. But Ogorodnikov saw the government transporting hundreds of officials by bus from one voting station to the next without any supervision; they kept casting votes for Putin in multiple stations.

Ogorodnikov had spent the previous months busily distributing articles and information. Despite attempts by the government to do all it could to keep potential demonstrators out of the cities where demonstrations were being held, the opposition succeeded in mobilizing more people every time. Most of the demonstrators, who come mainly from the urban middle class, are between the ages of seventeen and twenty-five. They take full advantage of what the Internet has to offer, especially Facebook and other social networks. Although the government has great difficulty controlling this communication, it employs every known means to sabotage it. Ogorodnikov and other leaders of the resistance noticed repeated disruptions in their e-mail service. And for reasons that could not be explained, Alexander's computer crashed.

Because the street protests were getting so much international attention, the government was careful not to deal too harshly with the demonstrators at first. "One plus point is that the sheer size of the protest is keeping the ruling elite from lording it over everyone and everything,"

Ogorodnikov says. He compares the youth revolt in Russia today with the uprisings of May 1968 in western Europe. "What is happening today," he says, "will leave a deep impact in the long term. The new generation that is now emerging will keep on fighting for its dignity and for full civil rights, in defiance of the official lies." In the meantime, he went on his own hunger strike to support the hunger strike of Oleg Shein, who was fraudulently deprived of his electoral victory as mayor of the city of Astrakhan.

On May 6, 2012, the day before Putin's official inauguration as president, the massively mobilized riot police came down especially hard on demonstrators. They swept the streets around the Kremlin clean and arrested 120 demonstrators, including the liberal opposition leader, Boris Nemtsov. Where is this uprising leading?

"No one knows the answer to that," Ogorodnikov insists.

> Not even the young people themselves. Most of those who spent hours chanting the slogan "Putin is a thief" did not act out of ideological motives. But whatever the reason, that protest will mark their lives — despite the government's attempts to nip the uprising in the bud by minimizing the protest in the media, which they control, and by placing Putin's "Day of Victory" fully in the spotlight.

One mitigating factor, however, is that the opposition is extremely divided. The country is in need of a new leader who could stand as an alternative to Putin. But many people distrust a great number of today's opposition leaders because they used to cooperate with the regime. "When new leaders arise, they are not given permission to organize meetings. I know many valuable people at the base, but they are not widely known," says Ogorodnikov, who hopes that the Moral Russia movement will play a significant role in the future.

Bursting with New Plans

What does Alexander Ogorodnikov's future look like at the moment? He has no shortage of plans. Now that the grounds in Buzhorova have been fenced off, he wants to ensure the safety of the residents of the Island of Hope shelter by using watchdogs. He hopes that the shelter will gradually become largely self-sufficient by cultivating its own potatoes and vegetables and by raising its own pigs, chickens, and rabbits. He has purchased an extra piece of adjacent land, increasing the size of the existing grounds so that a hundred residents can be accommodated in the future. The Catholic Comenius University in Bratislava, Slovakia, would like to enter into structural collaboration with the shelter and to send volunteers on a permanent basis. Volunteers worked on the reconstruction of the building in the summer of 2009 (an extra floor was added during that renovation), which was completed in November 2009 with financial support from the Belgian town of Herzele.

Despite persistent difficulties and constant obstruction from the local government, the renovation of the Buzhorova shelter was finally completed in 2011. Each floor now has furnished rooms as well as common toilets and showers. And for the first time, the shelter has permanent electricity — a basic need for the residents. But the power is not supplied via the existing electrical grid because, since 2002, Alexander has refused to pay bribes to corrupt officials. When you've done nine years in the Gulag and survived, you don't make those kinds of deals. Ogorodnikov had no other choice than to supply the electricity himself by means of two wind turbines and solar panels.

But the heart of Ogorodnikov's activities has always been in the social sector. For example, he has plans for a project for ex-convicts: in 2005 he purchased (again with foreign assistance) about fifty-two acres of land that had once been a *kolkhoz*, a collective farm from the Soviet period, located in the Tver region, on the main route from Moscow to Saint Petersburg. But the allocation of the lots has involved legal proceedings that have already gone on for four years. Ogorodnikov has been engaged in a struggle in the Tver region with Vekselber, an oligarch who has links with Putin and is the owner of the Skolkovo Innovation Center. Vekselber paid a judge named Kimry six million rubles in bribes to seize land that belonged to Ogorodnikov. After the possibilities of appeal in Russia are exhausted, the case will finally be settled by the European Court of Human Rights in Strasbourg, which is now recognized by Russian law. Ogorodnikov's hope is to create a sustainable project in the not-too-distant future for one of the most forgotten groups in society.

Epilogue

Over the past forty years, Alexander Ogorodnikov has been working nonstop for religious freedom and the creation of a more humane society in "his" Russia. How does he himself look back on his efforts?

The battle that I am still waging every day may seem somewhat one-sided and hopeless. Naturally, there are times when my spirits wane. I become disillusioned and desperate, and I ask myself whether everything I've done so far hasn't just been totally unnecessary and pointless, all the more so because the prospects are sometimes so bleak. How could it have come so far? Why is it that not a single dissident who survived the hell of the Gulag and contributed to the fall of Communism has yet succeeded in turning the tide? Actually, *the* dissident movement never existed. Even I just stumbled into the milieu by chance because, unlike most of the other intellectuals, I could no longer accommodate my conscience to the immoral Communist regime. The more we were oppressed, the more important we became — not in our own country, but in the West. The more we protested against the repression and arrests, the more dissidents were apprehended. No one at that time wondered what would happen the day the regime suddenly collapsed, because it seemed as if it would hold out for another hundred years at least.

After my unexpected release from the Gulag in February 1987, I couldn't just look on from the sidelines when people needed me most, even after freedom of religion had become a fact in 1990. Despite the continuous opposition — the KGB ruined my family twice, and murdered my brother and my secretary — I tried, with great drive and dedication, to relieve the intense suffering of all those in Russia who fall between the cracks. But the former dissidents became each other's rivals, all the more so because — as so often happens in history — no red carpet was rolled out for us. Even the few who managed to work their way to the political top did not manage to achieve success. Andrei Sakharov, with his moral standards, could hardly hold his ground in the Supreme Soviet, and as soon as the former Georgian dissident Zviad Gamsachurdia came to power, he emerged as a cruel dictator who ended his life fighting a civil war.

In no time at all our country was taken over by a new criminal-political elite, and I, too, was unable to do anything to prevent it. The gap between rich and poor only increased under the regime of Boris Yeltsin, and so did the corruption. Yet my struggle continues unabated. Why? I'm not a man of overly emotional or pretentious words, but I do this because it is my duty. I regard myself as a kind of martyr who offers the other cheek, as Jesus did. I do this because, as Fyodor Dostoyevsky so beautifully put it, "compassion" is in fact the highest Christian feeling. Christians possess this feeling by nature, as a kind of special innate gift. In the Bible, John 15:13 says: *Greater love has no man than this, that a man lay down his life for his friends.* If we want love to exist between us, between human beings, then we have to show it as well — through our deeds and through our mercy. *That* is the highest human calling.

ACKNOWLEDGMENTS

"This Story Ought to Be Told to *All* Generations"

I was put on the trail of Alexander Ogorodnikov in 2005 by Jan De Volder, my colleague at *Tertio,* the Flemish Catholic news magazine. De Volder is active in the Saint Egidius Community, which has supported Alexander Ogorodnikov's charity work for many years. In the summer of 2007 I came to know Ogorodnikov personally when he came to the Belgian village of Sint-Lievens-Esse for the commemoration of the 1,350th anniversary of the martyrdom of Saint Livinus. The theme of the event was "eternal martyrdom."

Ogorodnikov may not be a very gifted speaker, but he radiates inspiration and inner strength all the more. His witness made such a deep impression on me that I decided to publish his life story in book form. A good friend of mine, the Belgian filmmaker Roland Ottoy, also came up with the idea of making a documentary about Ogorodnikov's life and work.

In connection with this project, I have spent the past two years studying the available literature and visiting hundreds of websites. It was no easy matter supplementing these basic facts with original source material. Over the years, scores of documents were seized or destroyed when the KGB carried out searches in Ogorodnikov's home or the homes of his family members and friends. And when the British Keston Institute of Oxford moved in 2007 to Baylor University in Waco, Texas, their source material was impossible to consult because it was packed up in boxes. After months of contact with the main office of the Memorial historical society in Moscow, which manages the archive of the Gulag, the Russian historian Gennadi selected about six hundred documents on Ogorodnikov and the activities of the Christian Seminar — all of them from the private collections of the KGB archives — and had them scanned and burned onto CD ROMs.

All these materials were not enough, however, to serve as a basis for thorough research, analysis, and description. So in 2008, I decided to visit Russia myself in order to make personal contact with Memorial and to look for extra source material, if at all possible — including in the Perm-36 concentration camp. Roland Ottoy decided to travel to Russia with me to make "salient" recordings for his documentary.

In February-March 2008 we had the opportunity of becoming acquainted with the "democratic content" of Russian society during the presidential election campaign — or what was supposed to pass for that. There was absolutely no indication on the streets of Moscow that an election campaign was in progress. Not a single election poster could be seen, with the exception of one: a gigantic billboard put up by Putin's United Russia party, which featured an image of a bear and the Russian flag, and which covered the entire width of a large building just opposite the Kremlin, the power center of Russia. It could not have been more symbolic: with the Russian flag in the background, the retiring president, Vladimir Putin, was presenting "his" favorite candidate, Dmitri Medvedev. The campaign was limited to exaggerated attention on television and in the newspapers to Medvedev's "administrative qualities," which are, of course, under government control. The three opposition candidates — the Communist Gennadi Zhuganov, the ultranationalist Vladimir Zhirinovsky, and the unknown Andrei Bogdanov — posed no real threat. Mikhail Kashanov of the liberal opposition wasn't even allowed to run. So it was hardly accidental that no foreign observers were sent by the Organization for Security and Cooperation in Europe (OSCE) to monitor these elections.

In Moscow we interviewed Archpriest Vsevolod Chaplin, a senior official of the Russian Orthodox Church, and Father Georgy Kochetkov, director of the Saint Filaret Orthodox Christian Institute, a theological training center. During our visit to Perm-36, the former concentration camp — the journey of about 680 miles from Moscow by plane and taxi took almost an entire day — we slept on authentic prisoner mattresses. We were also the first foreigners to visit the shelter that Ogorodnikov runs in Moscow, where seventy refugees from the former Soviet republics are staying. And on Sunday, March 2, 2008, we visited the Island of Hope shelter in Buzhorova. There we had a firsthand experience of the secret service surveillance to which Ogorodnikov is constantly subjected.

A half hour after our arrival, much to our bewilderment — and at the special request of "a highly-placed official in Moscow" — the equally perplexed local police showed up to investigate the "irregularities" that were supposedly taking place in the shelter at that moment. Roland Ottoy immortalized on film this somewhat embarrassing and hilarious confrontation with Russian law enforcement.

That same evening, our return trip to Moscow ended in complete chaos. The center of the city was sealed off because of the major open-air festivities being held at the foot of the Kremlin. All the popular Russian pop groups were there to enliven the electoral victory of Dmitri Medvedev. We were able to get our hands on admission tickets and, after being checked by an impressive police cordon, to witness the boundless spectacle of glamour and glitter. Putin and Medvedev arrived at 11 p.m. to greet their thousands of supporters — long before the election results were officially announced.

I also had a number of in-depth interviews with Ogorodnikov during his visit to Belgium, November 27 to December 8, 2008. This monograph is almost unavoidably subjective to a certain extent, and some of the sources of the stories could no longer be verified. Yet, in my capacity as a historian, who by virtue of his profession is both accustomed and obliged to approach historical facts with a critical eye, I have attempted to be as objective as possible. During these intensive and confidential discussions — Ogorodnikov once jokingly called them "KGB cross-examinations" — I never once caught him in a fabrication or found him guilty of exaggeration.

Will Russia ever come clean about its evil past? In August 2007, seventy years after Stalin's terror and twenty years after the gates of the Gulag had shut behind Ogorodnikov, a national monument was finally erected at the execution trenches of Butovo, a former shooting range just outside Moscow. At the place where, in 1937 and 1938, during Stalin's Great Purge, more than 20,000 suspected enemies of the Communist regime were shot dead and buried in mass graves, the Russian Orthodox Church built a monumental white stone church: the Church of the Resurrection and the Holy New Martyrs and Confessors of Russia. The building was consecrated by Patriarch Alexei II on May 19, 2007, the birthday of Nicholas II, the last czar of the Russian Empire, who was canonized, along with his wife and five children, on August 14, 2000, by the Russian Orthodox Church. On that occasion the czar and his family were given the title *Strastoterpets* (passion bearers).

In October 2007, Vladimir Putin also visited the church and the museum in Butovo. "Such tragedies are not unique events in history," he declared. "They always take place when ideals that seemed so attractive at first glance ultimately degenerate into an empty shell and place themselves above our basic values — human life, human rights and freedom."

But doesn't history seem to be repeating itself? Under President Dmitri Medvedev a somewhat more liberal wind seems to be blowing through the Kremlin for the first time in a while. On April 19, 2009, in *Novaya Gazeta*, one of the last independent newspapers, an interview with the president was printed, which would have been unthinkable under Putin. There Medvedev emphatically denies "that Russians, in exchange for a higher standard of living, are expected to be loyal to the Kremlin and to keep their criticism to themselves." But does his denial reflect the truth? Throughout Russian history, the concept of "freedom" has remained something of an unknown phenomenon — under the authoritarian regime of the czar, under Communism, and equally under the current rulers. May we conclude that Russia today is once again turning into a totalitarian state — but in luxury wrappings? Voices of opposition and dissent are increasingly being restrained. Since Putin took office in 1999, eighteen journalists have been murdered — five from *Novaya Gazeta*. Only one of those cases has been solved. On October 14, 2009, during her visit to Moscow, Secretary of State Hillary Clinton insisted that these murders be cleared up. Will justice ever be served?

Getting to know the history of the Soviet Union and Russia at a deeper level and conducting a thorough analysis of the Soviet system and its gradual implosion have been extremely enriching experiences. As a historian, I was aware of the broad outlines, but the more deeply I delved into the subject, the more I came to realize how much Russian society in all its dimensions and facets differs fundamentally from Western European society. The thread running through it is a barbarity that is almost impossible for us Westerners to comprehend.

But I only became aware of the most important lesson as I was completing the final editing of this book. In October 2009, I sent the Russian translation of my book to Alexander, and for a long time I heard nothing from him. Later I learned that at that moment his main priority had been the renovation of the shelter in Buzhorova, which had been partially destroyed by fire in May 2008, and for which he had finally raised enough money. He wanted to finish the work before winter set in so "his" people would have a roof over their heads — literally. Unfortunately, reading through my text would have to wait. These were circumstances beyond his control. He had no other choice.

This incident is typical of Ogorodnikov. The accumulation of prestige, fame, and honor — such things are totally wasted on him. They leave him cold. I should note that I did not write this book at his request; he is far too modest for that. As a Russian Orthodox, but chiefly as a true Christian, his constant occupation is to spread Jesus' message, not with words so much as with deeds. It's easy to say beautiful things about that message when we are at a safe distance. But Ogorodnikov decided not to talk, but to act, with his whole life since his conversion — thirty-five years long.

Besides the physical torture — of which the partial paralysis of his face is a lasting reminder — Ogorodnikov also suffered psychological terror during his stay in the Gulag that drove him to the brink of the abyss. But he never broke. The years of incarceration only left him more stubborn and resolute. He made not a single concession, and he never agreed to compromise with the camp leadership. When Ogorodnikov left the Gulag after eight and a half years, he was neither embittered nor frustrated. Armed with an almost inexhaustible energy, he continued his struggle despite the unending intimidation: his two marriages broken by the KGB; the murder of his brother and secretary; and the attempt on his own life.

Always with the same affability, discretion, modesty, and inner peace, far from the floodlights and full of confidence and optimism, Ogorodnikov works steadily on building a better society. Why does he do it? Bolstered by indestructible expectations, a deep faith, and inner certitude — the three corners of his belief — Ogorodnikov's daily experience teaches him that what he is doing is not pointless. He lives in the firm conviction that all shall be well. Is it against his better judgment?

After his release in 1987, it seemed as though Communism would hold out for at least another hundred years. But less than five years later it imploded, much earlier than anyone had dared to predict. Even now, despite all the setbacks, he remains a valiant and imperturbable fighter for "his" people who are in danger of falling between the cracks. He does not act out of desperation, but with the firm conviction that all shall be well for them, too. Such inner confidence gives him the strength to carry on this seemingly one-sided fight. Getting to know Ogorodnikov — his person as well as his remarkable willpower and optimism — has made a deep impression on me, and it is forever engraved in my memory. He has changed my life and the way I think.

Acknowledgments

In the documentary on Alexander Ogorodnikov completed by Roland Ottoy in December 2008, the British parliamentarian David Alton says this: "His name ought to be written in capital letters for his courage and bravery. We must tell this story to all generations." After the fall of Communism, remarkably little was published about the Gulag, undoubtedly one of the blackest pages in the history of the twentieth century, certainly Russia's. Now that the Russian economy is faring somewhat better after Boris Yeltsin's dramatic clearance sale, no one wants to be reminded of the past. The aim of this book, in all modesty, is to raise the lid on this sordid "cesspool" — not only because history has a right to it, but also because we ought to draw lessons from history for the future.

On December 2, 2008, Ogorodnikov was made an official honorary citizen of the Flemish town of Herzele. The composer Michel Vangheluwe, of the Belgian folk group Ishtar, came up with the brilliant idea of writing an oratorio about Ogorodnikov's life and work for the occasion. On January 31, 2010, the Belgian Catholic television and radio broadcasting company KTRO broadcast Roland Ottoy's twenty-eight-minute TV film on the Belgian television stations Eén (in the morning) and Canvas (in the evening) on the life and work of Ogorodnikov, based on the penetrating film images of Ottoy's production and accompanied by the original music from Michel Vangheluwe's oratorio.

FINALLY, I WOULD LIKE to express my thanks to everyone who contributed to the creation of this book, directly or indirectly. My special appreciation goes to the translators Benjamin Bossaert and Katya Zelinskaja; to the filmmaker Roland Ottoy; to Gennadi from the Memorial association in Moscow; to Bert Claerhout and my colleagues at *Tertio;* to the members of "Vriendenkring Aleksandr Ogorodnikov"; to Cera, Lieven Sercu, Maarten Van Steenbergen, and Sonja Stock of the Lannoo publishing company; to the town council of Herzele; and to Ludo Van den Eynden, Michel Vangheluwe, and Prof. Emmanuel Waegemans. Last but not least, I would like to mention those who are most dear to me, my wife and my children, who, each in his or her own way, walked this long road with me.

KOENRAAD DE WOLF

Bibliography

Archives

KGB Archive (Moscow)
Memorial Archive (Moscow)
Archive of Camp Perm-36 (Perm)
Person archive of Alexander Ogorodnikov (Moscow)

Magazines

Tetradi Samizdata — Cahiers du Samizdat. Périodique Mensuel, Brussels, 1973-1989
Christianskaja Demokratija — Démocratie Chrétienne. Bulletin de l'Internationale Démocrate-Chrétienne sur l'Europe de l'Est, Brussels, 1989-1991

Newspapers

De Morgen (1978-2009)
De Standaard (1962-1992)
De Tijd (1989-1992)

Interviews

David Alton (London)
Vsevolod Chaplin (Moscow)
Leo Delcroix (Genk)
Georgy Kochetkov (Moscow)

Bibliography

Alexander Ogorodnikov (Moscow)
Danny Smith (London)

Books

Alexeyeva, L. *Soviet Dissidents: Contemporary Movements for National, Religious and Human Rights.* Middletown, 1985.

Alexeyeva, L., and P. Goldberg. *The Thaw Generation: Coming of Age in the Post-Stalin Era.* Pittsburgh, 1993.

Almarik, A. *Haalt de Sovjetunie 1984? Met bijdragen van prof. K. van het Reve en prof. dr. J. W. Bezemer.* Utrecht-Antwerp, 1984.

Applebaum, Anne. *Goelag: Een geschiedenis.* Amsterdam, 2003.

Balliauw, J. *Het verloren paradijs: De ontwrichting van Rusland.* Antwerp-Baarn, 1994.

Barron, J. *KGB: The Secret Work of Soviet Secret Agents.* New York, 1974. Dutch translation: *KGB: Werkwijze, organisatie en machtsbereik van de Russische Geheime Dienst.* Amsterdam, 1975.

Bloch, S., and P. Reddaway. *Psychiatric Terror.* New York, 1977.

Blommaert, S. *Niets is mogelijk. Alles kan. De wondere wereld achter het ijzeren gordijn, of hoe heet dat tegenwoordig?* Leuven, 1992.

Bonner, J. *Samen alleen. De vrouw van de Sovjetfysicus en Nobelprijswinnaar Andrej Sacharov vertelt het volledige, ongecensureerde verhaal van hun leven in ballingschap.* Amsterdam, 1986.

Bourdeaux, M. *Religious Minorities in the Soviet Union.* London, 1984.

Davis, N. *A Long Walk to Church: A Contemporary History of Russian Orthodoxy.* San Francisco and Oxford, 1995.

De Boer, S. P., E. J. Driessen, and H. L. Verhaar. *Biographical Dictionary of Dissidents in the Soviet Union, 1956-1975.* Amsterdam: Brill, 1982.

Detrez, R. *Rusland: Een geschiedenis.* Antwerp-Amsterdam, 2008.

Duncan, P. *Russian Messianism: Third Rome, Revolution, Communism and After.* London/New York, 2000.

Ellis, J. *Letters from Moscow: Religion and Human Rights in the USSR.* Oxford, 1978.

Ellis, J. *The Russian Orthodox Church: A Contemporary History.* Bloomington: Indiana University Press, 1986.

Felshtinsky, Y., and V. Pribylovsky. *De onderneming: Rusland onder Putin.* Amsterdam, 2008.

Goldfarb, A., and M. Litvinenko. *Death of a Dissident: The Poisoning of Alexander Litvinenko and the Return of the KGB.* New York, 2007. Dutch translation: *Dood van een dissident: Aleksandr Litvinenko en het einde van de Russische democratie.* Utrecht, 2007.

Gorbatsjov, M. *O perestrojke i novom mysjlenii.* Moskou, 1987. Dutch translation: *Perestrojka. Een nieuwe visie voor mijn land en de wereld.* Utrecht/Wijnegem, 1987.

Hofland, H. J. A. *De wording van het Wilde Oosten. Het Sovjet-rijk 1984-1990. Kroniek van een wereldhistorische verandering.* Amsterdam, 1991.

Knox, Z. *Russian Orthodoxy and Religious Pluralism: Post-Soviet Challenges.* In *CERC Working Papers Series* (Contemporary Europe Research Centre, The University of Melbourne), No. 1/2003.

Knox, Z. *Russian Society and the Orthodox Church: Religion in Russia after Communism.* London/New York, 2005.

Laqueur, W. *The Long Road to Freedom: Russia and Glasnost.* New York, 1989. Dutch translation: *De lange weg naar vrijheid: Rusland en de glasnost.* Naarden, 1990.

Lesnik, R. *V efire Moskobskoe Radio.* Dutch translation: *Radio Moskou roept U. Getuigenis.* Antwerp, 1985.

Luykx, T. *Evolutie van de communicatiemedia.* Brussels, 1973.

Luykx, T. *Geschiedenis van de internationale betrekkingen sedert het Congres van Wenen.* Brussels, 1971.

Naarden, B., and A. P. Van Goudoever, eds. *Gorbatsjov en Stalins erfenis. Witte plekken in de sovjetgeschiedenis,* Utrecht, 1980. *Prisoners of Conscience in the USSR: Their Treatment and Conditions; Report of an Amnesty International Mission to the Republics of the Soviet Union.* Dutch translation: *Gewetensgevangenen in de USSR. Een rapport van Amnesty International.* 1980.

Remnick, D. *Lenin's Tomb: The Last Days of the Soviet Empire.* New York, 1993. Dutch translation: *Lenins laatste adem. De ondergang van het Sovjetrijk.* Haarlem, 1994.

Riccardi, A. *De eeuw van de martelaren. Geschiedenissen van christenen uit de twintigste eeuw vermoord omwille van hun geloof.* Tielt, 2002.

Sacharov, A. *Vospominanija.* Moscow, 1990. Dutch translation: *Mijn leven.* Amsterdam, 1990.

Solzjenitsyn, A., *Archipelag Gulag.* Paris, 1973. Dutch translation: *De Goelag Archipel 1918-1956.* Baarn, 1974.

Urban, E., S. Mitrokhin, and V. Igrunov. *The Rebirth of Politics in Russia.* Cambridge, 1997.

Van De Voorde, H., J. Blomme, D. Coninckx, L. Reychler, J. Neckers et al. *Supermachten 2. Geschiedenis en instellingen van Rusland en de Sovjetunie.* Brussels: BRT-Instructieve Omroep, 1988.

Van Putten, J. *Democratisering in de Sovjetunie.* Utrecht, 1990.

Wesselman, F. *Ingenieurs van de ziel.* Amsterdam, 2005.

Wollants, A. *Voor het venster weer dichtgaat — relaas van de sovjet-dissidentie.* Leuven, 1977.

Academic Articles

Arnold, J. "Patriarch Aleksi II: A Personal Impression." *Religion, State and Society* 20 (1992): 237-39.

Bibliography

Badham, P. "Religion and the Fall of Communism." In *Religion and Global Order.* Cardiff, 2000 (pp. 133-48).

Clement, O. "Martyrs and Confessors." *The Ecumenical Review* (July 2000).

Krypton, C. "Secret Religious Organizations in the U.S.S.R." *Russian Review* 14, no. 2 (1955): 121-27.

Marsh, C. "Russian Orthodox Christians and Their Orientation toward Church and State." *Journal of Church and State* 47 (2005): 545-61.

Parravicini, G. "La Isla de la Esperanza." *Ecclesia* 17, no. 2 (2003): 239-52.

Rock, S. "Fraternal Strife: Nationalist Fundamentalists in the Russian Orthodox Brotherhood Movement." In *Orthodoxy, Christianity and Contemporary Europe.* Leuven, 2003 (pp. 319-42).

Van Der Veerde, E. "Fundamentalisme in Orthodox Rusland." In *Fundamentalisme Face to Face.* Kampen, 2007 (pp. 109-30).

Verchovskij, A. "The Role of the Russian Orthodox Church in Nationalist, Xenophobic and Antiwestern Tendencies in Russia Today: Not Nationalism, but Fundamentalism." *Religion, State and Society* 30 (2002): 333-45.

Magazine Articles

De Wolf, K. "De eeuwige dissident." *Tertio,* June 20, 2007, p. 1.

———. "Pausbezoek Moskou niet voor morgen: Aleksandr Ogorodnikov over recente ontwikkelingen in Rusland." *Tertio,* June 20, 2007, p. 7.

———. "'Alleen de bijbel hield me overeind.' Aleksandr Ogorodnikov over zijn opsluiting in de goelag in Siberië." *Tertio,* June 20, 2007, pp. 8-9.

Ellis, J. "USSR: The Christian Seminar." *Religion in Communist Lands* 8, no. 2 (1980): 92-102.

Harris, J. A. "The Kremlin vs. the Church." *Reader's Digest,* September 1981.

Ogorodnikov, A. "From Marx to Christ: An Interview with Aleksander Ogorodnikov." *Epiphany Journal* 11, no. 1 (1990): 41-46. This article was first published in *Again* 13, no. 1 (1990).

———. "Moscow's Island of Hope." *In Communion,* Sept. 13, 1998.

———. "Pis'mo Ogorodnikova Doktoru Filippu Potteru, July 26, 1976." *Vestnik* 119 (1976): 305.

Ogorodnikov, A., and B. Razveev. "Young Soviet Christians Form Seminar." *Religion in Communist Lands* 7, no. 1 (1979): 48-50.

Okada, T. "Supreme Soviet Member Speaks about Draft Law on Religion." *The Ukrainian Weekly,* Dec. 31, 1989.

Ostling, R. "Cross meets Kremlin." *Time Magazine,* Dec. 4, 1989.

Ostling, R. "Religion: Giddy Days for the Russian Church." *Time Magazine,* June 20, 1988.

Philips, W. "From Community to Isolation: Aleksander Ogorodnikov." *Frontier Magazine* 1 (1987): 2-5.

"Political Prisoners Seek Reagan's Aid in Urging Inspection of Soviet Camps." *The Ukrainian Weekly* 12, no. 51 (March 20, 1983).

Rodgers, B. "The Conscience of Lord David Alton." *CRISIS: Politics, Culture and Church,* October 26, 2004.

Roslof, E. E. "The Myth of Resurrection: Orthodox Church in Postcommunist Russia." *Christian Century,* March 17, 1993.

Walters, P. "The Ideas of the Christian Seminar." *Religion in Communist Lands* 9, nos. 3-4 (1980): 111-26.

Wooding, D. "Aleksander Ogorodnikov Continues His 'Island of Hope' Ministry to Homeless Girls in Moscow Despite Legal Setback." *ASSIST News Service,* April 21, 2001.

Index of Names

Index of Places